W9-CBN-561

PROTECTING YOUTH AT WORK

Health, Safety, and Development of Working Children and Adolescents in the United States

Committee on the Health and Safety Implications of Child Labor

Board on Children, Youth, and Families

Commission on Behavioral and Social Sciences and Education
National Research Council

Institute of Medicine

NATIONAL ACADEMY PRESS
Washington, D.C. 1998

NATIONAL ACADEMY PRESS • 2101 Constitution Avenue, N.W. • Washington, D.C. 20418

NOTICE: The project that is the subject of this report was approved by the Governing Board of the National Research Council, whose members are drawn from the councils of the National Academy of Sciences, the National Academy of Engineering, and the Institute of Medicine. The members of the committee responsible for the report were chosen for their special competences and with regard for appropriate balance.

This study was supported by Contract No. 200-96-2544 between the National Academy of Sciences and the National Institute for Occupational Safety and Health, Centers for Disease Control and Prevention, U.S. Department of Health and Human Services; by Grant No. 030461 between the National Academy of Sciences and the Robert Wood Johnson Foundation; by Purchase Order No. 7W-0522-NANX between the National Academy of Sciences and the U.S. Environmental Protection Agency; by a grant from the Wage and Hour Division of the U.S. Department of Labor; and by Contract No. 98-0168(P) between the National Academy of Sciences and the Maternal and Child Health Bureau of the U.S. Department of Health and Human Services. In addition, the National School-to-Work Office of the U.S. Departments of Education and Labor supported this study through an interagency agreement with the Centers for Disease Control and Prevention. Any opinions, findings, conclusions, or recommendations expressed in this publication are those of the author(s) and do not necessarily reflect the view of the organizations or agencies that provided support for this project.

Library of Congress Cataloging-in-Publication Data

Protecting youth at work : health, safety, and development of working children and adolescents in the United States / Committee on the Health and Safety Implications of Child Labor, Board on Children, Youth, and Families, Commission on Behavioral and Social Sciences and Education, National Research Council, Institute of Medicine .
    p. cm.
    Includes bibliographical references and index.
    ISBN 0-309-06413-9
    1. Children—Employment—Health aspects—Government policy—United States. 2. Teenagers—Employment—Health aspects—Government policy—United States. 3. Industrial hygiene—Government policy—United States. 4. Industrial safety—Government policy—United States. I. Board on Children, Youth, and Families (U.S.). Committee on the Health and Safety Implications of Child Labor.
    HD6250.U3 P73 1998
    331.3′1′0973—dc21   98-40159

Additional copies of this report are available from National Academy Press, 2101 Constitution Avenue, N.W., Washington, D.C. 20418. Call 800-624-6242 or 202-334-3313 (in the Washington Metropolitan Area). This report is also available on line at http://www.nap.edu.

iii

The National Academy of Sciences is a private, nonprofit, self-perpetuating society of distinguished scholars engaged in scientific and engineering research, dedicated to the furtherance of science and technology and to their use for the general welfare. Upon the authority of the charter granted to it by the Congress in 1863, the Academy has a mandate that requires it to advise the federal government on scientific and technical matters. Dr. Bruce M. Alberts is president of the National Academy of Sciences.

The National Academy of Engineering was established in 1964, under the charter of the National Academy of Sciences, as a parallel organization of outstanding engineers. It is autonomous in its administration and in the selection of its members, sharing with the National Academy of Sciences the responsibility for advising the federal government. The National Academy of Engineering also sponsors engineering programs aimed at meeting national needs, encourages education and research, and recognizes the superior achievements of engineers. Dr. William A. Wulf is president of the National Academy of Engineering.

The Institute of Medicine was established in 1970 by the National Academy of Sciences to secure the services of eminent members of appropriate professions in the examination of policy matters pertaining to the health of the public. The Institute acts under the responsibility given to the National Academy of Sciences by its congressional charter to be an adviser to the federal government and, upon its own initiative, to identify issues of medical care, research, and education. Dr. Kenneth I. Shine is president of the Institute of Medicine.

The National Research Council was organized by the National Academy of Sciences in 1916 to associate the broad community of science and technology with the Academy's purposes of furthering knowledge and advising the federal government. Functioning in accordance with general policies determined by the Academy, the Council has become the principal operating agency of both the National Academy of Sciences and the National Academy of Engineering in providing services to the government, the public, and the scientific and engineering communities. The Council is administered jointly by both Academies and the Institute of Medicine. Dr. Bruce M. Alberts and Dr. William A. Wulf are chairman and vice chairman, respectively, of the National Research Council.

Contents

Preface

The common statement that "Children are our future" reflects the priority long placed on the health and welfare of children in American society. More than 75 years ago, President Theodore Roosevelt established the U.S. Children's Bureau in the Department of Labor, placing it there because the problem of child labor was so salient at that time. Our nation has taken pride in how we provide for our children through a variety of social policies, such as the right to a high school education and protection from hazardous working conditions. In general, many of the components of our social policy designed to promote growth and development of children have been operating with apparent effectiveness for many years, but recent evidence suggests that a review of the current status of these policies is in order.

The most public evidence of this need is the increasing number of reports in news media that highlight dangerous, illegal, or exploitative use of children as workers. Although these news reports have often featured work settings outside the United States, there have been some U.S. stories that raise troubling questions about the effectiveness of existing policies to protect the nation's children. There is clearly a new awareness and sensitivity to the fact that mistreatment of children, in whatever form or place, must be discovered and dealt with quickly and decisively.

At the same time, it should be recognized that the problems that have caught the attention of the news media represent only a small part of youth employment in the United States. Youth employment, in fact, has become the norm in our society. Thus, it is important to recognize that youth employment includes a broad mix of positive and negative features. And it is critical that parents, teachers, policy makers, and youths themselves consider carefully the consequences of employment on children and adolescents who are still growing intellectually, socially, physically, and emotionally. If we restrict our concern to illegal child labor or to the mistreatment of working children in other countries, we risk denying the large majority of working youth in this country adequate consideration of their needs and protection of their health.

These concerns led the National Institute for Occupational Safety and Health (NIOSH) to ask the Board on Children, Youth, and Families to undertake a study on the health and safety implications of child labor, which has been done by this committee. The study was supported by NIOSH, the Robert Wood Johnson Foundation, the U.S. Environmental Protection Agency, the National School-to-Work Office, the Wage and Hours Division of the U.S. Department of Labor, and the Maternal and Child Health Bureau of the U.S. Department of Health and Human Services.

The committee included 16 members selected to represent a broad range of expertise that included adolescent social and biological development, public agency programs and practice, law, economics, sociology, psychology, occupational medicine, and rural health programs. Such an unusually broad range of backgrounds for the committee members was necessary to bring the proper attention to the complex issue of child labor. It was, therefore, immensely rewarding that, throughout the committee's deliberations, there was an eagerness on the part of all members to learn from one another. This proved essential in order that the intricacy and complexity of the committee's charge could be met and that the recommendations could reflect the needs of children, with proper respect for properly guided growth as they evolve their appropriate independent place as adults.

It should be noted that approximately half of the committee members are receiving or have received funding from NIOSH in support of their own research work. About midway through the project, I took a sabbatical from the university for work at NIOSH, but on a completely unrelated topic, health and safety issues of aging workers.

Throughout our deliberations, we sought a common understanding of the value of work to personal and social growth of youth as well as to learning from the "real world." We also examined the importance of work during adolescence to training for a lifetime of work and to what extent it is possible and effective to integrate and cross-fertilize classroom learning with practical experience. We synthesized the limited information about unintended health risks at work, about means and effectiveness for training of youth about health risks, and about what should be considered appropriate work tasks and jobs for young workers. Finally, we attempted to determine what was known about the effects of work on educational attainment. Throughout, our intention was to identify ways to maximize the benefits of work for young people while targeting for elimination the adverse consequences that could be identified.

The charge given the committee was intentionally broad so that both the positive and negative effects of work for youth would be given adequate consideration. The committee met four times over 10 months, with very active deliberations both during and between meetings.

The committee's efforts were enhanced by the input from many researchers, agency personnel, and representatives of interested groups who provided input during the committee's deliberations. The committee also consulted informally with other experts as issues arose and commissioned a paper on child labor regulations and analyses of some data from the Current Population Survey. Through this process, the committee sought to synthesize the relevant research, characterize the adverse consequences and extent of work for youth, assess the current status of regulation and information available from public data systems, and develop appropriate recommendations to guide development of a modern public policy on youth employment. These individuals are acknowledged by name and affiliation in Appendix A.

Several agency personnel deserve special mention for their helpfulness and availability to the committee and staff throughout the project. At the very beginning, Linda Rosenstock, director of NIOSH, played a key role in the formulation of the study charge, and she continued her interest and support throughout. Dawn Castillo, of NIOSH's Division of Safety Research and Leader, Child Labor Working Team, gave unselfishly of her time and knowledge by attending meetings of the committee, answering countless email queries from committee members and staff, sharing bibliographies and background materials, and keeping the committee informed about the work of the NIOSH Child Labor Working Team. John Ruser, Bureau of Labor Statistics, U.S. Department of Labor, presented information at the committee's workshop, shared his work on the use of full-time employee equivalent measures, and was extremely patient in assisting staff with analyzing data from the Current Population Survey. William Fern and Art Kerschner, Wage and Hour Division, U.S. Department of Labor, helped the committee understand the intricacies of child labor law and its enforcement, and Kevin Keaney, Office of Pesticide Programs, U.S. Environmental Protection Agency, did the same for pesticide regulations and that agency's Worker Protection Standards.

Special thanks are due to a panel of high school students in the Washington, D.C., area who were willing to devote an afternoon to meeting with the committee. The committee gained a great deal of insight into the adolescent work experience from the students' discussion about their interests in working, their experiences (both good and bad), their knowledge about work risks and benefits, and their desire to both work and learn. In reviewing the research, committee members often were reminded of comments made by these high school students, some of which are highlighted in the report.

Appreciation is also extended to those individuals who served as internal reviewers of the report. Many thanks are due to Aletha Huston, University of Texas at Austin, who offered helpful comments on behalf of the Board on Children, Youth, and Families, and to Robert Fullilove, New York University, who provided helpful input on behalf of the Board on Health Promotion and Disease Prevention.

This report has been reviewed by individuals chosen for their diverse perspectives and technical expertise, in accordance with procedures approved by the Report Review Committee of the National Research Council. The purpose of this independent review is to provide candid and critical comments that will assist the authors and the NRC in making the published report as sound as possible and to ensure that the report meets institutional standards for objectivity, evidence, and responsiveness to the study charge. The content of the review comments and draft manuscript remain confidential to protect the integrity of the deliberative process.

We thank the following individuals, who are neither officials nor employees of the NRC, for their participation in the review of this report: Darlene Adkins, National Consumer's League, Washington, D.C.; Eula Bingham, Department of Environmental Health, University of Cincinnati; Mark R. Cullen, Occupational and Environmental Medicine Program, Yale University School of Medicine; Kristine M. Gebbie, School of Nursing, Columbia University; Harry Holzer, Department of Economics, Michigan State University; Lyle V. Jones, L.L. Thurstone Psychometric Laboratory, University of North Carolina, Chapel Hill; Jonathan D. Klein, Division of Adolescent Medicine, University of Rochester Medical Center; Robert Lerman, Urban Institute, Washington, D.C.; Robert A. Moffitt, Department of Economics, Johns Hopkins University; and Christopher J. Ruhm, Bryan School of Business and Economics, University of North Carolina. Although these individuals have provided many constructive comments and suggestions, responsibility for the final content of this report rests solely with the authoring committee and the NRC.

Chairing this committee has been a rewarding experience, the task made much easier by the friendly and supportive atmosphere of the meetings. During the life of the committee, I and the entire committee depended heavily on the high quality intellectual and administrative skills of National Research Council (NRC) staff, under the able direction of study director Nancy Crowell. Her energy for the task was evident from the first day and her background work, research, and regular interactions with all committee members has left its positive stamp throughout this report. She was ably assisted by project assistant, Cindy Prince, whose new baby was a wonderful reminder of the task at hand. Additional thanks are owed to Anne Meadows for carefully editing and improving the structure of sections of the report, to Christine McShane for coordinating the editing, and to Eugenia Grohman for final editing and overseeing the review and publishing processes. Much credit is due Deborah Phillips, former director of the Board on Children, Youth, and Families, and to Karen Hein, former executive officer of the Institute of Medicine, for their contributions to the initial conceptualization of this project, as well as their support and encouragement throughout the study.

Finally, thanks and acknowledgment are due to the members of the committee, all of whom gave generously of their time. Several members took primary responsibility for drafting chapters of this report. I thank Letitia Davis for her work on Chapters 2 and 3; Jeylan Mortimer for her work on Chapter 4; Doris Slesinger and Barbara Lee for their work on Chapter 5; Ellen Widess for her work on Chapter 6; and Stephen Hamilton for his contributions to Chapters 1 and 6. Mostly, I thank all my colleagues for an intellectually stimulating and challenging task; I am confident our conclusions and recommendations will help ensure more rewarding work experiences for the nation's children and adolescents.

David H. Wegman, *Chair*
Committee on the Health and
Safety Implications of Child Labor

PROTECTING YOUTH AT WORK

Executive Summary

Today, work is a common part of the lives of many children and most adolescents in the United States. In general, the U.S. public believes that work is beneficial—and at worst, benign—for children and adolescents. Indeed, working provides many young people with valuable lessons about responsibility, punctuality, dealing with people, and money management, while increasing their self-esteem and helping them become independent and skilled. Working during high school may contribute to increased rates of employment and better wages up to a decade after high school completion.

Yet working can be dangerous. Each year, tens of thousands of young people are seen in hospital emergency departments for work-related injuries; hundreds of them require hospitalization; and more than 70 die of work-related injuries. Long work hours during the school year are also associated with problem behaviors, including substance abuse and minor deviance, and with insufficient sleep and exercise. Young people who worked long hours during high school also are more likely to have lower educational attainment a decade later than those who did not.

The Committee on the Health and Safety Implications of Child Labor was established by the Board on Children, Youth, and Families of the National Research Council and the Institute of Medicine, at the request of the National Institute for Occupational Safety and

1

Health, to examine the research on the positive and negative consequences of working for children and adolescents in the United States. The committee was charged with reviewing the available data on the extent to which children and adolescents work and on the number and types of work-related injuries and illnesses sustained by children and adolescents; reviewing the research on how working during school affects education, development, and behavior; and examining whether the laws and regulations that govern labor by children and adolescents in the United States are adequate to ensure the health and safety of young people at work.

FINDINGS

Scope and Patterns of Work

The U.S. Department of Labor estimates that about 44 percent of 16- and 17-year-olds work at some time during the year, either while in school or during the summer or both. The government estimates do not include children younger than 16 who may work, although the National Longitudinal Study of Adolescent Health found that about 40 percent of 7th and 8th graders were employed during the school year. Children of *any* age may work in family-owned businesses and on family farms. But even the official numbers for 16- and 17-year-olds are likely to be underestimates because they are based on reports by parents or other adults in the household. Research has found that parents systematically understate the involvement in the work force of their children. Department of Labor estimates are also limited by rather specific definitions of work. When high school students are interviewed directly through research surveys, about 80 percent report that they hold jobs during the school year at some point during high school.

A notable characteristic of working adolescents is that they move in and out of the labor market, changing jobs and work schedules frequently, in response to changes in employers' needs, labor-market conditions, and circumstances in their own lives. Children and teens, like adults, work mainly for the money. Children's income, however, no longer goes primarily toward family support, as it once did: The majority of working adolescents spend most of their incomes on discretionary items or on their individual needs.

The biggest employer of adolescents is the retail sector—restaurants, fast-food outlets, grocery stores, and other retail stores—which employs more than 50 percent of all working 15- to 17-year-olds. The next biggest employer is the service sector (e.g., health-care settings such as nursing homes), which accounts for more than 25 percent of working adolescents, followed by 8 percent employed in agriculture. Several of the industries in these sectors of the economy have high rates of injury for all workers. Rates of injury are high, for example, in grocery stores and nursing homes, and agriculture is among the most dangerous industries in the country, with a high rate of fatal injuries.

Some parts of the youth population face unique problems related to work. Children and adolescents who are poor, minority, or disabled are far less likely than white, middle-class young people to be employed and, therefore, to reap the potential benefits of work experience. Furthermore, the jobs that poor and minority young people have tend to be in more dangerous industries. When they do work, the hours they work and the wages they receive are comparable to those of other youngsters.

Consequences and Risks of Work

Adolescence occupies a crucial role in contemporary human development, for several interrelated reasons. It is a period of potentially great malleability and tremendous variability. It is an especially important formative period, during which many developmental trajectories become established and increasingly difficult to alter.

Working has been shown to be associated with both positive and negative consequences for adolescents. Working may increase responsibility, self-esteem, and independence and may help children and adolescents learn valuable work skills. Employment that is limited in intensity (usually defined as 20 hours or less per week) during high school years has been found to promote post-secondary educational attainment. Many studies show positive links between working during high school and subsequent vocational outcomes, including less unemployment, a longer duration of employment after completing schooling, and higher earnings.

However, high-intensity work (usually defined as more than 20 hours per week) is associated with unhealthy and problem behaviors, including substance abuse and minor deviance, insufficient sleep and exercise, and limited time spent with families. Moreover, a high level of investment in work during adolescence has been found to be associated with decreased eventual educational attainment. It should be noted that researchers have often chosen the dividing point of 20 hours of work per week as a convenient way to subdivide hours of work into "low-intensity" and "high-intensity" employment; that division is not based on specific research about 20 hours per se.

Children and adolescents may be exposed to many work-related hazards that can result in injury, illness, or death. About 100,000 young people seek treatment in hospital emergency departments for work-related injuries each year. The average of 70 documented deaths that occur among children and adolescents each year as a result of injuries suffered at work is believed to be an underestimate.

The rate of injury per hour worked appears almost twice as high for children and adolescents as for adults—about 4.9 injured per 100 full-time-equivalent workers among adolescents, compared with 2.8 per 100 full-time-equivalent workers for all workers. The industries with the highest injury rates for young workers are retail stores and restaurants, manufacturing, construction, and public-sector jobs. There is virtually no information on the extent to which young people are exposed to toxic or carcinogenic substances in the workplace, exposures that may cause illnesses many years later.

Work-related deaths of workers 17 years and younger are highest in agriculture, followed by retail trade and construction. The most common causes of work-related deaths among 16- and 17-year-olds involve motor vehicles, electrocutions, and homicides.

Many of the industries that employ large numbers of children and adolescents have higher than average injury rates for workers of all ages, but young workers do not receive adequate health and safety training at work—training that has been linked with reduced injuries and acute illnesses when provided to adult workers who are young or inexperienced. Furthermore, children and adolescents often work with inadequate supervision and at tasks for which they may be developmentally unprepared.

Inexperience, as well as physical, cognitive, and emotional developmental characteristics, may also play a part in the risk of injury faced by young workers. Research on adults finds that inexperience on the job contributes to occupational injuries. It should not be surprising, then, if the inexperience of children and adolescents turns out to be an important factor in their work-related injury rates. Injury may also result from a physical mismatch between the size of the child or adolescent and the task: For example, machinery that was designed for adult males may be too large or heavy for children or adolescents to handle safely.

Child Labor Laws and Regulations and Education

Work by children and adolescents is regulated at both the federal and state levels. The 1938 Fair Labor Standards Act (FLSA), administered by the Employment Standards Administration of the U.S. Department of Labor, is the primary federal law governing child labor. The FLSA sets limits on the number of hours that those younger than 16 may work and restricts those under 18 from being employed in certain hazardous nonagricultural occupations. The standards are much less restrictive for children and adolescents working in agriculture than for those employed in nonagricultural jobs, reflecting the social norms of six decades ago. Each state also has its own child labor standards, which vary widely, with some states permitting 50 or more hours of work per week during the school year for youths under the age of 18. The Occupational Safety and Health Act of 1970, which regulates workplace health and safety protections for workers in the United States, makes no special provisions for the health and safety needs of working children and adolescents.

Education and training is a complement to laws and regulations. Education about the employment of children and adolescents has three purposes: informing young people, parents, educators, employers, and others about child labor laws and regulations; training them to prevent work-related illness and injury and to respond appropriately to workplace hazards; and improving the quality of youngsters' work experiences, minimizing the harmful consequences and maximizing the benefits.

CONCLUSIONS AND RECOMMENDATIONS

Working provides benefits to children and adolescents, but the benefits do not come without potential risks to the workers' physical, emotional, educational, and social development. Because so many children and adolescents participate in the U.S. work force, and undoubtedly will continue to do so, the issue is not whether they *should* work, but what circumstances cause working to be detrimental, what can be done to avoid those circumstances, and how working can be made more beneficial.

Guiding Principles

The committee's recommendations are guided by the scientific evidence on working and a set of principles. The principles are based on a developmental framework, which recognizes that the needs and abilities of children and adolescents differ from those of adults: The tasks in which children and adolescents engage should be commensurate with their physical, cognitive, emotional, and social abilities. The committee believes that these principles, which represent the judgment and values of the committee, form the basis for ensuring that the work performed by children and adolescents will be safe and healthful.

Guiding Principle 1: Education and development are of primary importance during the formative years of childhood and adolescence. Although work can contribute to these goals, it should never be undertaken in ways that compromise education or development.

Guiding Principle 2: The vulnerable, formative, and malleable nature of childhood and adolescence requires a higher standard of protection for young workers than that accorded to adult workers.

Guiding Principle 3: All businesses assume certain social obligations when they hire employees. Businesses that employ young workers assume a higher level of social obligation, which should be reflected in the expectations of society as well as in explicit public policy.

Guiding Principle 4: Everyone under 18 years of age has the right to be protected from hazardous work, excessive work hours, and unsafe or unhealthy work environments, regardless of the size of the enterprise in which he or she is employed, his or her relationship to the employer, or the sector of the economy in which the enterprise operates.

With these principles in mind, the committee's recommendations are designed to protect young people in the workplace through updated, enhanced, and adequately enforced laws and regulations and through education and training. Because such efforts require adequate data, the committee also recommends improving data and surveillance systems and more general research. The major recommendations are included below in their entirety; the remaining recommendations in the report are summarized.

Surveillance Systems and Data

The combination of federal data sources and national and local survey research provides a fair amount of information about teenagers who have jobs, where they work, and how much they work. However, definitions and nomenclature often vary from source to source, making it difficult to compare information. Furthermore, little information is available about the extent of work by those under the age of 15, despite evidence that many youngsters begin working for pay before that age. Nor is there much information on subpopulations of young people, such as those who are disabled, poor, or members of minority groups. Information on the quality of the work in which young people engage is also lacking. And the limited data that do exist are not detailed enough to be used for state-level analysis of working children and adolescents, analysis that is needed for targeting prevention and training efforts as well as for regulatory enforcement efforts.

Likewise, information on the adverse health consequences associated with youth employment is limited. The occupational injuries, illnesses, and hazardous exposures to which working youth are subjected can be prevented by proper public health actions. Surveillance systems that provide information about where and how young workers are injured or made ill on the job is essential both for targeting and for evaluating prevention efforts. The current occupational illness and injury surveillance systems are limited and poorly coordinated, and they have not been evaluated to assess the extent to which they may systematically omit young workers or subgroups of young workers.

Recommendation: The Bureau of Labor Statistics should routinely collect and report data on the employment of young people aged 14 and older. Such data should be reported by informative age groupings, by school status (e.g., school year or summer and in-school or not-in-school), and by hours worked per job. For the decennial census, the Bureau of the Census should collect and report similar data on employment for young workers.

Recommendation: The Bureau of Labor Statistics should periodically conduct special studies to document the employment of children under the age of 14 and of special populations of children and adolescents, such as minorities, immigrants, migrant farmworkers, and those who are poor or disabled. Also needed are periodic studies of children and adolescents who are illegally employed.

Recommendation: The Bureau of Labor Statistics should develop methods to generate reliable estimates of youth employment at the state level.

Many agencies—including the National Center for Health Statistics, the Bureau of Labor Statistics, the National Institute for Occupational Safety and Health, the National Center for Education Statistics, the Bureau of Justice Statistics, and the Occupational Safety and Health Administration—collect much information on children and adolescents. Many of these agencies include information on the work experiences of children and adolescents, but there is no standard for what information is gathered or how it is reported. Standard definitions and nomenclature, on such items as work status, age groupings, and hours of work categories, are needed to make the various sources of information more complementary.

Recommendation: Federal agencies that collect data related to work by children and adolescents should establish standardized nomenclature and definitions for such variables as work status, age groups, and hours of work. Those agencies that collect data for health, education, and development purposes should also collect data on the employment of youngsters in their surveys.

Many young workers' occupational injuries, illnesses, and exposures to hazardous substances are preventable if proper public health actions are taken. Surveillance that provides information about where and how youngsters are injured or made ill while working is essential for both targeting and evaluating prevention efforts. Over the past decade, government agencies have substantially improved the surveillance of illnesses and injuries sustained by adult workers; more recent surveillance initiatives have begun to provide information regarding young workers, at least with respect to their work-related injuries. However, these activities are limited and poorly coordinated. The lack of specific attention to the need for data regarding issues related to the protection of young workers as a special population has often meant that even data on relevant age groups are not available to the public.

> **Recommendation: The National Institute for Occupational Safety and Health, in collaboration with the Bureau of Labor Statistics and other relevant federal and state agencies, should develop and implement a comprehensive plan for monitoring work-related injuries and illnesses sustained by workers under the age of 18 and for monitoring hazards to which these young workers are exposed. Additional resources should be allocated to the appropriate agencies to implement plan components not currently funded.**

Education

Information and Training

The health and safety hazards that children and adolescents face in the workplace and the protections to which they are entitled under the law are little known or understood by children and adolescents themselves, by their parents, and by other adults who are in a position to give them guidance. Although a number of efforts are currently under way around the country to provide information and training related to making workplaces safe and healthy environments for young people, they are scattered and uncoordinated. The committee proposes several plans to begin to remedy the lack of knowledge and to promote understanding of the conditions necessary for safe and meaningful work experiences for children and adolescents.

Recommendation: A national initiative should be undertaken to develop and provide information and training to reduce the risks and enhance the benefits associated with youth employment. Adequate resources should be allocated to an agency to lead this effort.

Occupational Health and Safety in School-to-Work Programs

The purpose of the School-to-Work Opportunities Act of 1994 (to run to October 2001) is to leverage other resources to foster partnerships, at the state and local levels, that will build systems to support the transition of adolescents from school into lifelong careers. An evaluation of the School-to-Work Opportunities Act is under way, but it is unclear if that evaluation will adequately assess the presence and effectiveness of health and safety training or the safety of workplacements under the act.

Recommendation: The Departments of Education and Labor, in their evaluation of the School-to-Work Opportunities Act, should make certain that the evaluation includes comprehensive assessment of the success of different programs in conveying appropriate and effective workplace health and safety information and training. Those practices found to be effective should be continued after the School-to-Work Opportunities Act expires.

Commendable Workplaces for Youth

Commending employers that provide healthy, safe, and beneficial workplaces for young people may be equally as important as fining those that do not. The committee envisions the establishment of a seal of approval for such workplaces, based on nationally developed criteria, but administered at a local level. All workplaces where young people receive publicly supported education and training could be required to be meet the criteria (e.g., internships, cooperative education, youth apprenticeship, and placements subsidized by Job Training Partnership Act and other federal funds), with participation by other employers on a voluntary basis.

Recommendation: The Secretary of Labor should convene a prestigious group representing all affected parties to develop criteria for designating "commendable workplaces for youth." These criteria would be used by local groups to identify who would earn the designation and to determine employers who are eligible to employ young people in school-related publicly supported programs.

Protective Measures

Hours of Work

The Department of Labor is not authorized to establish restrictions on working hours for 16- and 17-year-olds. As the vast majority of 16- and 17-year-olds are still attending school, the historical reasons that justified the exemption of those 16 and older from the hour limitations no longer apply. Furthermore, high-intensity work (usually defined as more than 20 hours per week) has been associated with unhealthy and problem behaviors, including substance use and minor deviance, insufficient sleep and exercise, and limited time spent with families, and it is associated with decreased eventual educational attainment.

Care will have to be taken in setting an upper limit in number of work hours for 16- and 17-year-olds. Some circumstances may warrant exemptions from limitations on work hours during school, such as for adolescents in extreme financial need or for emancipated minors. There may also be special circumstances, related to an individual student or to the quality of the work (e.g., high-quality school-to-work placements), under which long hours may be determined to have fewer negative consequences. In addition to the number of hours worked per week, the number of hours per day and start and stop times of work, particularly on school nights, should also be considered for regulation.

Recommendation: The Department of Labor should be authorized by Congress to adopt a standard limiting the weekly maximum number of hours of work for 16- and 17-year-olds during the school year. This standard should be based on the extensive research about the adverse effects of high-intensity work while school is in session.

Hazardous Work

Under FLSA, the Secretary of Labor may prohibit young people under 18 (under 16 in agriculture) from jobs designated as hazardous. The regulations that list these hazardous jobs are referred to as hazardous orders. Many existing hazardous orders refer to machinery and processes that are no longer used, and they fail to address the full range of health and safety hazards and technologies in the contemporary workplaces in which youngsters are now employed. None of the current hazardous orders takes into account the special risks to young workers caused by exposure to carcinogens, biohazards, reproductive toxins, and ergonomic hazards, the health effects of which may not be evident until adulthood; nor are the orders based on research and data on jobs that pose hazards to children and adolescents.

> **Recommendation: The U.S. Department of Labor should undertake periodic reviews of its hazardous orders in order to eliminate outdated orders, strengthen inadequate orders, and develop additional orders to address new and emerging technologies and working conditions. Changes to the hazardous orders should be based on periodic reviews by the National Institute for Occupational Safety and Health of current workplace hazards and the adequacy of existing hazardous orders to address them.**

Minimum Levels of Protection

State regulations vary widely on the maximum weekly hours minors under the age of 16 may work. Although some states have enacted regulations that are consistent with FLSA regulations, 16 states allow minors under age 16 to work more than the federal maximum. A few states regulate the maximum weekly hours that 16- and 17-year-olds may work, and these rules also vary, ranging from 20 to 54 hours per week. States' hazardous orders also differ with regard to coverage and interpretation from the FLSA hazardous orders. Although some states have incorporated the federal standards, other states have adopted their own definitions, as in the case of operating power-driven machinery. Consistent with the principle of equal protection for all children, federal hour limitations and hazardous orders should be considered the minimum safe requirements for working children and adolescents.

Recommendation: All state regulations regarding working hours and hazardous orders for child labor should be at least as protective as federal child labor rules.

Agriculture

Children are permitted to work many more hours and at younger ages in agricultural than in nonagricultural workplaces. Activities that are hazardous for those under the age of 18 in nonagricultural settings are equally hazardous in agricultural settings, yet current regulations do not protect 16- and 17-year-olds on farms from performing hazardous tasks, nor do they protect youths of any age on their parents' farms. The only appropriate justification for a lower minimum age for performing hazardous work would be demonstrably lower risks in the industry. This is not the case for work in agriculture; agriculture is one of the most dangerous industries in the country.

Recommendation: The current distinctions between hazardous orders in agriculture and nonagricultural industries should be eliminated from child labor laws. Furthermore, the minimum age of 18 should apply for all hazardous occupations, regardless of whether the adolescent is working in an agricultural or non-agricultural job and whether the minor is employed by a stranger or by a parent or other person standing in for the parent.

Recommendation: The current distinction in federal child labor restrictions on the total maximum weekly hours youngsters are allowed to work in agricultural and nonagricultural industries should be eliminated in favor of the more stringent nonagricultural restrictions.

Under current law, young workers in agriculture are not entitled to the same health and safety protection as those in other businesses. Only a few Occupational Safety and Health Administration (OSHA) standards apply to agriculture: For example, standards that regulate such things as electrical hazards, unguarded machinery, confined spaces, heat stress, carcinogens, and access to medical and exposure records in other industries do not apply in agriculture. Furthermore, although the enforcement of OSHA standards is more limited in general industry for businesses that employ 10 or fewer workers, the businesses must nonetheless comply with the standards, but farms that employ 10 or fewer workers (and do not have labor camps) are completely exempt from enforcement.

No health and safety justification for the distinction between agricultural and nonagricultural settings appears to exist. It should be a priority to protect the large number of youngsters working in agriculture to the same extent that young workers are protected in other industries. The committee acknowledges that extending OSHA coverage to agriculture is a complex issue with many possible ramifications. However, the fact that agriculture is one of the most dangerous industries in the country suggests the need to examine health and safety issues in agriculture more closely.

> **Recommendation: To ensure the equal protection of children and adolescents from health and safety hazards in agriculture, Congress should undertake an examination of the effects and feasibility of extending all relevant Occupational Safety and Health Administration regulations to agricultural workers, including subjecting small farms to the same level of OSHA enforcement as that applied to other small businesses.**

Other Regulations and Enforcement

The committee makes a number of other recommendations pertaining to regulations and enforcement, including:

• That the National Institute for Occupational Safety and Health, in consultation with the Occupational Safety and Health Administration and the Environmental Protection Agency, report on the extent to which existing occupational health and safety and pesticide standards take into account special risks to children and adolescents;

• That the Task Force on Environmental Health Risks and Safety Risks to Children, which was created by the President's Executive Order Number 13045, should ensure that its definition of children include older children and adolescents and include exposures to children and adolescents at work.

• That additional resources be provided for the enforcement of child labor and health and safety regulations, as well as for an evaluation of strategies for dealing with serious, willful, and repeated violators;

- That the names of serious, willful, and repeated violators and violations that jeopardize the health and safety of young workers be published;
- That inspectors (compliance officers) receive interagency cross-training;
- That the adequacy of states' workers' compensation systems for young workers be examined; and
- That the potential for work permit or registration systems to enhance the health and safety of young workers be examined.

Research

The committee identified several critical areas in which there is need for increased research in order to adequately protect young workers. Agencies that fund research on children and adolescents should be provided adequate resources to fund the types of initiatives discussed below.

The major focus of research on child and adolescent employment has been on the effect of number of hours worked. Little attention has been paid to the quality of the work environment and its effect on development, workplace injuries, and educational goals. These topics include:

- Longitudinal studies of how individuals who have worked in their youth function as adolescents and adults and how various outcomes are associated with the quality of the work experiences.
- Research to determine whether the developmental characteristics of children and adolescents put them at increased risk from factors in the work environment, including chemical, physical, ergonomic, and psychosocial conditions (such as stress or type of supervision).
- Research on the most efficient and effective strategies to protect working children and adolescents, with an emphasis on primary prevention of injury and other negative outcomes.

Because so many young people in the United States are in the workplace, it is important to determine the strategies that will best serve to make their work experiences safe and healthful.

1

Introduction

Work is a fact of life for many children and adolescents in the United States. The U.S. Department of Labor estimates that almost one-half (4.26 million) of the 10 million teenagers between the ages of 15 and 17 work at some time during the year (U.S. Department of Labor, 1998). While some periods of work occur during the summer, surveys of high school students indicate that about 80 percent of them work during the school year at some time during their 4 years of high school (Bachman and Schulenberg, 1992; Light, 1995; Steinberg and Cauffman, 1995).

There are potential benefits associated with engaging in work during adolescence. Some amount of work in high school has been shown in some studies to be associated with increased self-esteem, independence, and higher levels of employment and income in the years following high school. The general view that good work experience is part of growing up and that work serves youth well is probably true. However, insufficient attention has been directed to what constitutes good work experiences.

There are dangers associated with working (see Box 1-1). For example, more than 70 youngsters under the age of 18 die each year in work-related incidents (Castillo et al., 1994; Derstine, 1996), hundreds are hospitalized with work-related injuries and illnesses, and tens of thousands seek treatment in hospital emergency rooms for

---

BOX 1-1: CHILDREN INJURED AND KILLED AT WORK

A 15-year-old boy died in a bakery accident in Pennsylvania. He was killed while cleaning a horizontal dough mixing machine, although he was hired supposedly only to bag rolls. He had been employed in violation of the state's child labor laws. He didn't have working papers, he stayed on the job after permitted hours, and he was paid in cash, under the table (Meltzer, 1994).

A 16-year-old crew cook in a fast-food restaurant was pushing a container of hot grease from the kitchen to the outside for filtration. When he reached to open the door, his foot slipped, the lid fell off, and hot grease spilled over much of his body. He sustained second- and third-degree burns to his ankles, arms, chest, and face and was hospitalized for two weeks. Scarring occurred on all the burned areas (Heinzman et al., 1993:715).

A 12-year-old girl was killed when a car struck her while she was riding her bicycle delivering newspapers. The incident occurred just after 4 p.m. on an undivided two-lane road, where speeding is reportedly a problem. She was wearing a reflective white vest and white jacket, but not a bicycle helmet. Federal child labor laws, which limit hours and conditions of youth employment, do not apply to news carriers, who are considered independent contractors (Massachusetts Department of Public Health, May 1995).

A 14-year-old high school boy was killed when the tractor he was driving overturned on an icy county road and pinned him (Wisconsin State Journal, January 6, 1998:3B).

---

injuries incurred on the job (Layne et al., 1994). Furthermore, working long hours while attending school has been associated with other undesirable outcomes, such as an increased risk of alcohol, tobacco, or drug use (Bachman and Schulenberg, 1993; Mortimer et al., 1996; Resnick et al., 1997; Steinberg and Cauffman, 1995; Steinberg et al., 1993).

For many years the United States has judged it important to protect youth against bad work experiences by restricting both the types of work permitted and the hours that young people of different ages can work. By bringing together the best information about the health and safety dangers of work to youth, as well as the benefits of work, rational social decisions can be made. The intent of this study is not to discourage young people from work experiences, but, rather, to improve the understanding of how and when work may be harmful so that wise decisions are made by individuals, families, and society as a whole.

Attention to the potential for injuries and illnesses, as well as to potential positive and negative psychosocial effects among children and adolescents who work, has been growing since the late 1980s. More and more is known about the developmental needs and vulnerabilities of children and adolescents. At the same time, concern has mounted over the poor educational attainment of American youngsters, their lack of preparation for the job market, and their involvement in a variety of delinquent behaviors. Work is often suggested as an antidote to what ails the nation's young people. Parents of working youth often say that employment promotes a sense of responsibility, time-management skills, and positive work values (Aronson et al., 1996; Phillips and Sandstrom, 1990). Politically, the United States is in the midst of a strong antiregulatory period that has generated calls for reducing current regulations that deal with child labor. In the face of these competing social tensions, this study objectively looks at what is known about the work done by children and adolescents and the consequences of that work for their physical, emotional, and social health; their well-being; and their educational attainment.

The term *child labor* conjures images of Dickensian sweatshops in early industrial America or in underdeveloped countries today. In this report, the term is used as it is used in the Fair Labor Standards Act and subsequent regulations: Child refers to any individual under 18 years of age. Because it is common to identify the word *child* only with prepubescent individuals, however, this report frequently refers to child and adolescent labor to underscore the fact that the report is about teenagers as well as younger children. For the purposes of this report, the terms *teens*, *teenagers*, *youth*, and *adolescents* are used interchangeably to refer to individuals from the ages of 13 through 17. The terms *youngsters*, *young workers*, and *young people* refer to all children under the age of 18.

This report covers labor (rather broadly defined) about which there is a reasonable amount of data and information. By labor, or work, the report refers to activities that contribute to the production of a marketable product, good, or service, whether that activity is done for pay or not. This definition of work includes tasks performed in family businesses and on family farms, even when those enterprises are not covered under current U.S. child labor laws. The study does not cover children who are not working: Children may be injured, and even killed, as visitors or bystanders in workplaces, but unless the children are actually engaged in work, incidents that befall them simply by virtue of their proximity to a workplace are not covered. This is not to say that structural factors in the workplace, such as the provision of child care, might not decrease such incidents. Also excluded from this report's definition of work or labor are nonmarket tasks done solely within the family, such as household chores, mowing the lawn, or babysitting for a sibling. This type of informal work within the family is seldom characterized as employment, and so, little information has been collected on it.

Children and adolescents engaged in illegal activities—such as pornography, prostitution, or illegal drug sales—receive very little coverage in this report. Although young people are employed in such activities, their illegality makes gathering information about them difficult; hence, little is known about the extent to which children are involved. The overall estimates of hazards in the workplace reported in this volume are likely to be underestimates because of this exclusion.

With respect to the consequences of child labor, the committee understands the term *health* in a broad sense, encompassing not only physical health and well-being, but also social, psychological, and educational health and well-being. Thus, this report examines not only physical injuries or illnesses that result from working, but also the effects, both positive and negative, that various types and amounts of work may have on such things as educational attainment, self-esteem, independence, and interaction with peers.

HISTORICAL CONTEXT

Various social and economic forces have led to changes in the amount of time spent by children and adolescents in school and at work in the United States. For much of the nation's history, school and work were mutually exclusive activities. In the late 1700s, it was not unusual for children as young as 7 or 8 to be placed outside the home to earn income for their families. Schooling was sporadic for most children and adolescents, who spent the better part of the year in agricultural work or apprenticed to craftsmen and only attended school during nonwork seasons (Kett, 1977). The importance of children's contributions to the family economy is reflected in our traditional long summer vacations, which were originally intended to free school children to work on their families' farms. During industrialization in the early nineteenth century, the importance of children's contributions to family income continued. The rise of workers' associations to protect adult jobs coincided with other mid-century social forces that promoted the idea of adolescence as a special period in life that should be dedicated to education and protection from the adult world. From these movements arose calls for universal free and compulsory education and an end to child labor. Economic conditions, however, forced many families to continue to depend on income from the work of their children (Greenberger and Steinberg, 1986). The first half of the twentieth century saw the decline of children's full-time participation in the U.S. labor force. Reduced demand for poorly paid, unskilled laborers, coupled with compulsory education laws, led many youngsters to spend more years in school.

The passage of the Fair Labor Standards Act of 1938 (FLSA) included restrictions on child labor intended to protect "young workers from employment that might interfere with their educational opportunities or be detrimental to their health and well-being." For the first time, federal limitations were placed on the types of nonagricultural work permitted for children and adolescents under the age of 18. Hours of nonagricultural work were also limited for those under the age of 16. These legal restrictions played a part in the movement of American adolescents from workers to students. In 1900, fewer than 10 percent of 18-year-olds graduated from high school; of those between the ages of 14 and 19, 70 percent of males and 35 percent of females worked full time. By 1940, 50.8 percent of American 18-year-olds finished high school; of those between the ages of 14 and 19, only 40 percent of males and 25 percent of females worked full time (Kett, 1977; Greenberger and Steinberg, 1986).

The second half of the twentieth century has seen more young people remain in school. In 1990, only 9 percent of 16- and 17-year-olds were not attending school (1990 U.S. census data). By the

1970s, a substantial number of high school students combined school with part-time employment, as they continue to do today (Ruhm, 1997). As noted above, surveys of high school students have found that about 80 percent are employed at some point while attending school. Moreover, in contrast with the past, the earnings of few of today's student workers appear to contribute to the support of their families (Greenberger and Steinberg, 1986; Johnston et al., 1982; U.S. Department of Education, 1996; Yeatts, 1994).

School and Work

The relationship between school and work is fluid, and the two institutions interact in a number of ways. School has traditionally been seen as preparation for employment, teaching both skills and attitudes that will, among other benefits, make young people better workers. Working can also teach young people skills and attitudes, show the value of lessons learned in school, and provide an additional learning environment.

Most work requires some basic academic skills—knowing the multiplication tables and how to read, for example—that few youngsters would master simply by being in work settings. It is far more efficient to teach both academic knowledge and some general work skills, such as keyboarding, in classrooms than on the job. However, people also learn from hands-on activity and by performing concrete tasks.

Relating academic subjects more closely to employment contributes to the foundation for many subjects and can open some subjects to a wider range of students. For example, Hull (1993) compared the performance of college-bound students in traditional physics classes to that of vocational education students following a curriculum that taught principles of physics through technology. The vocational students not only made up the deficit in knowledge of physics that they had demonstrated at the beginning of the course, but after 1 year they had surpassed the students in college preparatory classes.

Vocational education emerged as a way of teaching young people knowledge and skills for employment in specific fields. However, as jobs have changed at an accelerating rate and as more jobs have required a deeper understanding of fundamental processes—of why as well as how—a new emphasis on enhancing academic learning has emerged among vocational educators (Parnell, 1985). Beginning in the late 1980s, the school-to-work movement expanded in response to the perception of a growing gap between what adolescents were learning in school and what businesses expected of new workers. At the same time, studies of high school students have found that they see little connection between school and life outside of school, are bored in school, and consequently are not putting much effort into school (Steinberg et al., 1996). What they are required to learn in school seems unconnected with the real world. Jobs that require no academic skills reinforce this skepticism: Store clerks are never asked to solve geometry problems. But exposure to more demanding adult jobs may motivate young people to return to the classroom: They may be more willing to learn geometry when they know it is needed to survey a plot of land or design a building.

The workplace can also be an alternative learning environment where young people can learn facts and principles that they did not grasp when presented in textbooks and lectures. This potential benefit of work experience has not been established empirically, but accounts of workers with minimal education successfully coping with complex phenomena suggest that it does exist (Scribner, 1984). From the school side, classroom reflection about work experiences can also open broad issues traditionally addressed in social studies and literature courses. Such issues might include the functions of profit in a free-enterprise economy, the distribution of power in a democratic society, and the multitude of perspectives and perceptions different people bring to the same situation. When used in this manner, work experience contributes to education in the broadest sense.

Occupational Safety and Health

The relationship between certain diseases and occupational exposures has been recognized by physicians for at least 400 years (Rom, 1992). With the advent of industrialization, work was performed in many new and different work environments, and the nature of occupational health and safety risks experienced by workers became more complex. In response to workplace injuries and illnesses, England created a centralized system of factory inspections in 1878; Germany followed at the beginning of the twentieth century. Although Massachusetts had created the first factory inspectorate in the United States in 1867, most other states did not follow this path.

After 1900, the increasing numbers of work-related injuries experienced in modern factories resulted in the passage of state workers' compensation acts (essentially no-fault insurance systems) to pay injured workers limited disability and health benefits. Although these programs filled an acute need by providing some support for the injuries workers experienced at work, they were primarily designed to protect companies from tort liability that had begun to be assessed when injured workers took their cases to the civil courts.

The first national legislation to protect the health of U.S. workers was the Walsh-Healey Public Contracts Act of 1936, which required federal contractors to comply with health and safety standards; at the same time, the Social Security Act funded the establishment of industrial hygiene programs in many states. Concern over a "spreading epidemic of occupational injuries and disease" (Bingham, 1992:1325) led to the passage, in 1969, of the Coal Mine Health and Safety Act (MSHA) and, in 1970, of the Occupational Safety and Health Act (OSH Act), giving the federal government broad responsibility for worker health and safety. The 1970 OSH Act established an employer's general duty to provide a healthy and safe work environment and ". . . to furnish to each of his employees employment and a place of employment which are free from recognized hazards that are causing or likely to cause death or serious physical harm . . . ." Today, debate is most frequently centered on defining "recognized" hazard and "serious physical harm," with employers generally arguing for narrow interpretations and workers arguing for broad ones.

Companies appear to focus most of their attention on control or prevention of injury risks since the negative impacts of injuries are easily and directly measured in terms of production delays and the costs of workers' compensation. Much less attention is devoted to preventing chronic diseases, such as occupational cancer, since the latency of these diseases results in little direct evidence of costs at the time the risks are incurred. During the 1970s and 1980s, many larger companies developed medical or nursing units to provide health-related services to workers, and only a few developed comprehensive occupational health and safety programs targeting prevention. The recent trend toward "lean" companies has resulted in a reduction or elimination of many such programs.

WHY U.S. CHILDREN AND ADOLESCENTS WORK

Historically, children and adolescents left school (and sometimes home) to enter the work force at relatively early ages in order to help support their families and to be trained for the jobs they would hold as adults. In the latter half of the twentieth century, the vast majority of young people in the United States remain full-time students until age 18, and the jobs typically held by adolescents provide little or no systematic preparation for later careers. Yet, most adolescents in this country work while going to school, and many of their parents, and adults in general, believe that working exerts a positive influence on adolescents (Aronson et al., 1996; Greenberger and Steinberg, 1986; Phillips and Sandstrom, 1990).

I am working basically so I would have my own money.

High school student,
Youth panel for the committee

Little research has been done on why children and adolescents seek paying jobs, but the primary reason seems to be money. Whether the money young people earn goes toward helping pay family bills or toward their own needs, income, rather than the work experience, itself, seems the main motivating factor. Greenberger and Steinberg (1986) report that 74 percent of the employed high school students in their sample say money is the primary reason for having a job: About half of them say that the money is for necessities and half say it is for "extras." In a large national survey of high school seniors, a majority of the employed students said that they spent between half and all of their income on their own personal needs and activities (Johnston et al., 1982). More than 80 percent of high school seniors say that "none or only a little" of their earnings go toward family expenses (U.S. Department of Education, 1996). Similar responses were found in 1981, 1991, and 1992. Yeatts (1994) reports that 69 percent of working high school seniors spend some of their earnings for car expenses, 97 percent use their earnings to "buy things," and 44 percent save some for college. Having money of their own not only allows adolescents to purchase items for their own use, but it may also give them a sense of independence.

My father said you're always asking me for money, so why don't you get you a little job so you can make your own?

High school student,
Youth panel for the committee

Parents encourage adolescents to get jobs, because doing so will enable them to buy the things they want or because work is seen as an inherent good. A common belief in the United States is that holding a job builds character and teaches a young person what real life is like. Interviews with parents support this idea; parents expect that jobs will teach their adolescents to be dependable, punctual, and responsible (Greenberger and Steinberg, 1986). Working adolescents also describe themselves as more punctual, responsible, and dependable than those who are not employed (Greenberger, 1984).

I first started a job because my parents thought it would teach me responsibility.

High school student,
Youth panel for the committee

INTERNATIONAL CONTEXT

The discussion of child labor in America is taking place at a time of intense debate over the legitimacy of child labor throughout the global economy. It is interesting to note that the issues that have emerged in the United States differ substantially from those addressed by the International Labour Organization (ILO). In the United States, the primary concerns have been the availability of work for low-income teenagers, the health and safety of the work environments of children and adolescents, and the compatibility of that work with young people's educational needs. On the international front, in contrast, it is the legitimacy of child labor itself that is debated. The most recent ILO convention on child labor (No. 138) was adopted in 1973 and ratified by 55 countries (excluding the United States); its stated objective is "the effective abolition of child labour." To this end, it mandates a minimum age of 15, to be relaxed only in exceptional cases, and a minimum age of 18 in hazardous jobs. The only exceptions envisioned for developed countries are employment in conjunction with vocational education programs and "light work" that impinges minimally on youngsters' physical, social, and educational development. The convention does not make a case for the benefits of child labor, nor does it view improvements in health and safety as preconditions for extending these benefits to more young people. Despite the large differences in emphasis, however, it can be argued that U.S. objectives are consistent with Convention No. 138 if there is stricter adherence to the "light work" model—healthy work that does not interfere with education and development.

A major difference between the United States and other industrialized countries appears to be the lack of a coordinated system for helping young people make the transition from student to worker. In countries such as Germany, for example, young people enter apprenticeships that are closely linked to their education and that lead to specific adult jobs. German apprenticeship is formally structured, with a contract that specifies the rights and obligations of the employer and the apprentice and a curriculum that specifies the opportunities for learning that the firm will provide and the knowledge and skills that the apprentice must acquire. Apprentices' learning is tested by a national examination and documented by their employers; on completion, the young workers have credentials that are recognized by all employers. Austria, Denmark, and Switzerland have comparable systems. In contrast, the jobs held by most U.S. children and adolescents, as noted above, are usually disconnected from school curricula and are usually not seen as career stepping stones.

It appears that the proportion of adolescents working in the United States is relatively high compared with other developed countries; see Table 1-1. Caution must be exercised in comparing data among countries, however. What groups are included in the labor force and how terms such as "employed" and "unemployed" are defined differ by country. Methods of data collection, classification, and tabulation differ. Countries also use different reference periods for determining who is employed: Some countries ask about employment on the specific day of the census, and others ask about

TABLE 1-1 International Comparison of Working
Adolescents

Country	Age Group	Active in Labor Force (%)[a]
Argentina	14-19	34.4
Finland	15-19	27.1
France	16-19	6.8
Germany	15-19	32.6
Greece	15-19	16.6
Ireland	15-19	21.8
Japan	15-19	17.0
Mexico	15-19	45.0
Norway	16-19	37.9
Spain	16-19	25.1
United Kingdom[b]	13-17	43.0
United States	16-19	53.5

[a]Being active in the labor force includes both employed youth
and those looking for work.
[b]United Kingdom data from Heptinstall et al. (1997).

SOURCE: Data from International Labour Office (1996).

usual employment with no reference to time. For adolescents, the
ages included also vary from country to country.

THIS STUDY AND REPORT

At the request of the National Institute for Occupational Safety
and Health, the Board on Children, Youth, and Families of the
National Research Council and the Institute of Medicine organized a
study on the health and safety implications of child labor. The study
was asked to:

- synthesize the relevant research on the positive and negative
consequences of child labor in both agricultural and nonagricultural
settings;
- characterize the conditions under which adverse consequences
are most likely to occur, and the extent to which children and youth
are exposed to these conditions, including pesticides and other toxins;

- assess the current status of regulation, monitoring, surveillance, and data collection associated with child labor in the United States; and

- provide a set of recommendations regarding the collection of health and safety data related to child labor, the coordination of monitoring and surveillance activities to assure that adequate, reliable, and useful data are collected; the identification of conditions of child labor that appear to pose particular risks to the health, safety, education, and development of children and youth; and the identification of research needs and opportunities.

To fulfill these requests, the study committee and staff gathered information in a number of ways. Relevant research studies were collected through targeted literature searches of Medline, Educational Resources Informational Center (ERIC), and UnCover, as well as through searches of the past 10 years' indexes of journals devoted to the health or development of children or adolescents and journals devoted to occupational health and safety. The committee met four times between February 1997 and December 1997 to discuss data availability and research findings, identify critical issues, analyze the data and issues, seek additional information on specific concerns, formulate conclusions and recommendations, and refine this report. At two of these meetings, invited guests spoke to the committee about various data and issues pertinent to child labor and about relevant research findings. Prior to one meeting, several committee members had the opportunity to interview a group of high school students concerning their attitudes towards and experience with work and workplace risks. A paper on child labor regulations was commissioned for the study, and experts on various relevant topics were consulted informally between meetings. In addition, Current Population Survey data for 1995 and 1996 available on the World Wide Web were analyzed.

Chapter 2 discusses what is known about the extent to which children and adolescents are working in the United States, where they are working, and how much time they spend at work. Included is a discussion of the various sources of data and their respective strengths and weaknesses.

Chapters 3 and 4 examine outcomes associated with work by children and adolescents. Chapter 3 concentrates on work-related fatalities, injuries, and illnesses and the sources of data that track them. Chapter 4 reviews what is known about the educational, psychological, and social effects of working on school-age youngsters.

Chapter 5 discusses work in agriculture, which is treated differently from other industries under child labor laws and regulations. Issues specific to migrant workers, who are primarily agricultural workers, are also discussed.

Chapter 6 reviews child labor laws and regulations in the United States and their implementation and enforcement. The chapter deals primarily with federal laws and regulations. A thorough review of state laws was beyond the scope of this report; some state laws are presented as examples of approaches to regulating child labor. This chapter also presents information on some educational and training programs that are aimed at improving health and safety for young people at work. A thorough review of the issues involved in school-to-work transition would require a report unto itself (see, for example, National Research Council, 1994); the committee confined its review primarily to health and safety issues involved in the recent school-to-work programs instituted under the 1994 School-to-Work Opportunities Act.

Chapter 7 presents the committee's recommendations.

2

Scope and Patterns of Work by Children and Adolescents

How many young people in the United States work? Who are they? Where do they work? According to the Bureau of Labor Statistics, 34.5 percent of 16- and 17-year-olds—more than 2.6 million youths—were employed at any given time during 1996 (Bureau of Labor Statistics, 1997).[1] Because young people's jobs are often temporary, and teens move in and out of work, the proportion of teens employed at all during the year is most likely to be greater than the proportion employed at any given time. In 1996, more than 44 percent of 16- and 17-year-olds had worked at some point during the previous year.[2] Likewise, the proportion of teens who work for at least some of their high school years is greater than those who work in any given year. While some periods of work occur during the summer, surveys of youth suggest that about 80 percent of teens work at some time during the school year in their junior or senior

---

[1]Unless otherwise noted, this report uses employment figures rather than labor-force-participation figures: The (civilian) labor force includes all people 16 years of age or older who are employed or are unemployed but available for and seeking work. If labor-force-participation rates were used, the 1996 figure for 16- and 17-year-olds would be 42.5 percent.

[2]Based on committee analysis of data from the 1996 Current Population Survey March Supplement. This is a conservative estimate because it does not take into account the fact that the individuals surveyed were younger during the previous year. If the shift between age groups is taken into account, the estimate is approximately 52 percent.

years in high school (Bachman and Schulenberg, 1992; Light, 1995; Steinberg and Cauffman, 1995).

Whether young people are employed or not may be less important than where they work and how much time they devote to work. Retail trades and services employ the vast majority of working 15- to 17-year-olds (51 percent and 26 percent, respectively). Agriculture—one of the three most dangerous industries in the country—is the next largest employer of this age group, employing 8 percent of them. Young people spend a significant amount of time each week working. In 1995, working 15- to 17-year-olds averaged about 18 hours of work in weeks that they worked (data from 1995 Current Population Survey).

Both cross-sectional and longitudinal data paint a general picture of the employment of adolescents in the United States. But that picture lacks many details. This chapter examines the information about the number of children and adolescents who work, who they are, where they work, and how much they work. The strengths and weaknesses of the data sources that provide this information and reasons for differences among the data sources are discussed.

DATA ON WORK

Statistics from the U.S. Department of Labor

Official estimates of employment (and unemployment) in the United States are derived from the Current Population Survey (CPS), which is conducted by the Bureau of the Census for the Bureau of Labor Statistics (BLS). The CPS is a monthly survey of about 50,000 households, scientifically selected to be representative of the civilian, noninstitutionalized population of the United States.[3] Households are in the sample for 4 months, retired for 8 months, and then return for 4 more months. The first and fifth interviews are face-to-face interviews; the other interviews may be conducted by telephone. Labor-force information that includes employment status and hours worked during the previous week is collected in the Basic Monthly Survey for each household member aged 15 or older. In addition, an

---

[3]Prior to 1996, about 60,000 households were surveyed; funding cuts resulted in the smaller survey.

extended survey each March, the Annual Demographic Survey or "March Supplement," collects other information about work experience during the previous calendar year, including earnings, number of weeks worked, average hours worked per week, occupation and industry classifications, and demographic information. The CPS Base Monthly Surveys for 1993 to 1996 indicate that about one-third of 16- and 17-year-olds are employed at any given time during the year. Data from the decennial census, which also collects information on employment, found similar results: About one-third of U.S. 16- and 17-year-olds were employed in the spring of 1990.

In 1996, for the first time, young women were more likely to be employed than young men: 35.7 percent for 16- and 17-year-old females; 33.3 percent for 16- and 17-year-old males. As with adults, there was a marked contrast in employment by race: Only 18.8 percent of young African Americans were employed, compared with 38.6 percent of white youths (Bureau of Labor Statistics, 1997). Likelihood of employment increased with age, ranging from 17.5 percent for 15-year-olds to 51.9 percent for 17-year-olds.[4]

There are advantages to relying on official statistics because they are regularly collected over a long period of time on a representative sample of the population. For information about children and adolescents' work experience, however, using the Current Population Survey has drawbacks. The Department of Labor's definition of the labor force automatically excludes people under the age of 16. The CPS data exclude those under the age of 15—youngsters who, under child labor laws, are allowed to work as news carriers, on family farms, in other family businesses, and in certain other jobs.

Even though data are collected on 15-year-olds, those data are not used in official BLS estimates, nor are they included in published tables. Furthermore, in all but the most detailed published tables,[5] data for 16- and 17-year-olds are aggregated with those for older age

---

[4]This finding is based on committee analysis of data from the 1995 CPS March Supplement.

[5]It is possible to purchase CPS Monthly Survey data tapes to analyze the data on 15-, 16-, and 17-year-olds. The U.S. General Accounting Office (1991) did such an analysis of 1988 data and found that 28 percent of 15-year olds and 51 percent of 16- and 17-year-olds were employed at some time during 1988. In addition, data from the CPS Monthly Survey and the CPS March Supplement are available on the World Wide Web for analysis (http://ferret.bls.census.gov).

groups; thus, BLS publications cannot be used to track work experience of minors, for whom the legal restrictions on child labor have been imposed. Furthermore, 19-year-olds and many 18-year-olds have finished high school, so their employment patterns can be expected to differ from those of adolescents still in high school. Aggregating the data for 16- to 19-year-olds obscures these differences. The official figures also exclude individuals who work fewer than 15 hours per week without pay in family-operated enterprises, a group that is likely to include many children and adolescents.

The CPS collects information on all the members of each household from one responding adult, so information about hours of work by adolescents does not come from adolescents themselves. It is possible that adults and adolescents would give different answers, not only for the number of hours worked by the adolescent, but also for whether the adolescent worked or not. In fact, Freeman and Medoff (1982) found that parents systematically reported that their children worked fewer weeks per year than the children reported. Obtaining information from the CPS on subpopulations of adolescents is also problematic. Pallas (1995) notes that the number of minorities enrolled in grades 10 to 12 in the sample in any given year is not large; therefore, statistical estimates about them are subject to large sampling errors. Disabled youngsters are not identified in the CPS, so no estimates are available for them.

National Longitudinal and Other Surveys

A number of national longitudinal surveys, such as the National Longitudinal Survey of Youth, the National Educational Longitudinal Survey, and the National Longitudinal Study of Adolescent Health, collect information on young people, including their employment experience (see Table 2-1 and Appendix B for details about these surveys). Unlike the CPS, which provides a snapshot of youngsters' employment at a particular time, longitudinal surveys allow researchers to study the complex patterns of young people's employment over time. Youngsters may start to work in informal jobs (e.g., mowing lawns, babysitting) or in family businesses and family farms at fairly young ages. As they move through their teens, they are likely to move from job to job, working different numbers of hours at different times.

Surveys suggest that most youth are employed at some time during their high-school years and that many of them work during the school year. These surveys find a higher percentage of young people working than reported in the CPS. For example, one-third of 10th-grade and two-thirds of 12th-grade participants in the 1987 National Assessment of Economic Education Survey reported that they were employed at some time during the school year (Lillydahl, 1990). Surveys of parents of 16- to 18-year-olds in the nationally representative National Survey of Families and Households (conducted between March 1987 and May 1988) found that 70 percent of the teenagers had worked during the past month (Manning, 1990).

Surveys of representative samples of young people themselves, such as Monitoring the Future and the National Longitudinal Survey of Youth, give estimates that about 80 percent were employed at some point during the school year in their high-school years (Bachman and Schulenberg, 1992; Light, 1995; Steinberg and Cauffman, 1995). Such employment may begin early. Data from the National Longitudinal Study of Adolescent Health found that 30.6 percent of 12-year-olds worked during the school year, as did 36.9 percent of 13-year-olds, 35.4 percent of 14-year-olds, and 44.2 percent of 15-year-olds (Kruse, 1997). Table 2-2 shows the hours of work by 7th through 12th graders in this survey.

Early involvement in work may be associated with a greater amount of time spent working in later teen years. Schoenhals et al. (1997) found that students who worked more than 5 hours per week at a formal job during the school year as 8th graders had the highest labor-market participation rates of any group by 10th grade. They were more likely to be employed in 10th grade than those who had less or no work experience in 8th grade and, on average, they worked more than 20 hours per week when they were in 10th grade.

Differences Among Findings

A number of factors may account for the discrepancies between data from CPS and data from survey results, and among surveys themselves. The employment questions sometimes refer to different periods of time (e.g., during the current school year, during the last month, during the last calendar year) and sometimes to employment at a single date (e.g., when the survey is administered). The longer the period of time under consideration, the higher will be the proportion of employed youngsters identified among those surveyed. In

TABLE 2-1 National Surveys Containing Data on Youth
Employment in the United States

Survey Name	Respondent	Ages	Sex	Definition of work
National Survey of Families and Households (NSFH), 1987-1988	Parent	12-18	Yes	Amount earned in last month
National Educational Longitudinal Survey (NELS) 1988	Child	14 in 1988 (8th grade); follow-up in 10th and 12th grades	Yes	Work for pay
National Longitudinal Study of Adolescent Health (Add Health) 1994-95	Child and Parent	7th-12th graders	Yes	Work for pay in last 4 weeks
Panel Survey of Income Dynamics (PSID)	16+	16+	Yes	Weeks worked
Monitoring the Future	Child	12th graders; 8th and 10th graders added in 1991	Yes	Work during school year
National Longitudinal Survey of Youth (NLYS), 1979	Child	14-21 in 1979; annual follow-up	Yes	Work for pay, in own business, or more than 15 hours without pay in family business
Monthly Current Population Survey (CPS)	Adult	16+	Yes	Work for pay, in own business or more than 15 hours without pay in family business in week of survey

Employment Paid/Unpaid	Employment Full/Part-Time	Employment School/Vacation	Occupation/ Industry
Paid	Hours worked in past week	Determined by date of interview	No/No
Paid	Hours worked in present or most recent job	School vs. summer	Yes/No
Amount earned per week	Hours per week	Nonsummer vs. summer	No/No
Paid	Hours worked		
Paid and unpaid	Hours worked per week		
Paid; unpaid only if more than 15 hours per week in family business	Hours worked per week	Start and stop dates of employment	Yes/No
Paid; unpaid only if more than 15 hours per week in family business	Hours worked per week	May be determined by month of survey	Yes/Yes

TABLE 2-2 Hours Worked per Week by Grade (in percent)

Hours Worked per Week	Grade 7		Grade 8	
	School Year	Summer	School Year	Summer
0	58.82	46.62	53.93	40.70
1 to 4	22.22	16.88	21.55	14.60
5 to 9	10.91	13.80	13.59	13.58
10 to 14	3.49	6.67	4.59	7.17
15 to 19	0.80	2.82	1.20	2.99
20 to 24	1.61	3.98	2.03	5.64
25 to 29	0.40	0.88	0.53	2.59
30 to 39	0.22	3.66	0.88	5.68
40 or more	0.37	2.90	0.75	5.57
Missing data	1.15	1.80	0.96	1.49

SOURCE: Special tabulation for the committee. Data collected by the National Longitudinal Study of Adolescent Health, J. Richard Udry, principal investigator,

some studies, students must be working a minimum number of hours per week to be considered employed. Some studies include only paid work, and others also include unpaid work. Some studies include informal work, such as babysitting or lawn-mowing, but others do not. Because of these varying definitions, estimates of employment vary considerably across surveys (Kablaoui and Pautler, 1991). Determining the extent of labor by children and adolescents at the state or metropolitan-area level is even more problematic, making geographical comparisons within and among states difficult (National Institute for Occupational Safety and Health, 1997). The CPS publishes state-specific data only for the age group of 16- to 19-year-olds.

Results are influenced by whether the respondent is the child, the parent, or another household member. As noted above, parents systematically understate their children's labor force attachments, particularly for children who are still in school. The nature of the sample may also have an effect. Samples drawn from school populations miss teenagers who have dropped out of school. About 9 percent of all 16- and 17-year-olds are not in school (based on 1990 census data), so studies done in schools miss a group of young people

Grade 9		Grade 10		Grade 11		Grade 12	
School Year	Summer	School Year	Summer	School Year	Summer	School Year	Summer
52.72	40.71	44.35	32.33	35.78	24.05	26.42	18.53
16.15	9.41	10.59	5.44	5.87	2.56	4.52	1.61
11.60	9.21	9.48	7.33	7.21	3.89	5.02	3.17
6.96	7.58	7.46	5.19	8.68	4.04	6.98	1.74
2.87	3.56	6.62	3.94	9.88	4.05	10.29	2.44
4.06	7.42	9.34	8.71	14.17	7.99	15.39	8.53
0.94	2.40	3.62	4.96	5.78	5.46	8.63	6.63
1.84	7.65	4.82	13.32	8.25	19.08	14.25	18.78
1.92	10.37	2.41	16.12	3.50	26.88	7.37	36.41
0.93	1.70	1.30	2.68	0.88	2.00	1.11	2.16

funded by the National Institute of Child Health and Human Development, National Institutes of Health, and 17 other federal agencies.

whose background characteristics and employment experience may be quite different from those of their counterparts who remain in school.

INTENSITY OF WORK

Not surprisingly, both the percentage of youngsters employed and the hours of employment apparently increase with age. In 1988, according to an analysis of CPS data, 28 percent of all 15-year-olds and 51 percent of all 16- and 17-year-olds held jobs; 15-year-olds with jobs worked an average of 17 hours a week and 19 weeks a year; working 16- and 17-year-olds averaged 21 hours a week and 23 weeks a year at work (U.S. General Accounting Office, 1991). Because these annual data do not differentiate between the school year and summer vacation, the analysis could not estimate the amount of time youngsters worked during the school year. An analysis of 1995 data files from the CPS found that 15-year-olds with jobs worked an average of 11 hours per week during the school year and 19 hours per week during the summer. For 17-year-olds with jobs, the numbers were an average of 18 hours per week during the school year and 26 hours per week during the summer.[6] Figure 2-1 shows employment in the summer versus the school year, by age group, and Figure 2-2 shows the number of hours worked for summer months versus the school year, by age group.

Surveys and studies other than the CPS provide more information on the amount of time young people spend working. Data from the National Longitudinal Survey of Youth show that 3 percent of all sophomores, 10 percent of all juniors, and 19 percent of all seniors worked more than 20 hours per week in the week the survey was conducted (Ruhm, 1997). The recent National Longitudinal Study of Adolescent Health found that 17.9 percent of all high-school students worked more than 20 hours per week during school (Resnick et al., 1997). Tables 2-3 and 2-4 summarize the findings of various studies on how much adolescents work.

An additional factor that may lead to different estimates of work in different studies is erroneous recall, which can complicate data on the number of hours worked, particularly if the respondents are estimating their average hours worked during some previous period. How best to estimate actual work hours is a matter of debate. Studies using detailed time diaries find lower hours of work than surveys that ask people the average number of hours worked in a previous period (Robinson and Godbey, 1997). Unfortunately, the time-diary data available on work by children and adolescents lump together data for ages 12 to 17, making them impossible to compare with other survey data.

Several potentially important aspects of work intensity are not well accounted for in most studies, such as the number of hours per day, the timing of those hours, and the variability of the work schedule. For example, working two 8-hour days over the weekend may be qualitatively different than working four 4-hour days after school. How late a youngster works on school nights may be as important as how many hours he or she works in a week. Working many hours for a short period of time (such as the Christmas holidays) may have

---

[6]These numbers were generated by project staff using 1995 CPS data made available by the Bureau of Labor Statistics. Since the monthly survey asks only about work in the previous week and the March supplement asks for average hours worked in the previous year, the annual and monthly figures are not necessarily comparable.

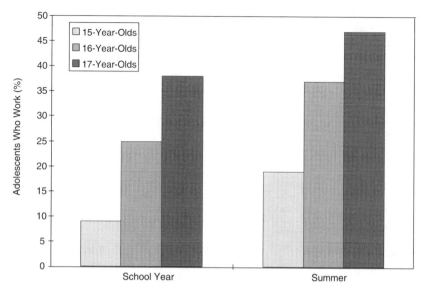

FIGURE 2-1 Percentage of adolescents who work, by time of year.
SOURCE: Data from 1995 Current Population Survey and census population estimates.

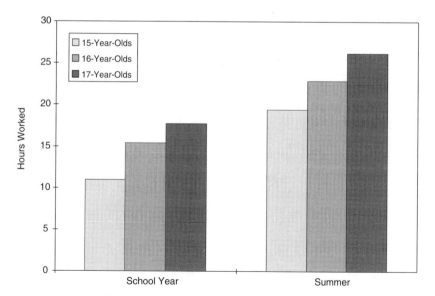

FIGURE 2-2 Average hours per week worked by adolescents, by time of year.
SOURCE: Data from 1995 Current Population Survey.

TABLE 2-3 Studies of Employment and Hours of Work During School Year

Study	Survey Name	Ages
Bachman and Schulenberg (1992)	Monitoring the Future	High-school seniors; 8th and 10th graders added in 1991
Light (1995)	National Longitudinal Survey of Youth (NLYS), 1979	11th-12th graders
Resnick et al. (1997)	National Longitudinal Study of Adolescent Health ("Add Health") 1994-1995	9th-12th graders
Schoenhals et al. (1997)	National Educational Longitudinal Survey (NELS) 1988	10th graders
Sweet (no date)	National Survey of Families and Households (NSFH) 1992-1994 follow-up	9th-12th graders
Special tabulations prepared by Jo Jones, Carolina Population Center, for National Research Council, 1998	National Longitudinal Study of Adolescent Health ("Add Health") 1994-1995	7th-12th graders

Findings

How Many Work	Amount of Work
74.9% of males for pay	53.5% of working males ≤ 20hrs/wk
6.3% of males unpaid	46.5% of working males >20 hrs/wk
72.7% of females for pay	61.6% of working females ≤ 20 hrs/wk
6.7% of females unpaid	38.4% of working females >20 hrs/wk
80% of males	Males averaged 12.8 hrs/wk
73% of females	Females averaged 11.1 hrs/wk
	17.9% worked 20 hrs/wk or more during the school year
43.3% of males	Males averaged 17.5 hrs/wk
37.7% of females	Females averaged 15.0 hrs/wk
37% of males for pay	20% of males < 10 hrs/wk
45% of females for pay	17% of males ≥10 hrs/wk
	27% of females < 10 hrs/wk
	18% of females ≥ 10 hrs/wk
40% of 7th graders	2.6% of 7th graders work 20 or more hrs/wk
45% of 8th graders	4.2% of 8th graders work 20 or more hrs/wk

TABLE 2-4 Findings on the Extent to Which Work and School are Combined

Study	NLS Cohort	Measure of Sample
D'Amico (1984,1986) D'Amico and Baker 1984)	Y, 1979-1982	Grades 9-12 during school year
Griliches (1980)	YM, 1966-1970	Complete at least grade 10 by 1970
Light (1994)	Y, 1979, 1991	First leave school in 1978-1991
Michael and Tuma (1984)	Y, 1979	Ages 14-17, in school in 1979
Ruhm (1997)	Y, 1979-1991	Grades 9-10 in 1979
Steel (1991)	Y, 1979-1981	Ages 17-18 in 1979
Stephenson (1979, 1981a, 1982)	YM, 1966-1971	In school one year, out of school next
Stephenson (1981b)	YW, 1968-1978	In school one year, out of school next
Stern and Nakata (1989)	Y, 1979-82	High-school senior in 1979; terminal high-school grads

NOTE: Y, youth; YM, young men; YW, young women; FT, full time; PT, part time

SOURCE: Light (1994:47)

In-School Work	Selected Findings
Percent of weeks worked	50% (75%) of white males work in grade 10 (12), 15% (57%) for more than half the year; less for minorities and females.
Cumulative work experience while in school	48% work in high school, 63% in college; 24% average at least 20 hours per week.
Whether employed at time of last observed exit from school	48% of white males hold jobs, work 60% of last year of school, on average; college students work more than others.
Whether employed week prior to 1979 interview	25% of 14-year-olds work, 51% of 17-year-olds; males work more than females, whites more than blacks or Hispanics.
Whether employed interview week, grades 10-12; hours/week and weeks/academic year	28% of sophomores, 43% of juniors, 50% of seniors work; seniors work 19 hours per week, 52% of academic year, on average.
Whether employed at time of 1979 interview	58% of whites work, 41% of Hispanics, 35% of blacks; all average about 25 hours per week.
Whether working FT or PT or unemployed while in school	29% of whites work FT, 33% PT, 7% unemployed; less FT, PT work for blacks, more unemployment.
Whether working FT or PT or unemployed while in school	46% work FT, 11% PT, 9% unemployed; (blacks and whites combined).
Whether employed week prior to interview	51% work; average about 16 hours a week in 1978-79.

different effects than working many hours for many months. Few surveys collect adequate details about these facets of work. The manner in which data are collected in the CPS also makes it difficult to distinguish work during the school year from work during summer months.

WHERE YOUNG PEOPLE WORK

As shown in Figure 2-3, more than one-half of 15- to 17-year-olds are employed in the retail sector (e.g., restaurants, grocery stores, other retail stores) and more than one-quarter work in the service sector (e.g., recreation, health, education). Agriculture is the next largest employer of this age group, employing 8 percent of them. Restaurants employ more young people (28 percent) than any other industry. These patterns vary somewhat by age, with more than

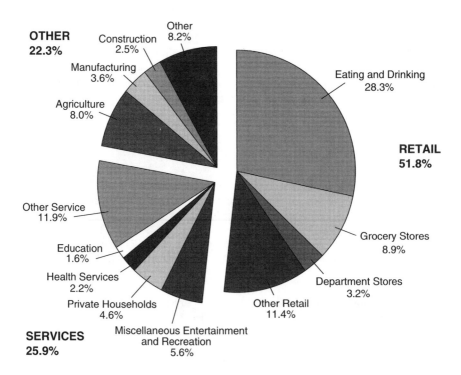

FIGURE 2-3 Working adolescents aged 15 to 17, by industry (in percent).
SOURCE: Data from 1996 Current Population Survey March Supplement.

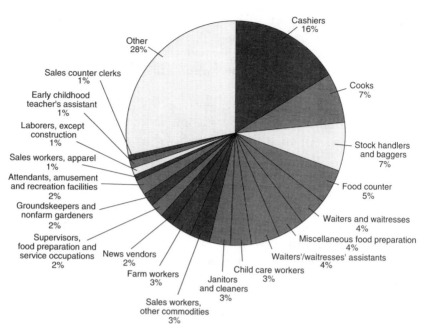

FIGURE 2-4 Working 15- to 17-Year-Olds, by occupation (in percent).
SOURCE: Data from 1996 Current Population Survey March Supplement.

twice the percentage of employed 15-year-olds working in agriculture than 16- and 17-year-olds (based on data from 1995 CPS March Supplement).[7]

The types of jobs that adolescents hold are varied. As shown in Figure 2-4, the most common job held by 15- to 17-year-olds, is cashier (16 percent), followed by cook (7 percent), stock handler (7 percent), food-counter worker (5 percent), waiter (4 percent), waiters' assistant (4 percent), and food-preparation worker (4 percent). However, the job titles youngsters have may not reflect the actual nature of the tasks they perform (Massachusetts Department of Public Health, 1997). For example, youngsters hired as cashiers may also clean and perform other tasks that are not associated with

---

[7]The actual number of 15-, 16-, and 17-year-olds employed in agriculture is similar: 60,000, 61,000, and 67,000, respectively. However, many more 16- and 17-year-olds than 15-year-olds are employed: 444,000 15-year-olds, 1,028,000 16-year-olds, and 1,450,000 17-year-olds.

operating a cash register. This phenomenon makes it difficult to estimate the kinds of hazardous exposures adolescents may experience on the job. Furthermore, inappropriate job titles could obscure the fact that adolescents are performing tasks prohibited by child labor laws.

Adolescents' type of employment appears to vary by family income, with youngsters from low-income families working in more hazardous jobs. An analysis by the U.S. General Accounting Office (1991) found that 20 percent of 15- to 17-year-olds from low-income families worked in hazardous industries, such as agriculture, mining, manufacturing, construction, and wholesale trade, compared with 14 percent of those from high-income families.[8]

Determining the extent of illegal employment among children and adolescents is difficult. By analyzing CPS data available on the number of hours worked and the occupations and using a number of assumptions, Kruse (1997) estimated that nearly 3 percent of working 15- to 17-year-olds were employed in violation of child labor laws: One-third of those were working more hours per week than allowed by law, and two-thirds were working in prohibited hazardous occupations. More than 12 percent of 15-year-olds in the National Longitudinal Study of Adolescent Health were found to be working more than the legally allowed 18 hours per week during the school year (Kruse, 1997).

Children employed in "sweatshops" and other illegal activities are likely to be underrepresented in survey data. Sweatshops are defined as businesses that regularly violate safety-and-health, wage-and-hour, or child-labor laws and are believed to be concentrated in the apparel, restaurant, and meat-processing industries. Although no good data exist on their number or the extent to which children and adolescents are employed in them, Kruse (1997) extrapolated from child labor violations found in New York City apparel firms (U.S. General Accounting Office, 1989), to estimate that about 13,000 minors a year might be employed in sweatshops.

Young people's employment in criminal activities, such as prostitution or drug dealing, has been documented only among children and adolescents who have run away from home, been thrown out of

---

[8]In this study, a low-income family was defined as one with annual income of $20,000 or less, a high-income family as one with annual income of more than $60,000.

their homes, or been arrested. There were an estimated 1.5 million runaway children in 1988 (Children's Defense Fund, 1988). About 26 percent of runaways seen in a medical outpatient clinic reported that they had traded sex for drugs at some time (Yates et al., 1988). A study of homeless adolescents in Northern California found that those who chose to remain on the street and use no services reported high levels of involvement in illegal activities: 88 percent panhandled, 62 percent stole, 50 percent sold drugs, and 42 percent engaged in prostitution (Stanford Center for the Study of Families, Children, and Youth, 1991).

The Drug Use Forecasting Program of the U.S. Department of Justice collects information on drug use and other illegal activity from individuals who have recently been arrested.[9] In 1996, 19 percent of young arrestees reported that their primary source of income was from legal full- or part-time work; the primary source of income from drug dealing was reported by 5.8 percent, from other illegal activity by 3.2 percent, and from prostitution by 0.1 percent (Golub, 1997).

WORK-RELATED ISSUES FOR SPECIAL POPULATIONS

Minority and Poor Youth

Minority adolescents have consistently been found to be less likely to be employed than white adolescents. In 1995, 18.8 percent of young African Americans had jobs, compared with 38.6 percent of young whites (data from 1995 CPS March Supplement). Ahituv et al. (1997), using data from the National Longitudinal Survey of Youth, found that African Americans also had their first jobs at later ages than whites. By the age of 15, 22.2 percent of whites, 23.1 percent of Hispanics, and only 16.4 percent of African Americans had held their first job. By age 17, 82.8 percent of whites, 79.1 percent of Hispanics, and 69.5 percent of African Americans had job experience. However, the detailed analysis found that the racial and ethnic distinctions resulted largely from group differences in family socioeconomic characteristics. Adolescents from poorer families living in economically disadvantaged locales were less likely to have

---

[9]This program was replaced by the Arrestee Drug Abuse Monitoring Program in fall 1997.

paid jobs while attending high school. For minority youngsters with jobs, their number of hours worked are similar to those for whites (Ruhm, 1997; Steel, 1991). Similarly, for poor youngsters, their hours worked are similar to those worked by more affluent youngsters (data from National Longitudinal Survey of Adolescent Health).

Race, ethnicity, and socioeconomic status also appear to affect the types of jobs young people get. Although retail establishments provide the greatest number of first jobs for all youth, a greater percentage of minority than white youngsters are employed in services, such as janitorial work (Ahituv et al., 1997). And low-income youth, when employed, are more likely than more affluent youth to work in hazardous industries, such as agriculture, manufacturing, and construction (U.S. General Accounting Office, 1991).

Children and Adolescents with Disabilities

About 12 percent of those between the ages of 15 and 21 are considered disabled, as defined by the Americans with Disabilities Act (Public Law 101-336), which includes those whose actions or activities are limited because of physical, mental, or other health conditions (McNeil, 1997). About 10.5 percent of school-age children have disabilities as defined by the Individuals with Disabilities Education Act (U.S. Department of Education, 1996). These are children with impairments caused by physical, mental, or other health conditions requiring the provision of special education and related services. Slightly more than half (51.2 percent) of disabled school-age children have specific learning disabilities, 21.8 percent have speech or language impairments, 10.9 percent are mentally retarded, and 8.7 percent have serious emotion disturbances; the remaining 7.5 percent suffer have disorders or conditions, such as autism, deafness, blindness, hearing impairments, multiple disabilities, orthopedic impairments, other health impairments, traumatic brain injuries, or visual impairments (U.S. Department of Education, 1996).

Work-force participation is lower for disabled people of all ages, adolescents and adults, than for the general population; disabled women have particularly low rates of employment. The rate of employment for all disabled individuals over the age of 15 is about 67 percent for men and 21 percent for women (compared with 71 percent for men and 57 percent for women aged 16 and over in the general population). The rates are much lower for those with severe disabilities or combinations of chronic illness and physical or cognitive impairments (White, 1997). Among adults with severe disabilities, only 26 percent are employed (McNeil, 1997). Using data from the National Longitudinal Transition Study of Special Education Students for young people 3-5 years after leaving high school, Wagner et al. (1992) found that 57 percent of disabled individuals were employed and only 27 percent were enrolled in post-secondary education. Few disabled adolescents under the age of 15 are employed (White, 1997).

Not only do adolescents with disabilities lack work experience, but they also receive little preparation for work or careers. White and colleagues (White and Shear, 1992; White et al., 1990) have been studying a large sample of youngsters with chronic illnesses and physical disabilities. To measure their attitudes toward and knowledge of work, the subjects took a Career Maturity Inventory, which has been normed at each age group with adolescents who have no disabilities. The adolescents with chronic illnesses and physical disabilities scored high on involvement: They did not see themselves as hopeless in terms of work, and they saw their disabilities as less problematic than potential employers see them. But the subjects scored much lower on orientation: They knew little about workplaces and what would be expected of them. Career maturity was found to be highly associated with parental perception of readiness for work. Often parents or other caregivers postponed a disabled child's entry into the workplace, and in some cases they did not think a first job was needed until age 25. Socioeconomic status played no role in this phenomenon. Interestingly, the degree of disability was not associated with career maturity.

These factors can have important consequences for development and successful transition into adult roles. Benz et al. (1997) found that having two or more job experiences during high school was highly predictive of a disabled individual's being competitively employed after high school. Work may play a central role in acculturating young people with disabilities. In making the transition from school to work, social context—how the parent or employer sees the disabled young person—may be as important as the young person's functional status (White, 1997).

Immigrant Youth

Very little data on work among immigrants, in general, and immigrant youth, in particular, have been collected. Furthermore, there are problems with the data that do exist. For example, the census makes no distinctions between legal and illegal immigrants or between legal immigrants who have the right to work in the United States and those who are here legally but who are not allowed to work (as is the case, for example, with the spouse or child of a visiting professor). This makes it difficult to interpret the existing data (Jasso, 1997). For immigrants younger than 18 who are granted permanent residency in the United States, the vast majority are coded as students by the Immigration and Naturalization Service. In 1994, for example, only about 11 percent of 17-year-old male immigrants and 8 percent of 17-year-old female immigrants reported an occupational title (Jasso, 1997). A committee analysis of 1990 census data indicated that 16- and 17-year-olds who had at least one immigrant parent were less likely to be employed than were their counterparts whose parents were born in the United States. These data shed no light on the reasons for this difference. It is possible that adolescents with at least one immigrant parent are less likely to report employment, even if they are working. It is also possible that immigrant parents encourage their children to concentrate on school achievement rather than work. A New Immigrant Pilot Study currently under way is designed to test the feasibility of alternative methods of locating immigrants and maximizing their participation in surveys, and to test ways of tracking this highly mobile population.

CONCLUSIONS

The vast majority of adolescents in the United States have their first work experience prior to finishing high school. The combination of federal data sources and national and local survey research provide a fair amount of information about teenagers who have jobs, where they work, and how much they work. However, little information is available on the quality of the work in which young people engage. Information is lacking about the extent to which those under the age of 15 work, although it seems clear that many youngsters begin working for pay at a young age. There is also very little information on subpopulations of young people, such as disabled, minority, and poor youth.

3

Health and Safety at Work

Work may be an integral part of the lives of many children and adolescents, but how safe is the workplace for children? Despite child labor laws that are intended to protect children from hazardous working conditions, many young workers face health and safety hazards on the job. In fact, if one examines the major industries in which adolescents are employed, one finds that many of these industries—grocery stores, nursing homes, and agriculture—have higher-than-average injury rates for workers of all ages; see Table 3-1. In general, typical "teen jobs" cannot be assumed to be safe. Such factors as inexperience, developmental characteristics (physical, physiological, cognitive, and psychosocial), and the need to balance school and work may place younger workers at greater risk than adults confronted with similar hazards.

Injuries are the leading cause of death among children (over age 1) and adolescents (Rosenberg et al., 1996). In 1995, 1,612 children aged 5 to 9 died from unintentional injuries, as did 1,932 children aged 10 to 14, and 6,622 adolescents aged 15 to 19 (National Center for Health Statistics, 1995). Injuries also are the leading cause of hospital admissions for young people (National Center for Health Statistics, 1990) and account for numerous visits to emergency departments and physicians (Baker et al., 1992). Between 1992 and 1994, injuries accounted for 43 percent of 31,447,000 annual emer-

TABLE 3-1 Incidence Rates of Nonfatal Occupational Injuries and
Illnesses for All Workers in the Private Sector, by Industry

Industry	1992		1993	
	Total Injuries (per 100 FTE)	Lost Workday Cases (per 100 FTE)	Total Injuries (per 100 FTE)	Lost Workday Cases (per 100 FTE)
All Private Industries[a]	8.9	3.9	8.5	3.8
Agriculture[a]	12.2	5.5	11.5	5.3
Grocery Stores	12.7	5.0	11.3	4.7
Eating Places	9.1	3.1	8.5	3.0
Nursing Homes[b]	18.6	9.3	17.3	8.9

NOTES: The incidence rates represent the number of injuries and illnesses
per 100 full-time equivalent workers and were calculated as follows: (N/EH)
× 200,000, where N = number of injuries and illnesses; EH = total hours
worked by all employees during the calendar year; and 200,000 = base for
100 full-time equivalent workers (working 40 hours per week, 50 weeks per
year).
  Lost workday cases involve injuries or illnesses that result in days away from
work or days of restricted work activity or both.

gency department visits by children and adolescents. The highest
rate of injury-related visits occurred among 15- to 17-year-olds (H.B.
Weiss et al., 1997).

  Occupational injuries and illnesses among young people have
typically been overlooked in pediatric health care and pediatric public health. At the same time, occupational health experts have generally focused on the health and safety of adult workers. Consequently, until quite recently, the scientific literature has been notably
silent on the subject of occupational injuries and illnesses among
children and adolescents. Although information remains limited, a

1994		1995		1996	
Total Injuries (per 100 FTE)	Lost Workday Cases (per 100 FTE)	Total Injuries (per 100 FTE)	Lost Workday Cases (per 100 FTE)	Total Injuries (per 100 FTE)	Lost Workday Cases (per 100 FTE)
8.4	3.8	8.1	3.6	7.4	3.4
10.3	4.8	10.4	4.7	9.4	4.3
11.2	4.7	9.9	4.1	10.1	4.1
7.7	2.6	7.6	2.4	6.2	1.9
16.8	8.4	18.2	8.8	16.5	8.3

aExcludes farms with fewer than 11 employees.

bThese figures are for nursing and personal care facilities, the category that includes nursing homes, for which separate rates were not available.

SOURCE: Data from Bureau of Labor Statistics. Available at: http://stats.bls.gov/sahome.html#OSH [1998, February 2].

growing body of research now suggests that occupational injuries contribute to the overall burden of injuries among youth.

This chapter first examines the data on work-related injuries and illnesses among children and adolescents. It then examines the factors that may increase their risk of injuries and illnesses in the workplace. Finally, it includes a review of the available sources of surveillance data and their strengths and weaknesses. Although the information presented here is relevant to both agricultural and nonagricultural settings, the special concerns of agriculture are addressed in Chapter 5.

NONFATAL WORK-RELATED INJURIES

Since the mid-1980s, a number of descriptive epidemiological studies have characterized the extent and nature of occupational injuries to children and adolescents. Because there is no national system for monitoring occupational illness and injuries, researchers have largely relied on administrative data, such as workers' compensation records, for documentation. No single data source captures all injuries; thus, findings based on any single data source should be considered conservative estimates. Because these data sources are not complete, exhaustive, or mutually exclusive, it is difficult to compare the data or to determine an accurate number of work-related injuries to young people. In addition, most of these data sources are not based on representative samples of working children and adolescents. As is discussed in more detail below (see "Sources of Surveillance Data"), official Bureau of Labor Statistics figures from the Annual Survey of Occupational Injuries and Illnesses are estimated to miss at least 11 percent of workers under the age of 18; hospital emergency rooms are estimated to see only one-third of *all* work-related injuries (and it is not known what percentage of injuries to young workers are seen in hospitals). Data from administrative sources, such as workers' compensation, differs from state to state. Taken together, however, studies provide an important picture, albeit incomplete, of work-related injuries suffered by young people in the United States.

Even less information is available on the severity of injuries suffered by young workers. None of the data sources specifically rates injury severity, but the sources include only injuries that require multiple days away from work or require medical attention—both commonly used indicators of serious injuries.

Extent of the Problem

One approach to estimating the magnitude of the problem is to examine workers' compensation claims filed for children and adolescents. A review of data from 26 states in 1987 to 1988 identified 59,000 injuries to minors (U.S. General Accounting Office, 1990).[1]

---

[1]The twenty-six states that reported injury data were Arkansas, Colorado, Florida, Hawaii, Idaho, Iowa, Kentucky, Louisiana, Maine, Maryland, Michigan, Minnesota, Mississippi, Missouri, Nevada, New Jersey, New Mexico, Oklahoma, Oregon, Pennsylvania, Rhode Island, Tennessee, Texas, Washington, Wisconsin, and Wyoming.

New York state alone reported that more than 1,200 youths received compensation for occupational injuries that resulted in 8 or more days lost from work each year from 1980 to 1987; more than 40 percent of the injuries resulted in permanent disability (Belville et al., 1993). In Washington state, which collects data on all injuries regardless of lost work time, more than 4,400 young workers were awarded workers' compensation benefits annually from 1988 to 1991 (Miller, 1995). Brooks et al. (1993) report that in Massachusetts from 1988 through 1990 approximately 700 workers under the age of 18 filed claims annually for injuries resulting in 5 or more days away from work. These findings vary widely because eligibility requirements for worker's compensation vary by state. Table 3-2 summarizes the findings from the major studies of work-related injuries.

Injury logs maintained by employers in accordance with the requirements of the Occupational Health and Safety Act also shed light on the extent of injuries to young workers. Each year the Bureau of Labor Statistics (BLS) conducts the Survey of Occupational Injuries and Illnesses (SOII), based on the injury logs required of a sample of private employers throughout the United States. According to these official statistics, in 1993 youngsters in private-sector industries suffered an estimated 21,620 injuries and illnesses that necessitated days away from work. The median number of lost work days was 3. The survey excludes the self-employed, farms with fewer than 11 employees, private households, and government, which means that the survey does not cover at least 11 percent of working youth, according to one estimate (Centers for Disease Control and Prevention, 1996).

Emergency-department records are another key source of information about work-related injuries suffered by adolescents. These records document not only serious injuries, but also injuries that do not necessarily require time away from work. In the National Hospital Ambulatory Medical Care Survey, the National Center for Health Statistics of the U.S. Department of Health and Human Services annually collects information on a nationally representative sample of emergency department visits. Between 1992 and 1994, there was an annual average of 2,111,000 emergency department visits by 15- to 17-year-olds for injuries. For 1993 and 1994, the years for which data on place of injury were collected, 5 percent

TABLE 3-2 Studies on Work-Related Injuries of Adolescents

Study	Population/Source	Sample
Banco et al., 1992	14- to 17-year-olds/ Connecticut workers' compensation reports for 1989	796 workers' compensation reports for 14- to 17-year-olds (.05% 14-year-olds; 10.2% 15-year-olds; 34.7% 16-year-olds; 54.6% 17-year-olds)
Belville et al., 1993	14- to 17-year-olds/ Workers' compensation records for 1980-1987; New York state	9,656 work-related injury awards

Injury	Job Type	Event
35% cuts	42% food stores	30% case cutter, knife,
25% contusions	27.5% general	other sharp objects
22% sprains	merchandise stores	25% struck by object
7% burns	11.3% restaurants	17% overexertion
3% fractures,	7.4% professional	13% falls
dislocations	and related services	7% burns
8% other	3.6% manufacturing	8% other
	2.7% public admin	
	2.6% business and	
	repair services	
	1.4% personal services	
	0.4% construction	
	0.3% agriculture	
	0.8% other	
35% lacerations	52.3/1,000	
18% fracture	unskilled labor	
18% sprain, strain	39.5/1,000	
9% contusion, crush	building service	
9% other traumatic	38.9/1,000	
injuries	food service	
7% burns	26.3/1,000	
1% amputations	agriculture	
1% other skin	25.0/1,000	
conditions	construction,	
1% systemic injuries	mechanics	
	20.2/1,000 clerical	
	15.9/1,000 sales	
	14.0/1,000	
	amusement	
	and health	
	10.6/1,000	
	managerial,	
	professional	

Table continues on pages 60-69

TABLE 3-2 Continued

Study	Population/Source	Sample
Brooks et al., 1993	14- to 17-year-olds/ Emergency room and hospital admission records, 1979-1982; 14 Massachusetts communities	1,176 work-related injuries
Brooks and Davis, 1996	14- to 17-year-olds/ Workers' compensation records for 1987-1990; Massachusetts	2,551 work-related injury awards
Broste et al., 1989	872 high school vocational agriculture students in central Wisconsin/ Audiometric assessment	Noise-induced hearing loss in at least one ear
Cooper and Rothstein, 1995	Under 18 years old in Texas/ Workers' compensation reports, 1991	1,097 injuries and illnesses 2% 11-13 year olds; 7% 14-15 year olds; 90% 16-17 year olds

Injury	Job Type	Event
49.1% lacerations		41.7% cutting, piercing
12.2% contusions		objects
9.6% strains, sprains		12% struck by object
7.5% eye injuries		9.6% falls
6.4% burns		6.9% machinery
3.0% fractures		6.8% burns
2.0% concussion,		6.3% overexertion
cranial		4.5% caught in or
0.4% amputation		between object (s)
9.9% other		4.4% foreign object
		7.8% other
33.1% sprain, strain	55.4% retail trade	
24.3% laceration	20% services	
15.6%contusion,	11% manufacturing	
crushing	4.6% construction	
8.5% fracture	3.5% wholesale	
4.7% burn	trade	
0.7% amputation	2.0% transportation	
13.1% other	1.2% agriculture	
	2.2% other	
57.1% of students		
who live and work		
on farms		
54.5% of student		
who work on farms,		
but live elsewhere		
24% of students who		
live, but do not work		
on farms		
33% of students with		
no farm exposure		
	35% vehicle drivers,	
	material handlers	
	30% service laborers	
	19% sales workers	

Table continues on pages 62-69

TABLE 3-2 Continued

Study	Population/Source	Sample
Hayes-Lundy et al., 1991	15- to 19-year-olds/ Utah State Insurance fund data, 1982-1985	73 cases
Heinzman et al., 1993 (Minnesota Adolescent Occupational Injury Study)	13- to 17-year-olds/ Workers' compensation records for 8/90-8/91	742 injured adolescents 534 usable records
Heyer et al., 1992	17-year-olds and younger/Washington state workers' compensaton claims, 1986-1989	16,481 claims
Knight et al., 1995	14- to 16-year-olds/ Follow-up survey of all work-related injury cases seen in emergency rooms participating in NEISS, July 1 to Sept. 30, 1992	174 cases 146 interviews completed
Layne et al., 1994	14- to 17-year-olds/ Representative sample of emergency departments (NEISS), July 1 to Dec. 30, 1992	37,405 estimated injuries nationwide based on 679 injuries in sample

Injury	Job Type	Event
100% burns from hot grease	100% fast-food restaurants	25% adding, filtering, changing hot grease 16% splashed grease 14% cleaning grill 11% slipped on floor into grease 34% other
13% burns (44% had permanent scars)	39% fast food establishments	50% hot grease 25% grills, other cooking equipment
	37% full service restaurants	42% hot grease 35% hot water
5.2% serious injuries 12.8% disabling injuries	7% farm 43% food workers	
	34% eating places 7% schools 6% grocery stores 6% amusement, recreation services 3% hospitals 44% other	17% moving materials or freight 13% cooking, food preparation 12% janatorial work 10% stocking shelves, cutting up boxes
34% lacerations 18% contusion, abrasion 16% sprain, strain 12% burn 4% fracture, dislocation 15% other	38% eating establishments 7.8% food stores 7.6% other retail 6.7% health services 3.3% amusement, recreation 2.9% educational services 7.6% other services 6.7% agriculture 4% manufacturing 15% all other	

Table continues on pages 64-69

TABLE 3-2 Continued

Study	Population/Source	Sample
Miller, 1995	11- to 17-year-olds (rates for 16- to 17-year-olds only)/ Workers' compensation records, 1988-1991; Washington state	17,800 work-related injury awards
NIOSH analysis of Survey of Occupational Illnesses and Injuries; U.S. Department of Health and Human Services, 1996 (state-specific numbers also available)	Under 18-year-olds/ 1993 survey of national sample of employers	21,620 injuries or illnesses involving lost work days
Parker et al., 1994b (Minnesota Adolescent Occupational Injury Study)	3,051 10th-12th grade students in 39 Minnesota high schools/Self-completed questionnaire survey	379 work-related injuries reported (detailed information provided for 339)

Injury	Job Type	Event
	45.3% restaurants 18.8% food stores and other sales	50% struck by person or object 14.6% falls 10.1% overexertion 9.1% burns 4.9% toxic exposures 3.3% caught in machinery 0.7% moving vehicle
31% sprains, strains 17% cuts, lacerations 13% contusions, abrasions 8% heat burns 5% fractures, dislocations	39% eating, drinking establishments 14% grocery stores 6% nursing, personal care facilities 5% department stores	21% falls on same level 17% over exertion 10% striking against objects 9% contact with hot objects 7% struck by falling object 6% struck by slipping hand- held object, such as knife, razor, tool
29% burn 27% cut 23% sprain 10% bruise 3% puncture 12% other (36% of injuries met reporting criteria)		31.6% striking or struck by object 25.4% contact with hot object 17.1% lifting, carrying, pushing, pulling 10% falls

Table continues on pages 66-69

TABLE 3-2 Continued

Study	Population/Source	Sample
Parker et al., 1994a	Under 18-year-olds/ Injury reports to Minnesota Department of Labor and Industry, 8/15/90 to 8/14/91 and follow-up interviews of injured adolescents	742 injuries (complete information on 534)
Schober et al., 1988	17 years and younger/ Workers' Compensation claims in the BLS Supplemental Data System, 1980	23,823 claims

Injury	Job Type	Event
37.6% strains and sprains 24.2% cuts and lacerations 13.1% burns 12.5% bruises 8.8% fractures	[a] 3%/1% agriculture 4%/7% nurses aide 6%/7% dish buser 13%/8% carhop 14%/14% cashier (restaurant) 12%/14% fast food cook 11%/7% short order cook 13%/11% dishwasher 4%/5% waiter 43%/45% janitor 2%/2% sales clerk 16%/15% stock clerk 16%/15% bagger	
36.5% cut, laceration 17.3% sprains, strains 12.8% contusion, crush 9.7% burns 5.8% fracture 3.5% abrasions 0.7% dislocations 0.6% amputations 13.1% other	49.7% retail trade 20.9% services 9.1% manufacturing 6.1% agriculture, forestry, fishing 3.9% wholesale trade 3.7% construction 3.7% public admin 1.2% transportation, utilities 1.2% finance, real estate 0.3% mining 0.3% not classified	

Table continues on pages 68-69

TABLE 3-2 Continued

Study	Population/Source	Sample
Stueland et al., 1996	under 18 year olds living on farms in central Wisconsin/ Medical records from 5/90 through 4/92	60 injured farm children

*a*First percentage is for males, second is for females. Each interviewee could give up to 3 types of work so total adds to more than 100 percent.

(103,000) of those injuries were identified as work-related (H.B. Weiss et al., 1997). In comparison, 15 percent of the emergency department visits by 18- to 20-year-olds for injuries were identified as work-related. No place of injury was recorded for 19 percent of the emergency department visits by 15- to 17-year-olds, some of which may have been work-related injuries. A Massachusetts study based on emergency-department data collected in the early 1980s found that 7 percent to 13 percent of all medically treated injuries among 14- to 17-year-olds were work-related. For 17-year-olds, the estimate for work-related injuries (where the locations at which injuries occurred were known) was as high as 26 percent and exceeded the proportion of injuries attributed to motor vehicles or to sports (Brooks et al., 1993). The National Institute for Occupational Safety and Health (NIOSH), in collaboration with the Consumer Product Safety Commission, has used data from the National Electronic Injury Surveillance System (NEISS) to assess the scope of the problem. NIOSH reports that in 1992 an estimated 64,100 adolescents, aged 14 to 17, required treatment in emergency departments for work-related injuries (Layne et al., 1994). Research suggests that only one-third of work-related injuries are treated in emergency departments (Centers for Disease Control and Prevention, 1983; unpublished tabulations, Occupational Supplement, 1988 National Health Interview Survey). Applying this figure to the NEISS findings, NIOSH has estimated that 200,000 adolescents are injured on the

Injury	Job Type	Event
31.7% contusion, abrasion	31.7% observing farm work	
28.3% laceration	68.3% working on farm	
16.7% fracture		
8.3% puncture		
6.7% burn		
6.7% closed head injury		
5% sprain		
10% other		

job each year (National Institute for Occupational Safety and Health, 1995).

Surveys of young workers themselves highlight the extent of the problem. In several recent surveys of working high-school students, estimates of the proportion of teens who report having been injured at work range from 17 percent to 50 percent. Between 7 percent and 16 percent of teens who have worked report having been injured at work seriously enough to seek medical care (Bowling, 1996; Dunn et al., 1998; Parker et al., 1994b). For example, in a survey of 450 teens at a large urban high school in Massachusetts, 67 percent reported that they either were working currently or had worked in the past: Of these, 35 percent reported having been injured at work; 10 percent were injured seriously enough to seek medical care (Massachusetts Department of Public Health, 1997).

The numbers alone indicate a basis for considerable concern. Moreover, because teens typically work part-time, often in seasonal jobs, the numbers of injuries suffered by adolescent workers translate into high injury rates per hour worked. This fact is often lost in national statistics that cannot provide rates by age that are adjusted for hours of work. *Healthy People 2000* calls for the reduction of occupational injuries among adolescents to no more than 3.8 per 100 full-time workers (National Center for Health Statistics, 1996). The fact that this objective is substantially lower than the goal for adults—6 per 100 full-time workers—reflects a social policy decision that youth deserve special protection in the workplace. Although the limitations of the data regarding both the number of young workers injured (numerator for injury rate calculations) and the total number of young workers (denominator for injury rate calculations) make it difficult to calculate injury rates for young workers, studies in which injury rates have been computed for both youngsters and adults using the same methods suggest that the injury rate per hours worked for young workers is higher than that for adults (Coleman and Sanderson, 1983; Miller, 1995). Current injury rates also appear to be well above the target for adolescents. The National Center for Health Statistics (1997) reports an occupational injury rate for 15- to 17-year-olds of 4.9 per 100 full-time-equivalent workers in 1996. The injury rate for all workers 16-years-old and older in 1996, based on the same sample, was 2.8 per 100 full-time-equivalent workers (National Institute for Occupational Safety and Health, 1998).

The injury rates alone do not provide a sense of the consequences of occupational injuries for the injured adolescents or for the adolescent population in general. Adolescents who are injured seriously enough to miss work may also miss days of school. In an effort to examine the burden that adolescent work-related injuries place on the community at large, Brooks et al. (1993) computed the rate of occupational injuries among teens residing in the community, regardless of their work status. Using emergency-department data collected from 14 Massachusetts communities and towns from 1979 to 1982, they report that approximately 1 out of every 30 adolescents aged 16 to 17 was seen in emergency departments for a work-related injury each year. Among males, the figure was 1 in 20.

Who Is Injured at Work: Age and Gender Differences

Studies show remarkably consistent patterns of nonfatal occupational injuries by age. In general, studies at both the national and state levels find older adolescents to have more injuries than younger adolescents (Banco et al., 1992; Belville et al., 1993; Brooks and Davis, 1996; Brooks et al., 1993; Castillo et al., 1994; Cooper and Rothstein, 1995; Heyer et al., 1992; Layne et al., 1994; Miller, 1995; Schober et al., 1988; Suruda and Halperin, 1991; Toscano and Windau, 1995); older adolescents also have higher injury rates (Belville et al., 1993; Brooks et al., 1993; Layne et al., 1994). Overall, more than 85 percent of nonfatal work-related injuries to adolescents are sustained by 16- and 17-year-olds (Banco et al., 1992; Belville et al., 1993; Brooks and Davis, 1996; Layne et al., 1994; Miller, 1995; Schober et al., 1988). The reasons behind this pattern are not entirely clear. Federal child labor laws and many state laws have stronger restrictions on the work that may be performed by those under the age of 16. Therefore, younger workers may be in less hazardous jobs. Or, because of limits on their hours of employment, they may simply have less exposure to situations in which they could be injured. Employers also may give older teens more responsibility and more hazardous tasks to perform than their younger counterparts are given. And older teens may be more likely to perceive themselves as mature, and therefore, attempt tasks for which they are unprepared.

Studies also consistently show that adolescent males have greater numbers and higher rates of injuries than adolescent females (Banco et al., 1992; Belville et al., 1993; Brooks and Davis, 1996; Brooks et al., 1993; Layne et al., 1994; Miller, 1995; Parker et al., 1994a, 1994b; Schober et al., 1988). Some studies show an injury rate for males that is nearly double that for females (Brooks et al., 1993; Coleman and Sanderson, 1983; Miller, 1995; Schober et al., 1988). Until recently adolescent males were more likely than adolescent females to be employed, which could partly explain the disparity in the numbers of injuries, but not the difference in rates. Males are more likely than females to work in risky industries, such as construction (Jacobs and Steinbery, 1990; Reskin, 1993). Dunn et al. (1998) report that teenage boys are more likely to be exposed to occupational hazards than are teenage girls. They conclude that the high rates of injury in adolescent males likely reflect their job experience, their exposure to work-related hazards, and employers' expectations, rather than the boys' risk-taking behaviors. Anecdotal evidence suggests that within the same jobs, boys are frequently asked to do "heavier" tasks. In general, males tend to have higher rates of injury than those of females, at all ages. Baker et al. (1992) note that the annual rate of nonfatal injuries requiring medical treatment or at least one day of restricted activity for males is 1.4 times that for females. The extent to which the increased risk of occupational injuries among young males can be explained by gender-related differences in job and task assignments or to gender-related behavior remains to be more fully explored.

Types and Seriousness of Work-Related Injuries

The most common nonfatal injuries observed among working children are lacerations, sprains and strains, contusions, burns, and fractures (Banco et al., 1992; Belville et al., 1993; Brooks and Davis, 1996; Brooks et al., 1993; Bush and Baker, 1994; Layne et al., 1994; Miller, 1995; National Institute for Occupational Safety and Health, 1996; Parker et al., 1994a, 1994b; Schober et al., 1988) (see Figure 3-1 and Table 3-3). The rank ordering of these injury types varies depending on the data source. For example, studies based on emergency-department records indicate that cuts and lacerations are the leading type of injury, while studies based on workers' compensation claims for injuries resulting in lost work time and on Occupational Health and Safety Administration data from injury logs tend to report more sprains and strains (Brooks and Davis, 1996; Brooks et al., 1993; Centers for Disease Control and Prevention, 1996; Layne et al., 1994).

Although data on the extent of disability associated with these injuries are limited, the seriousness of these injuries should not be

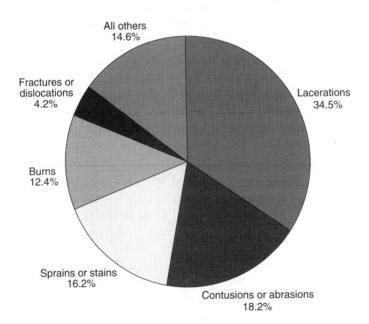

FIGURE 3-1   Work-related injures of 14- to 17-year-olds, by type of injury. SOURCE: Data from Layne et al. (1994).

TABLE 3-3 Typical Nonfatal Youth Work Injuries, for Selected
Industries

Industry	Injury	Circumstances
Restaurants	Cut fingers	Knife slips while cutting Finger contacts blade while using or cleaning power meat slicers
	Burns	Grease splatters onto worker from grill or deep fryer Hand contact with grill while cleaning Slips on a slick surface and contacts grill or fryer when trying to break fall Grease spills on worker when draining or transporting hot grease from a fryer Hot liquid or food spills on worker
	Strains	Slips on a slick surface and strains muscles trying to avoid the fall
	Bruises (contusions)	Slips on a slick surface and is bruised in fall
Grocery Stores	Cut arms or legs	Case-cutter slips while opening cardboard boxes
	Torso strains	Overexertion while lifting or moving inventory Overexertion while lifting customer bags Overexertion while retrieving carts from parking lot
Nursing Homes	Back strains	Overexertion while lifting patients

underestimated. The fact that the data come from hospital emergency rooms and workers' compensation claims indicates that the injuries were serious enough to require medical attention. Knight et al. (1995) report that 25 percent of adolescents who visit emergency rooms for work-related injuries experienced limitation in their normal activities for more than 1 week. Forty-four percent of adolescents who received workers' compensation payments in New York suffered permanent disabilities; younger teens (14- and 15-year-olds) were more likely than older teens (16- and 17-year-olds) to be permanently disabled (Belville et al., 1993). Parker et al. (1994a) found that sprains and strains were the most common causes of severe injury, with strains to the back accounting for 73 percent of all strain injuries. Back injuries were more common in smaller workers and were positively associated with the amount of weight lifted at work. Back sprains and strains made up 15 percent of all young workers' compensated injuries in Massachusetts (Brooks and Davis, 1996). Back pain is unusual among adolescents. Because a history of back pain has been identified as a risk factor for new back injuries (Mitchell et al., 1994; Venning et al., 1987), back strains among adolescent workers may have consequences for their long-term health.

It has been estimated that work-related injuries for all workers in 1993 cost $121 billion in medical care, lost productivity, and wages (National Safety Council, 1995). In 1993–1994, hospital emergency department visits by 15- to 17-year-olds for injuries identified as occurring at work resulted in medical costs of $522 million (in 1993 dollars) (H.B. Weiss et al., 1997). There is no information on the long-term human and economic burden of occupational injuries suffered by young workers. The effects of these injuries on their future health and employment status and the costs incurred by the workers, their families, employers, and society at large remain to be documented.

Work Settings and Injuries

From a prevention standpoint, information about the types of work settings and circumstances in which working children and adolescents are injured is crucial. Not surprisingly, most injuries occur in those industries in which the majority of young workers are employed. Without exception, in studies of nonfatal injuries, half of the injuries occurred among youth employed in retail trades, predominantly in restaurants and food stores (Banco et al., 1992; Belville et al., 1993; Brooks et al., 1993; Brooks and Davis, 1996; Layne et al., 1994; Miller, 1995; Schober et al., 1988). Nationally, nearly 40 percent of work-related injuries suffered by youngsters occur in restaurants, and between 8 percent and 14 percent occur in food stores. Other industries that experience relatively high numbers of such

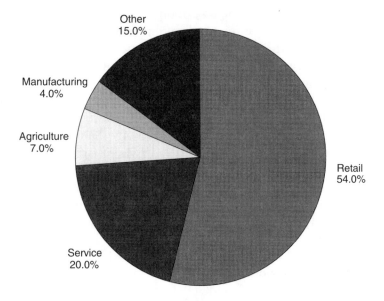

FIGURE 3-2 Work-related injuries of 14- to 17-year olds, by industry.
SOURCE: Data from Layne et al. (1994).

injuries include general merchandise stores, nursing homes, and agriculture (Centers for Disease Control and Prevention, 1996; Layne et
al., 1994); see Figure 3-2. Common occupations of youngsters who
are injured include food-preparation and food-service workers, cashiers, stock handlers, and baggers (Banco et al., 1992; Cooper and
Rothstein, 1995; Miller, 1995).

State-specific data reveal findings that are important for local
prevention efforts but are obscured in national statistics. In Alaska,
for example, laundry, cleaning, and garment services and the manu-
facture of specific food products each accounted for 16 percent to 17
percent of the injuries incurred by young workers. In Hawaii, nearly
one-fourth of the incidents resulting in injuries occurred in construction. In Vermont, hotels and motels were the most common site of
work-related injuries and illnesses (Centers for Disease Control and
Prevention, 1996).

In targeting industries for prevention activities, it is important to
consider not only those with high numbers of injuries, but also those
with high rates of injury. The rates indicate the probability or risk of
being injured at work. In a large industry that employs a lot of teens,

many may be injured, but the rate of injury may be low. By contrast, in a small but high-risk industry, the number of workers injured may be small, but the rate may be high. Limitations of data on both the number of young workers and the number of their work-related injuries pose significant challenges in calculating rates and comparing findings across studies, but injury rates reported in several state and national studies draw attention to high-risk industries, some of which are not necessarily highlighted solely by the numbers of injuries that occur in them. Layne et al. (1994) report that the retail-trade sector had not only the highest frequency of adolescent occupational injuries treated in emergency departments nationwide, but also the highest rate of such injuries. High rates of injuries have also generally been seen in the manufacturing and construction sectors (Belville et al., 1993; Brooks and Davis, 1996; Layne et al., 1994; Miller, 1995). In Washington state, 16- and 17-year-olds working in public administration had the highest rate of on-the-job injuries: Most of these youths were involved in summer job programs as trail-crew members, grounds keepers, and park maintenance workers (Miller, 1995). Banco et al. (1992) also reported high rates among young workers in public-sector jobs in Connecticut. The Massachusetts Department of Public Health (1998) reported that young workers employed in the trucking/warehousing industry had the highest injury rates. The injured workers were, for the most part, teens engaged in handling materials. Small numbers but high rates were also found among Massachusetts teens employed by temporary agencies and retail bakeries (Bowling, 1996; Massachusetts Department of Public Health, 1998).

An examination of the types of injuries, events, sources of injuries, and how these vary by industry provide information that is necessary for developing specific intervention strategies. The types of injury differ by industry. For example, lacerations and burns are the leading injuries among youth employed in restaurants (Miller, 1995), while contusions, lacerations, and sprains are the leading injuries among youth employed in service industries, such as nursing homes, recreational services, and hotels. Common events include falls on the same level, overexertion from activities like lifting, striking against objects, and contact with hot objects. Examples of commonly reported sources of injuries include case cutters (Banco et al.,

1992), hot water or oil (Miller, 1995), knives and slicers (Miller, 1995), and containers and surfaces (Schober et al., 1988).

Interviews with young workers demonstrate the prevalence of exposure to potential hazards at work. Of 562 North Carolina teens with work experience outside of farming, 36 percent reported using ladders or scaffolds at work; 31 percent reported using forklifts, tractors, or riding mowers on the job; and 27 percent reported working around very loud noises (Dunn et al., 1998). Of 300 Massachusetts high-school students who reported that they were currently working or had previously worked, 50 percent reported using cleaning chemicals at work, nearly 50 percent used case cutters, 37 percent used ladders, 19 percent used food slicers, and 13 percent used box crushers—despite the fact that child labor laws prohibit individuals under the age of 18 from operating either food slicers or box crushers. Twelve percent reported working alone at night (Bowling, 1996; unpublished tabulations, Massachusetts Department of Public Health).

FATAL INJURIES

Work-related injuries that result in death merit special attention. Each year from 1992 through 1995, approximately 70 youths younger than 18 died from injuries they received at work (Derstine 1996; Toscano and Windau, 1994). Table 3-4 summarizes findings from the major studies of work-related deaths. Estimates of the number of deaths, as well as where and how they occurred, vary from study to study. As discussed in more detail below ("Source of Surveillance Data"), there are many reasons for this variation. Most data sources rely on death certificates, but they capture only 81 percent of work-related deaths in general. For children and adolescents, the percentage may be even lower because it is less likely that the death will be recognized as work-related for them than for adults. A further difficulty in studying work-related deaths among youngsters results from the relatively small number of such deaths that occur each year. To have an adequate number of cases to analyze, researchers must aggregate data over a number of years and combine data for different ages. Differences in the years selected and the age groupings with a low base-rate phenomenon (such as children's work-related deaths) can result in fairly large differences among study findings. Of youths younger than 18, the majority of deaths

TABLE 3-4 Studies of Work-Related Deaths of Adolescents

Study	Population/Source	Sample	Job Type	Event
Castillo et al., 1994	16- and 17-year-olds/ National Traumatic Occupational Fatality Surveillance System, 1980-1987 death certificate data	670 nonmilitary deaths	16.4% agriculture, forestry, fishing 8.8% construction 8.4% services 6.3% retail trade 5.1% manufacturing 3.7% transportation, public utilities 2.1% mining 1.5% wholesale trade 0.6% other 47.2% not classified	24.2% motor vehicle related 16.9% machine related 11.9% electrocution 9.6% homicide 5.7% falls 4.6% struck by falling object 4.3% suffocation 3.7% drowning 3.0% poisoning 2.5% natural and environmental 13.6% other
Cooper and Rothstein, 1995	Under 18-years-old in Texas/Death certificates 1980-1990	125 work-related deaths, ages 6-17	23% farm 15% construction 10% mining/oil	24% motor vehicle injuries 17% machinery (usually agricultural)

Derstine, 1996	19-years-old and younger/1992-1995 Census of Fatal Occupational Injuries	720 deaths	22.1% retail 21.5% agriculture, fishing, farming 14.2% construction 12.5% services 10.3% manufacturing 8.2% public administration 11.3% other	19% homicide 18.8% motor vehicle, highway
	17-years-old and younger	269 deaths	21.9% retail 40.1% agriculture, fishing, farming 11.2% construction 10.0% services 5.9% manufacturing 2.2% public administration 8.6% other	
Dunn and Runyan, 1993	Under 20-years-old/Medical examiner's records for 1980-1989 in North Carolina	71 deaths	21% farm/forestry 20% nonfarm laborer 7% sales	51% motorized vehicles 14% homicide 11% electrocution 7% poisoning
Hayden et al., 1995	Agricultural fatalities in Minnesota, 9/1/81 to 8/31/86/Death certificates and Minnesota Newspaper Association Clipping Service	78 farm-related deaths of 19-year-olds and younger	100% agriculture	

Table continues on page 80

TABLE 3-4 Continued

Study	Population/Source	Sample	Job Type	Event
Suruda and Halperin, 1991	OSHA fatality investigations/ Integrated Management Information System and records from Michigan, California, and Washington for 1984-1987	104 deaths of 17-year-olds and younger	24% construction 21% wholesale, retail trade 15% manufacturing 15% services 15% farming	30% industrial vehicles, machines 16% electrocution 11% falls 11% asphyxiation 8% explosions 6% motor vehicle accidents 5% fire 3% drowning 10% other
Toscano and Windau, 1994	All work-related deaths in 1993/Death certificates, medical examiner records, other state and federal records (Census of Fatal Occupational Injuries)	29 deaths of under 16-year-olds		34% transportation 21% assaults 28% contact with objects 10% harmful substances
		39 deaths of 16- and 17-year-olds		38% transportation 28% assaults 21% contact with objects 8% falls

occurred among 16- and 17-year-olds, but younger workers accounted for a substantial proportion (40 percent) of those killed, and 19 percent of the victims were younger than 14. Approximately 90 percent of youths killed at work were males, which is similar to the findings for adults (Bureau of Labor Statistics, 1996; Castillo and Malit, 1997; Castillo et al., 1994; Cooper and Rothstein, 1995; Derstine, 1996; Dunn and Runyan, 1993).

In 1992-1995, employment in agriculture accounted for the largest proportion (40 percent) of youngsters' work-related fatalities; more than half of these children worked on family farms (Derstine, 1996). Among youth under the age of 16, employment in family agricultural businesses accounted for 71 percent of fatalities in agriculture. Among 16- to 17-year-olds, deaths occurred somewhat more frequently in retail trades (28 percent of the work-related deaths in this age group) than in agriculture (26 percent). Deaths in the construction industry were also relatively frequent among the older adolescents, accounting for 15 percent of work-related deaths. Figure 3-3 shows work-related deaths, by industry, for workers 17 and younger.

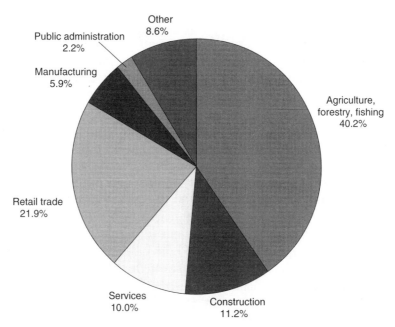

FIGURE 3-3 Work-related deaths of children 17 and younger, by industry. SOURCE: Data from Derstine (1996).

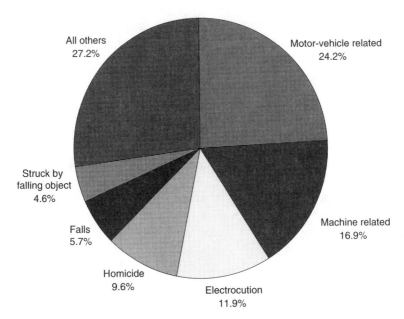

FIGURE 3-4 Causes of work-related deaths of 16- and 17-year-olds.
SOURCE: Data from Castillo et al. (1994).

The leading causes of fatal occupational injuries among youths are motor-vehicle-related events, homicides, machine-related events, and electrocutions (Belville et al., 1993; Castillo and Malit, 1997; Castillo et al., 1994; Cooper and Rothstein, 1995; Derstine, 1996; Dunn and Runyan, 1993; Suruda and Halperin, 1991); see Figure 3-4. Motor-vehicle-related events are the leading causes of work-related deaths for males; for females, it is homicides (Castillo and Malit, 1997; Derstine, 1996). Although federal law prohibits workers under the age of 18 from driving for work, except for incidental or occasional driving, one-third of the motor-vehicle-related deaths involve youths driving motor vehicles at work (Castillo and Malit, 1997; Castillo et al., 1994). Findings for workers of all ages indicate that the majority of work-related homicides are associated with robberies in retail trades (National Institute for Occupational Safety and Health, 1996). Firearms were used in 21 of the 24 homicides of workers between the ages of 16 and 17 between 1990 and 1992 (Castillo and Malit, 1997). Tractors and forklifts account for most of the machine-related deaths of young workers (Castillo and Malit,

1997; Castillo et al., 1994; Dunn and Runyan, 1993; Suruda and Halperin, 1991).

NIOSH reports that for the 3-year period from 1990 through 1992, the rate of fatal occupational injury among 16- to 17-year-olds was 3.51 per 100,000 full-time-equivalent workers (Castillo and Malit, 1997). This rate is only slightly lower than that for older workers (3.87 per 100,000 full-time equivalent workers age 20-24, 3.95 for ages 25-34, 3.93 for ages 35-44, and 4.56 for ages 45-54), which is cause for concern inasmuch as federal and state labor laws prohibit youngsters from working in the most hazardous jobs. Although violations of these laws are common, employment data suggest that, in general, young people are less likely than adults to work in especially hazardous jobs. Given this pattern, children and adolescents may actually be at higher risk of fatal injury than adults in similar work.

EXPOSURES TO POTENTIAL HEALTH HAZARDS

Although recent research has contributed to understanding work-related injuries suffered by young people, little is known about the extent to which they incur illnesses from exposures to health hazards—such as toxic chemicals, vibration, noise, and temperature extremes—in the workplace. However, the limited surveys of exposures that are available, plus case reports of acute poisonings, suggest that acute illnesses do occur and do result in the need for medical care. By combining data on the types of jobs and tasks in which young people engage with information from the research on occupational medicine on job-specific exposures for adults, it seems likely that young workers are exposed to a wide variety of health hazards.

Exposures to such hazards may result in immediate illnesses or in illnesses that are not manifest until years after the exposure. Workers' compensation data and employers' illness and injury logs include information about work-related illnesses, but it is well recognized that illnesses are undercounted in these data systems (National Research Council, 1987). Illnesses captured by these systems tend to be those with short latencies and those that have the most visible acute effects. Because the systemic effects of exposures to some chemicals may mimic diseases, their causes may go unrecognized. Pesticide-related illness, for example, may be difficult to distinguish from the flu. Furthermore, the exclusion of agriculture from many of the existing systems for gathering data results in significant under-counting of exposures.

Many chronic diseases that are related to work have long latency periods between the first exposure to the hazards and the onset of the disease, and they may also have causes other than hazards in the workplace. As a result, chronic occupational diseases frequently go unrecognized as work-related—for adults as well as youngsters. They certainly are not seen in young workers, either because they do not occur or because they will not be manifest until well into adulthood. Therefore, to address occupational health problems that may affect young people, it is essential to document the nature and extent of their exposures to health hazards in the workplace.

A number of hazardous substances or conditions at work could contribute to subsequent illnesses for young workers. Audiometric testing of vocational agricultural students in Wisconsin found that 57 percent of the students who lived and worked on farms had noise-induced hearing loss, a condition found in only 33 percent of the students who had little or no farm experience (Broste et al., 1989). To protect young people's health and safety, the Fair Labor Standards Act prohibits their working with hazardous agricultural chemicals. Yet in a survey of North Carolina teens, 38 percent of those who worked on farms reported using pesticides or other farm chemicals (Schulman et al., 1997). Similarly, a 1989 survey of migrant farmworkers under the age of 18 found that 10 percent had prepared or applied pesticides. Aside from gloves, no protective equipment was used, and the gloves were made of cloth and therefore inadequate as protection. More than 40 percent had worked in fields still wet with pesticides, in violation of regulations governing the time that must elapse between spraying and reentry by workers, and 40 percent had been sprayed while working in the fields, either directly by crop-dusting planes or indirectly by chemicals drifting from planes or tractors (Pollack et al., 1990). A recent Massachusetts survey, in which an industrial hygienist observed youth working in paid jobs and vocational shops, found young workers exposed to a wide range of potential hazards, including lead and asthma-causing agents in construction, ergonomic stressors in health-care settings, and reproductive hazards in a print shop.[2]

The paradigm used to establish exposure limits for many health

---

[2]Personal communication, E. Morse, Massachusetts Department of Public Health.

hazards assumes an 8-hour working day and a 40-hour working week over a lifetime of working. Because young people typically work part time, often in short-term jobs, many of their exposures to health hazards do not exceed existing standards. The short-term nature of their exposures may preclude or mitigate the potential long-term health effects, but there are challenging scientific questions about whether young people are more susceptible than adults, about how an individual's age at the time of first exposure affects the severity of any health consequences, and about the effects of multiple exposures over a working lifetime. There are also important policy considerations about what risks are acceptable for working children and adolescents.

DO CHILDREN AND ADOLESCENTS HAVE UNIQUE RISKS AT WORK?

It seems clear that work may pose substantial safety risks for young workers, and there is evidence of potential health risks as well. The overall injury rates suggest that young workers may be at greater risk than adults. Identification of the factors that place children and adolescents at risk in the workplace is essential for developing effective preventive efforts. These factors include characteristics of the work, the work environment, and the interaction between them and young workers.

This section examines factors that raise special concerns about working youth. It begins with a discussion of the concentration of young workers in certain types of work environments and addresses the issues of inadequate health and safety training, inadequate supervision, and inappropriate or illegal job assignments. The section then turns to the children and adolescents themselves and discusses the characteristics that may increase their risk of work-related injury or illness: inexperience, the need to balance school and work, fatigue, and developmental factors.

The Work: Types of Jobs

Many of the industries that employ large numbers of children and adolescents—grocery stores, hospitals and nursing homes, and agriculture—have higher-than-average injury rates for workers of all ages. Children and adolescents face the same workplace hazards faced by adults in similar occupations, ranging from hot grease, large machinery, and unstable ladders to pesticides and other toxic chemicals.

Young workers are congregated in jobs that are characterized by the absence of opportunities for significant promotion within the firm, high turnover, little on-the-job training, limited scope for worker discretion or application of skill, heightened job insecurity, wide variation and uncertainty in hours, low pay, and few benefits (Doeringer and Piore, 1971; Osterman, 1982, 1988; Tilly, 1991, 1996). Jobs with these characteristics are, in general, more danger-ous than those without them. For example, one study found the incidence of occupational injuries and illnesses positively associated with authoritarian work structures and negatively associated with on-the-job training, promotion opportunity, job security, and wages (Robinson, 1988). Using data from the Ontario workers' compensa-tion system, a third study linked high lost-work-time frequency rates to high rates of turnover, low amounts of worker autonomy, and low "long-term career commitment from employees" (Shannon et al., 1996). Finally, Robinson (1991) found that the risk of occupa-tional injury is weakly correlated with the absence of promotion opportunity, moderately correlated with lack of control over work, and strongly correlated with the lack of on-the-job training and job security.

Jobs with the above characteristics are likely to be in small busi-nesses. Researchers have found a negative relationship between a firm's size and its employees' risk of injury or death (Hunting and Weeks, 1993; Mendeloff and Kagey, 1990). There are many reasons that the safety records of small companies could be expected to be worse than those of large companies: Small firms tend to have high turnover, which means more inexperienced workers (Hunting and Weeks, 1993); they are more exposed to market pressure, which may lead them to cut corners on safety; and they have fewer resources to fall back on for improving their safety performance. NIOSH's 1988 National Occupational Exposure Survey, for instance, found that establishments with fewer than 100 workers took significantly fewer steps—such as providing training, conducting inspections, and using safety professionals—to ensure the safety of employees (National Institute for Occupational Safety and Health, 1988).

The Work Environment:
Health and Safety Training

Health and safety training for workers is considered an essential component of comprehensive occupational health-and-safety programs (Keyserling, 1995; U.S. Office of Technology Assessment, 1985). In fact, more than 100 standards promulgated by the Occupational Safety and Health Administration explicitly require employers to train employees in the safety and health aspects of their jobs (U.S. Department of Labor, 1992). Although rigorous evaluations of training programs are limited, studies of adult workers suggest that safety training may reduce injuries and acute illness among young or inexperienced workers (Jensen and Sinkule, 1988; Perkins, 1995; Van Zelst, 1954). It is reasonable to assume that lack of training could affect working children and adolescents, who are by definition inexperienced, to a greater extent than adults. Recent, consistent evidence shows that young workers do not receive adequate health and safety training at work. General surveys of working youth find that about half of the young workers surveyed report no such training (Bowling et al., 1998; Runyan et al., 1997). Of 180 students interviewed in California, few had received any information about job safety from anyone at their workplaces or schools (Bush and Baker, 1994).

When I worked at [fast food chain] I thought the grill was hazardous. . . . I didn't receive any training, I was just thrown into it because someone didn't show up for work that day.

High school student in focus group
Massachusetts Department of Public Health

Knight et al. (1995) surveyed 146 14- to 16-year-olds who were treated in hospital emergency rooms for occupational injuries: 54 percent of the respondents reported no safety training at all. These youngsters were much more likely to have serious injuries—involving eight or more days of restricted activity—than were those who had received such training. The Massachusetts Department of Public Health (1998) reports that only 50 percent of 300 teens injured at work indicated they had received health and safety training on the job. The few studies of the effects of training on injuries among adolescents have examined health and safety training, but they have not examined the importance of job-skills training. In adult workers, the incidence of work-related injuries and illnesses has been found to be negatively associated with on-the-job training (Robinson, 1988, 1991). Workers who report no on-the-job training are 1.5 to 2.5 times as likely as other workers to have hazardous occupations (Robinson, 1991). It would be interesting to examine whether the role of jobs-skills training is different from or complementary to that of health and safety training in reducing injuries among young workers.

The Work Environment:
Inappropriate Assignments and Structure

Work-related injuries and illnesses may also occur because children and adolescents are asked to or attempt to perform tasks for which they are developmentally not ready (see discussion of physiological development below). Very little research has been done on defining developmentally appropriate job tasks, which leaves employees to rely on Hazardous Orders, issued under the Fair Labor Standards Act, that prohibit young people from performing certain tasks (see Chapter 6). Studies indicate that working in legally prohibited occupations is a contributing factor to teens being injured or killed at work. For example, Knight et al. (1995) found that 19 percent of youth with work-related injuries who were treated in emergency departments appeared to have been injured in jobs declared to be hazardous or typically prohibited for their age by federal laws governing child labor. Of 104 deaths of children and adolescents investigated by the Occupational Safety and Health Administration from 1984 through 1987, 41 percent involved youths engaged in work prohibited by federal child labor laws (Suruda and Halperin, 1991). However, many youths are injured or killed while doing legally allowed tasks.

The structure of some work settings may also be inappropriate for teens. Greenberger and Steinberg (1986) noted a lack of adult supervision of young people on the job: The average young worker spent only 12 percent of his or her time in the presence of a supervisor. Inadequate supervision and certain aspects of work schedules have been associated with injuries on the job. Knight et al. (1995)

found that 80 percent of work-related injuries suffered by adolescents occurred when no supervisor was present. Some work schedules, such as those involving long or unusually late or early hours, may contribute to fatigue in adolescents, and fatigue is associated with an increased likelihood of injury (Miller, 1995; Rosa, 1995). Working alone or late at night may also be a risk factor for work-related assaults associated with robberies (National Institute for Occupational Safety and Health, 1996).

On one job, we were using these power saws. I knew how to use it, but if I ever got cut .... I mean I wasn't supposed to be doing it since I was only 15.

High school student
Youth panel for the committee

Another issue that is just beginning to be recognized is the assignment of youths to jobs other than the ones they were hired to perform. Davis and Frank (1997) reported a wide discrepancy between job titles and "tasks ever done" by the employees who held the jobs. For example, a cashier in a fast-food restaurant may also regularly be asked to cook or clean; see Table 3-5. Anecdotal reports indicate that when there is a shortage of staff, young workers are often assigned to fill in on a variety of tasks for which they have had no preparation. Even if all the tasks are age-appropriate and performing them provides opportunities to explore new responsibilities, the assignment of a multiplicity of tasks has important implications for job-skills training and health and safety training.

The Workers: Characteristics of Children and Adolescents

Injury-control experts understand that prevention of workplace injuries requires that primary attention be focused on the elimination of hazards. At the same time, it is important to examine factors specific to young workers that may place them at risk, which include inexperience, lack of physical or emotional maturity, and the need to balance school and work. The fact that developmental characteristics may play a role in young workers' injury rates in no way implies that children and adolescents are to blame for their own injuries.

TABLE 3-5 Job Titles, Tasks Ever Done, Equipment Ever Used, in percent

Job Title	%	Tasks Ever Done	%	Equipment Ever Used	%
Cashier	29	Cashier	50	Case cutter	47
Sales Clerk	10	Cleaning	50	Ladder	37
Office Worker	10	Stock shelves	43	Food slicer	19
Work with kids	7	Cook	18	Box crusher	13
Stock shelves	6	Shovel	15	Fat fryer	12
Cook	6	Load trucks	13	Motor vehicle	10
Cleaners	6	Landscape work	10	Power tools	10
Dietary Aide	3	Deliver food by car	4	Forklift	6

NOTE: Data are for students currently working or who had worked in the past.

SOURCE: Data from Massachusetts Department of Public Health and University of North Carolina Injury Prevention Research Center.

Instead, these characteristics must be taken into account so that work environments can be structured to minimize the risks to which young people are exposed.

Experience

Inexperience is not unique to children and adolescents, but it is an inescapable characteristic of young workers. Studies of occupational injuries provide no clear-cut answers about the relative influences of inexperience and an individual worker's personal characteristics (such as age) on the occurrence of hazardous incidents, but a number of studies have found a relationship between injury rates and adult workers' ages. Band and Pismire (1984) reviewed coal-mining injuries and found that younger adult workers had much higher rates of disabling injuries than did older workers. Jensen and Sinkule (1988) report that the risk of amputation while operating a power press is associated with age: The youngest press operators were at the greatest risk of amputation. In a study of factory workers, Van Zelst (1954) found that accident rates were highest in the first 5 months on a new job for all adult workers, but that younger workers consistently had accident rates above those of older workers. Based on workers' compensation data from nine states, Mitchell (1988) found higher rates of injury among workers under 25 years of age, although the more serious injuries were among older workers. LaFlamme et al. (1996) found similar results among Swedish miners.

In an examination of factors related to injury rates among petroleum-drilling workers, Mueller et al. (1987) found that age, rate of job changes, and rate of rig transfers each had independent effects on injury rates. Length of time on the job had little effect when the influence of age was statistically excluded from the analysis. The highest injury rates were observed among workers under the age of 25 when another risk factor, such as inexperience, job change, or rig transfer, was present. In contrast, Leigh (1986) studied a subset of a nationally representative sample of adult employees and concluded that job characteristics, including length of time on the job, were better predictors of hazardous incidents than were personal characteristics, including age. Age was only predictive when job characteristics were not taken into account.

None of these studies looked at children or adolescents. Because children and adolescents are, by definition, young, age most likely plays a role in their high rates of work-related injury. Findings like those of Mueller and colleagues (1987) suggest that it may be the interaction of age with job stressors, such as inexperience, that result in higher rates of injury for children and adolescents than for adults. The ways in which the relationship between injury rates and age, experience, and hazard exposure for children and adolescents differs from that of adults remains to be examined.

Developmental Factors

Adolescence is a unique period, marked by the second most rapid period of growth in an individual's life (infancy is first). Three aspects of development occur during adolescence—physical, cognitive, and emotional growth—each of which may affect young workers.

The issue central to concerns about adolescents' working and their potential physical vulnerabilities is whether anatomic and physiologic processes are mature in adolescence, or whether they are still developing. Considerable scientific study has been devoted to the issues of chemical exposures, toxicology, pharmacology, and metabolism among infants and young children. However, there are very few scientific data on these issues for the adolescent population, which is the group that encompasses most American young workers. Thus, one is left with minimal specifically relevant science and a great need for further research on these issues, and knowledge about adolescent growth, development, anatomy, and physiology.

The major points resulting from a review of the relevant literature are as follows:

• Some basic science literature documents small increments in growth in some body systems during adolescence; they include renal excretion and the size of alveoli in the pulmonary system.

• Pharmacokinetic studies and clinical experience make it apparent that, despite these increments in growth, adolescent body systems are similar to adult systems in most respects, and therefore, no inherent special vulnerability can be attributed to those systems. Exceptions to this include the endocrine system, which may be especially vulnerable during adolescence; the musculoskeletal system, which has special vulnerabilities in both childhood and adolescence as compared with adulthood; and the brain, in which altered learning capacity may have more serious implications for a teen who still has much to learn, than for an adult, who has more fully completed the task of learning the essentials facts of life.

• The fact that rapid cell growth occurs during adolescence has raised concerns that young workers may be particularly vulnerable to potential carcinogens, and to substances associated with diseases of long latency. There are no data at present to inform either of these concerns beyond the hypothetical.

• Because adolescents are of childbearing age, exposures to occupational hazards carry the same concerns about harm to reproductive functioning as they do for adults in the workplace.

With the exceptions noted above, the exposure to occupational chemicals appears to carry the same risks for adolescents as for adults. Any small differences in growth, anatomy, and physiology appear to have virtually no clinical relevance. Thus, the essential issue becomes how to minimize the exposure to chemicals that would be hazardous for any worker.

Musculoskeletal Development and Ergonomic Factors Approximately 15 to 20 percent of an individual's height is acquired between the ages of 10 and 20 years; about half of that growth occurs during a 2-year period that includes the phase of most rapid growth, the peak height velocity (Marks and Cohen, 1978), which girls reach at an average of 12 years of age and boys reach at an average of 14 years of age (Marshall and Tanner, 1969, 1970). During this period of rapid growth, adolescents are at particularly high risk of injury to ligaments and to bone growth plates (epiphyses)[3] (Nelson, 1992; Pendergrast and Strong, 1992). Because the body grows in a disproportionate pattern, with bone growth preceding muscle, tendon, and ligament growth, some joints may experience limited ranges of motion (Nelson, 1992), and injuries that would result in torn ligaments in adults may produce fractures of the growth plates in adolescents (Macy, 1992). Injuries to growth plates can result in various osteochondroses (degeneration and abnormal regrowth of the epiphyses), some of which may have significant long-term orthopedic consequences, including limbs of unequal length (Garrick, 1992).

Also of concern are other musculoskeletal disorders that have been found to be work-related among adults. There is strong evidence that various disorders of the neck, elbow, hand and wrist, and back are related to factors in the workplace (Bernard, 1997). In particular, carpal tunnel syndrome, tendinitis of the hand and wrist, and various elbow problems are related to a combination of repetitive motion, force, or posture. Although little research has focused specifically on adolescents, adolescents are commonly employed in a number of settings where work-related risk factors, such as awkward postures, high force, and repetitive motions, can add to similar stresses inherent in school and leisure activities, resulting in musculoskeletal disorders. Back strains represent a fairly high proportion of the work-related strains that cause adolescents to experience pain

---

[3]Growth in the long bones, such as those of the arms and legs, occurs at the ends of the bones in what is known as an epiphysis, or growth center. This area is separated from the main bone by cartilage until growth is completed in late adolescence or early adulthood, when the area becomes completely ossified and joins with the main bone.

and to miss work (Parker et al., 1994a). Inasmuch as back pain is rare among adolescents, and history of back pain has been identified as a risk factor for new back injuries (Mitchell et al., 1994; Venning et al., 1987), the long-term consequences of back strains among adolescent workers are of substantial concern.

Besides being vulnerable because of their rapid growth, children and adolescents may be at risk because of mismatches between their size and the dimension of equipment or machinery designed for adults. For example, the Consumer Product Safety Commission found that young, short, and light-weight operators of ride-on mowers were more likely than others to be injured (unpublished 1993 Consumer Product Safety Commission data, as cited in National Institute for Occupational Safety and Health, 1997). Specifically, operators were at increased risk of injury if their height was less than 60 inches, weight was less than 125 pounds, or their age was less than 15. Growth charts suggest that about half of all 15-year-olds weigh less than 125 pounds. The association of small body size with injuries from ride-on mowers raises concerns about the operation of other machinery by children and young teens.

Development of the Endocrine System   Puberty is central to the normal development that occurs in adolescence. The biological systems that lead to reproductive capacity are initiated and maintained by a complex system of hormones in the brain and reproductive organs. Although the time of onset and the speed with which each stage occurs vary widely among individuals, the events that mark puberty for both girls and boys occur in a predictable sequence. Although there are no data to demonstrate adverse effects on normal hormonal development, there are concerns that any chemical exposures that alter the delicate balance of these hormones and their feedback loops could have devastating effects, given the importance of the endocrine system during adolescence.

Cognitive and Behavioral Development   A number of changes occur in cognitive abilities as an individual moves from childhood through adolescence and into adulthood. In general, from early adolescence on, "thinking tends to involve abstract rather than merely concrete representation; to become multidimensional rather than limited to a single issue; to become relative rather than absolute in the conception of knowledge; and to become self-reflective and self aware" (Keating, 1990:64). Whereas younger children can focus on only one topic or problem at a time, adolescents are able to keep several dimensions in mind at once. This growth may be because of increased memory capacity, increased familiarity with a range of content knowledge, the automatization of basic processes, or some combination of these factors (Case, 1985).

Pertinent to the health and safety of young people at work is their ability to recognize and assess potential risks and to make decisions about them. The ability to generate options, to look at a situation from a variety of perspectives, to anticipate consequences, and to evaluate the credibility of sources increases throughout adolescence, with transitional periods falling at about 11 to 12 years, and again at 15 to 16 years (Mann et al., 1989). By midadolescence, most youngsters make decisions in ways similar to adults (Keating, 1990). It should be remembered, however, that adults are not perfect: Their decision making is subject to a number of well-studied biases and distortions (Fischhoff et al., 1981; Tversky and Kahneman, 1974, 1981). Research also consistently finds that reasoning is not separable from knowledge about content (Chi et al., 1982; Glaser, 1984; Resnick, 1986). Thus, adolescents may need specific information about the tasks they are asked to perform, in order to make reasoned decisions about safety. However, *possessing* knowledge and skills does not ensure their use in real situations; a number of influences besides decision-making skills and knowledge affect the actions of adolescents.

Focus group research with adolescents and interviews with teens injured at work suggest that some adolescents may undertake tasks on the job to demonstrate their responsibility and independence (Massachusetts Department of Public Health, 1996). Some indicated that they perform tasks they know to be dangerous or in violation of child labor laws out of fear of losing their jobs. Unfortunately, these may be tasks for which they are not developmentally ready.

Sleep Needs of Adolescents   As is now widely recognized, adolescents may actually need as much or more sleep as younger children. Sleep laboratory research has found that the amount of sleep needed by adolescents does not decrease significantly between ages 10 and 18, but remains at about 9.5 hours per night (Carskadon, 1990, 1997; Carskadon et al., 1980). Even though the total amount of sleep needed remains constant throughout adolescence, a change in the physiological circadian rhythms seems to occur (Carskadon et al., 1993). There appears to be a shift, beginning in mid-adolescence (Tanner Stage 3),[4] to a later timing of melatonin secretion, which is related to sleep onset. In addition, some new work suggests that adolescents may also have increased sensitivity to evening light, which would make them more likely to stay awake later (Carskadon, 1997; Carskadon et al., 1997). This pattern is accompanied by a tendency for mid-afternoon sleepiness, which occurs even in those youngsters who get adequate sleep at night, but it is exacerbated in those who get fewer hours of sleep.

Along with these biological changes, social and environmental factors affect the times at which adolescents go to bed and get up, which results in their getting less sleep than they may actually need. Parental regulation of bedtime decreases as children reach adolescence. More than half of 10-year-olds report that their parents set their bedtimes on school-nights; by age 13, only 19 percent report parental control of school-night bedtimes (Anders et al., 1978; Billiard et al., 1987; Petta et al., 1984). Bedtimes get later and later as youngsters age. By age 12, more than 70 percent of youngsters report that they no longer wake up spontaneously in the morning, but must rely on an alarm or parental awakening, which may indicate insufficient sleep.

Although adolescents' bedtimes get later with age, students in most school districts must start their schooldays earlier with age. This results in teens averaging about 7 hours of sleep on school nights, about 2 hours less than they need. Some school districts are experimenting with starting high school an hour later, at 8:30 a.m. Preliminary results suggest that students are more alert, exhibit fewer behavior problems, and earn better grades (R. Weiss, 1997) with a later starting time.

Having a job during the school week may decrease the amount of sleep an adolescent gets. Students who work more than 20 hours per week stay up later and sleep fewer hours per night than do those

---

[4]Tanner Stages rate maturation and secondary sex characteristics of adolescents. Tanner Stage 1 refers to prepubescent; at Tanner Stage 2, secondary sex characteristics are beginning to be manifest; at Tanner Stage 3, there are significant manifestations of secondary sex characteristics; Tanner Stage 5 refers to the fully mature adolescent.

who work fewer hours or not at all. Students who work more than 20 hours per week report more symptoms of daytime sleepiness, including tendencies to arrive at school late because of oversleeping and to have difficulty staying awake in school (Carskadon, 1990). They also report a higher use of stimulants, such as caffeine and cigarettes, possibly as an attempt to increase alertness.

Excessive sleepiness is associated with performance lapses and failures, which can interfere with learning (Carskadon, 1990). It is also possible that lapses in performance because of sleepiness play a role in the injury rates of adolescents. There is evidence that insufficient sleep is associated with moodiness, irritability, and difficulty in modulating impulses and emotions (Carskadon et al., 1989; Dahl, 1996; Pilcher and Huffcutt, 1996). An added risk arises from the tendency for sleepiness to increase the sedative effects of alcohol (Lumley et al., 1987; Roehrs et al., 1986; Zwyghuizen-Doorenbos et al., 1988). This effect may be particularly dangerous for adolescents who are experimenting with alcohol and other risky behaviors, as their sleepiness may increase their vulnerability.

SOURCES OF SURVEILLANCE DATA

Information about where, how, and under what circumstances young workers are injured or made ill is essential to both developing and evaluating prevention strategies. Surveillance systems can provide this information. Public health surveillance is generally defined as an ongoing systematic collection, analysis, and interpretation of health data that is essential to the planning, implementation, and evaluation of public health practice. Public health surveillance entails not only collecting data, but also using the data to take preventive action. In a surveillance system, the data collectors are responsible for providing information to those who set policy and implement programs and for following up to see how the data have been used.

A 1987 National Research Council report, *Counting Injuries and Illnesses in the Workplace,* concluded that the surveillance of occupational injuries and illnesses in the United States was inadequate; the report called for a number of changes. Since that time, federal and state agencies have substantially improved data collection and surveillance. Although no comprehensive national surveillance system for work-related injuries has been established and work-related illnesses remain undercounted, several ongoing occupational-injury surveillance efforts can be used to monitor injuries among young workers. These efforts are described in the rest of this section. Different systems monitor nonfatal and fatal work-related injuries.

Nonfatal Work-Related Injuries

Survey of Occupational Injuries and Illnesses

The official source of statistics on nonfatal work-related injuries and illnesses in the United States is the Annual Survey of Occupational Injuries and Illnesses (SOII) of the Bureau of Labor Statistics (BLS). Information is collected through an annual survey mailed to a stratified random sample of employers in private industry. Excluded from the sample are self-employed individuals; farmers and other employers with fewer than 11 employees; private households; and federal, state, and local government agencies. Employers who receive the survey are asked for information on all job-related injuries and illnesses for which they were required to maintain records by the Occupational Safety and Health Act. This requirement applies to any injury that results in death, loss of consciousness, restricted work activity, transfer to another job, or medical treatment beyond simple first aid (see 29 U.S.C. §657). There has long been a concern about the accuracy of the records kept by employers (for a full discussion of problems with the SOII, see National Research Council, 1987). The concern over the validity of the record-keeping, and thus the information submitted to BLS, increased in 1981, when the Occupational Safety and Health Administration exempted industries with below-average injury rates from its general-schedule inspections.

A redesigned survey was fully implemented in 1992. The SOII now includes the following information on nonfatal incidents involving days away from work: the occupations and demographics (including age and sex) of workers who sustain injuries and illnesses, the nature of the injuries or illnesses and how they occurred, and the amount of time workers were away from work (Bureau of Labor Statistics, 1997a). In 1993 the survey documented an estimated 21,620 injuries and illnesses involving days away from work among employees under the age of 18 (Centers for Disease Control and Prevention, 1996). Older adolescents accounted for almost all of the injuries and illnesses; only 4 percent of the reported injuries and illnesses were to youngsters under the age of 16. Males were somewhat more likely than females to be injured, accounting for 59 percent of reported injuries and illnesses.

Although the revised survey is an important source of information about young people's work-related injuries, it has a number of limitations. For several reasons, the survey's estimates may undercount incidents involving working children and adolescents. Because of the industries that are excluded from the survey, it has been estimated to miss at least 11 percent of working children and adolescents under the age of 18 (Centers for Disease Control and Prevention, 1996). Because most young people work only part-time, injuries or illnesses that might have prevented them from working on days they were not scheduled to work would not be counted, even though those injuries might have resulted in their missing school. For both children and adults, the survey is believed to undercount illnesses, especially long-latency illnesses, such as those caused by exposure to carcinogens (Bureau of Labor Statistics, 1997a).

Another limitation in using data from the SOII to assess the injuries suffered by working children and adolescents is that injury rates based on the survey's data are routinely computed using the information on hours of employment that is provided by the employers participating in the survey. This information is not broken down by age groups, which means that injury rates by age are not available. Also, data on the number of injuries suffered by young workers are aggregated with the data for adult workers in standard SOII reports, which makes them an inadequate source of information about the health and safety of working children and adolescents.

National Electronic Injury Surveillance System

The National Electronic Injury Surveillance System (NEISS), maintained by the Consumer Product Safety Commission (CPSC), collects information on product-related injuries from a national probability sample of 91 hospital emergency departments. The NEISS covers not only injuries sustained by individuals who are engaging in paid work, but also injuries suffered by those performing volunteer work for organized groups. Beginning in July 1992, NIOSH collaborated with CPSC to have this system collect information on work-related injuries to youngsters aged 14 through 17.

Based on an analysis of data from the NEISS, Layne et al. (1994) estimated that 64,100 adolescents aged 14 to 17 were treated in emergency rooms for work-related illnesses in 1992. Eating and drinking establishments (38 percent), followed by grocery stores (7.8 percent), accounted for the greatest number of injuries. Lacerations were the type of injury (34 percent) most likely to be seen in the emergency departments, followed by contusions and abrasions (18 percent), and sprains and strains (16 percent) (see Table 3.2, above, for more details).

One limitation of NEISS is that it covers only injuries treated in hospital emergency departments, which comprise only an estimated one-third of all work-related injuries (Ries, 1978; Unpublished tabulations, 1988 National Health Interview Survey, Occupational Supplement, NIOSH). Furthermore, for children and adolescents, emergency department personnel may not think to ask about the work-relatedness of an injury or may not note work-relatedness in the medical records. Comparing NEISS data to those from other systems is also difficult because NEISS uses unique coding systems and does not include the standard medical external-cause-of-injury coding (E-codes). Also, although the participating emergency departments are generally representative of emergency departments throughout the country, the youth populations served by the hospitals are not necessarily representative of the national population of young workers.

In spite of its limitations, NEISS data showed more than three times as many work-related injuries to adolescents for 1992 than were reported by employers in the 1993 SOII. Some of the injuries found by NEISS may not have met OSHA's reporting requirements, but that seems unlikely to account for all the differences. In fact, follow-up interviews with youngsters identified by the system found that 68 percent of them experienced limitations in their normal activities (including school, work, and play) for at least one day (Knight et al., 1995)—which requires reporting by employers.

National Hospital Ambulatory Medical Care Survey

Beginning in December 1991, the National Center for Health Statistics began collecting information annually on emergency department and outpatient department visits from a nationally representative sample of hospitals, through its National Hospital Ambulatory Medical Care Survey (NHAMCS). The survey collects information on patients' symptoms and demographic characteristics, diagnoses, services provided, drugs prescribed, referral status, and expected payment source. Although not limited to visits for injuries, NHAMCS data includes information on work-related injuries. The injuries are coded using the standard E-codes, allowing this data to be compared to those from other sources.

Weiss et al. (1997) used NHAMCS data to study the incidence, characteristics, and payments of child and adolescent emergency department visits by narrow age groupings. No work-related injuries were recorded for youngsters under the age of 15 in the 1993-1994 survey. For adolescents aged 15 to 17 years, 103,000 visits were for injuries identified as work-related, more injuries than found by either SOII or NEISS data. Work-related injuries represented 5 percent of the emergency department visits for injuries by this age group. This may be a conservative estimate as place of injury was unspecified for 19 percent of the injuries.

State-Based Surveillance Systems

State-based surveillance activities provide important opportunities to link data collection efforts with active intervention in the workplace and community and to identify local concerns that may be obscured in national efforts. The Massachusetts Department of Public Health, for example, has been working since 1992, with funding provided by NIOSH, to establish a model state-based surveillance system for work-related injuries to youth. Recognizing that no single data source captures the full extent of the problem, the department uses several data sources to identify cases. New state regulations require physicians and hospitals to report to the department all cases of young people being injured at work. These reports, together with data from the workers' compensation system, the Census of Fatal Occupational Injuries, and the Fatality Assessment and Control Evaluation program, are used to identify cases. Some of the injured youngsters are interviewed to obtain additional information, and their cases may be referred to other agencies for workplace follow-up. Summary data are used to target a variety of broad-based intervention efforts, ranging from a community-based education program to inform parents, teens, educators, and employers about the health and safety concerns of young workers to initiatives to update the state's child labor laws.

State-level data on the extent of work by young people and on work-related injuries could be helpful in targeting inspections and studying injury rates. Many states oversee health and safety inspections of workplaces, but do not have the resources to mount a surveillance system, so they need better information to target those inspections.

Other Data Sources

Information from workers' compensation reports and claims has been used to analyze injuries among workers under the age of 18 in several states, including California (Bush and Baker, 1994), Connecticut (Banco et al., 1992), Massachusetts (Brooks and Davis, 1996), Minnesota (Heinzman et al., 1993; Parker et al., 1994a), New York (Belville et al., 1993), Texas (Cooper and Rothstein, 1995), and Washington (Heyer et al., 1992; Miller, 1995). A study in Utah looked at work-related burns, using both data from a hospital burn center and the State Insurance Fund's industrial records (Hayes-Lundy et al., 1991). Emergency-department data in Massachusetts (Brooks et al., 1993), other medical records in Wisconsin (Stueland et al., 1996), and survey methodology in Minnesota (Parker et al., 1994b) have also been utilized in studying injuries of young workers (see Table 3-2, above).

The drawbacks to emergency department data have already been noted. Workers' compensation records also have some drawbacks. In no state are all employees covered; small-business employees, farm laborers, domestic servants, and casual employees are frequently excluded from workers' compensation. The self-employed are also excluded, and children working informally for family businesses are unlikely to be covered. The number of lost workdays required to qualify for workers' compensation payments differs by state, so comparisons of injuries across states are difficult. In addition, in many states, claims for medical treatment alone are not included in the computerized datasets, leaving only claims for lost worktime (indemnity claims) available for analysis. This exclusion may eliminate a large proportion of the cases. Between 1988 and 1991, for example, 76 percent of the claims for injuries to children and adolescents in Washington state were claims for medical benefits only (Miller, 1995). There is also evidence that workers' compensation claims are less likely to be filed for injuries to adolescents than for injuries to adults (Brooks and Davis, 1996; Fingar et al., 1992).

Fatal Work-Related Injuries

There are a number of sources from which information on work-related deaths among children and adolescents can be garnered. State workers' compensation records, death certificates, medical examiner's records, federal and state safety-inspection records, and newspaper clippings are among those commonly examined. A number of federal systems draw on many of these records for their information. These datasets are collected for different purposes and from different sources, so each yields different estimates of the number of work-related fatalities. Each of the datasets also contains slightly different information and has its own advantages and drawbacks for understanding fatal injuries among youngsters under the age of 18. The Census of Fatal Occupational Injuries, an important recent initiative by the Bureau of Labor Statistics, combines data from multiple sources to obtain a comprehensive count of fatal injuries at work. There are four key sources of federal data on work-related fatalities:

- Census of Fatal Occupational Injuries;
- National Traumatic Occupational Fatality Surveillance System;
- Fatality Assessment and Control Evaluation Program; and
- Integrated Management Information System.

Census of Fatal Occupational Injuries

The Census of Fatal Occupational Injuries (CFOI), begun in 1992, is a cooperative effort of the Bureau of Labor Statistics (BLS) and the states to develop a complete and accurate count of work-related deaths. Because no single source of data provides an exhaustive count of all workplace fatalities, CFOI uses multiple sources to identify, verify, and profile all work-related fatalities. At least two independent source documents are used to verify the work-relatedness and the circumstances of the incident for each death recorded in CFOI. Source documents come from both the state and federal levels and include workers' compensation records and claims, death certificates, newspaper articles, aircraft and highway transportation data, and other administrative records. Demographic information, the circumstances of each incident, the industry in which it occurred, the involvement of any equipment or machines, and the victim's occupation are recorded in CFOI. Data are available at the national, state, and metropolitan statistical area levels. BLS and the states share the costs and data-collection responsibilities.

From 1992 to 1996, CFOI recorded a total of 339 deaths of children and adolescents. There were annual averages of 27 work-related deaths of youngsters under the age of 16, and 41 work-related deaths of 16- and 17-year-olds (Bureau of Labor Statistics, 1997b; Derstine, 1996). The most common causes of death during the period from 1992 to 1995 (latest year available) were motor vehicle or other transportation-related incidents and homicides. Agriculture was the most deadly industry for younger teens: Some 80 percent of the fatalities of youngsters under the age of 14 were in agriculture, as were 46 percent of the fatalities of 14- and 15-year-olds (Derstine, 1996). For 16- and 17-year-olds, about a quarter of the fatalities occurred in agriculture and a quarter in retail. More than 25 percent of all fatalities of youngsters under the age of 18 occurred in family businesses (Derstine, 1996). As is discussed at greater length in Chapter 6, agriculture is exempt from many child labor and health and safety laws.

In 1993, homicides accounted for 28 percent of the work-related deaths of 16- and 17-year-olds recorded in CFOI (Toscano and Windau, 1994), compared with 10 percent of the work-related deaths from 1980 to 1989, as recorded in the National Traumatic Occupational Fatality surveillance system (NTOF) (Castillo et al., 1994). The differences between NTOF and CFOI, however, make it impossible to determine whether homicides at work have been increasing for this age group or were underreported in NTOF during the 1980s.

A strength of CFOI is its use of multiple data sources to develop a relatively complete count of fatalities. However, the final count still depends on the recognition, in individual cases, that the deceased was working at the time of the fatal incident. Young people are not typically thought of as workers. It is, therefore, reasonable to assume that deaths among children and adolescents who are fatally injured on the job may not be identified as work-related deaths and may be undercounted in the CFOI system. This undercounting may be particularly true of young workers on family farms and in family businesses, where the boundaries between work and family life are blurred. Information about whether safety or child labor laws were being violated during the fatal incidents is not systematically recorded.

Another problem in using data from CFOI to assess the fatal injuries among young workers is that the rates presented by BLS in its standard reports are misleading. These rates are routinely computed using estimates of the number of employed persons in the denominator (e.g., deaths per 100,000 workers). For populations of workers who are employed part-time or temporarily, such as teens, calculating the rate using the number of workers overestimates the true period of exposure to job risks. In computing rates, the use of employment figures rather than numbers of full-time-equivalent workers results in underestimates of the risk-per-hour-worked for part-time workers. Exposure would be more closely approximated by hours of work. Ruser (1998) reports that the fatality rate for 15- to 19-year-olds is 4.0 per 100,000 full-time-equivalent workers, compared with a rate of 2.5 per 100,000 employed persons. (The rates for workers aged 20 to 64, who are more likely than youngsters to work full-time, remain substantially the same regardless of the denominator.)

National Traumatic Occupational Fatality Surveillance System

The National Traumatic Occupational Fatality Surveillance System (NTOF) is a census of all U.S. death certificates that have an external cause of death noted (i.e., are E-coded) and for which the certifier checked "injured at work" on the death certificate. The National Institute for Occupational Safety and Health collects and automates death certificates from the 52 vital statistics reporting units (the 50 states, New York City, and Washington, D.C.) for workers 16 years of age and older. This system includes information on the victim's industry, occupation, cause of death, and a description of the injury, taken from the death certificate.

Between 1980 and 1989, NTOF listed 673 deaths of 16- and 17-year-olds (Castillo et al., 1994). The leading causes of death were incidents involving motor vehicles (24 percent), machines (17 percent), electrocution (12 percent), and homicide (10 percent). The industries with the most deaths were agriculture (110), construction (59), and services (56). Nearly half of the death certificates for 16- and 17-year-olds did not contain information on industry or occupation, however, so these numbers should be interpreted with caution.

This surveillance system has a number of other limitations. Studies have found that, on average, death certificates capture only 81 percent of work-related deaths (Stout and Bell, 1991). Certain types of deaths are more likely to be undercounted by NTOF, including work-related homicides and motor-vehicle-related deaths—important causes of occupational fatalities among children and adolescents. Furthermore, only a 60-76 percent agreement exists between the "usual occupation" and "usual industry" entries on death certificates and the victim's actual employment at the time of death (Bell et al., 1990). For adolescents, the agreement may be even worse. Castillo et al. (1994) found the "usual occupation" of a high percentage of young people was listed as "student," even though other information on the death certificate indicated that the fatality was work-related.

The NTOF surveillance system predates the CFOI by 10 years. The National Institute for Occupational Safety and Health and the Bureau of Labor Statistics are working to merge the two systems.

Fatality Assessment and Control Evaluation Program

The Fatality Assessment and Control Evaluation (FACE) program was developed by NIOSH to obtain more detailed information about the interactions of the worker, work environment, and work processes in work-related fatalities, details that are necessary to devise prevention strategies. This program provides an important follow-up component to the occupational fatality surveillance system. It involves in-depth, research-oriented investigations of targeted occupational fatalities, including fatal falls and machinery-related deaths. Confined-space deaths and electrocutions have been targeted in the past. NIOSH staff investigate deaths due to targeted causes in West Virginia and five surrounding states. With the assistance of NIOSH, 14 states enumerate all work-related fatalities occurring within their borders and conduct investigations of targeted deaths. For each investigation, a FACE report is prepared; it includes recommended measures to prevent similar deaths in the future. These reports are widely disseminated to relevant trade associations, workers' organizations, and health and safety professionals. Because only certain causes of death are targeted, not all deaths of young people are investigated in participating states. Massachusetts is an exception, in that it targets all deaths of young people. Even though not all work-related deaths are included in the FACE program, it provides important contextual information that is unavailable in the other systems and can be vital to prevention efforts.

Integrated Management Information System

The Integrated Management Information System (IMIS) is maintained by OSHA. It is an inspection-based system, containing only information obtained as a result of visits by agency inspectors. Employers are required to report work-related fatalities to OSHA within 48 hours of their occurrence, but only the information on fatalities that are investigated is entered into IMIS. This information is the basis for annual reports by the agency on the number of inspections it has undertaken, the number of violations cited, the penalties imposed, and so forth.

From 1984 through 1987, the database included 104 deaths of individuals under the age of 18; of these, 14 (13 percent) involved youngsters under the age of 15 (Suruda and Halperin, 1991). Incidents involving industrial vehicles or machines accounted for 30 percent of the deaths of children and youth under the age of 18. The other most frequent causes of death were electrocution (16 percent), falls (11 percent), and asphyxiation (11 percent).

It should be noted that OSHA investigates less than 30 percent of all work-related deaths (Stout and Bell, 1991; Suruda, 1992). It does not investigate work-related homicides or most transportation accidents—neither of which is under OSHA jurisdiction—deaths in industries regulated by other federal agencies, deaths among federal workers, or deaths among the self-employed. In many states, all state and local public-sector workers are also excluded. Although a large number of young workers' deaths occur in agriculture, the industry is little investigated by OSHA. Although IMIS does not include all work-related deaths of children, it offers the ability to match violations of safety and child labor laws with deaths. Of 104 children whose deaths were identified through this system for the period from 1984 to 1987, Suruda and Halperin (1991) found that

41 percent were doing work prohibited by federal child labor laws. Citations for safety violations were issued in 70 percent of these deaths.

CONCLUSIONS

Based on currently available data, injuries that are identified and specified as related to work appear to represent only a small percentage of all the injuries suffered by children and adolescents. Nevertheless, work-related injuries are widely recognized to be underreported. As a national policy, the United States treats workplaces differently than other places. The Occupational Safety and Health Act was passed "to assure so far as possible every working man and woman in the Nation safe and healthful working conditions" (29 U.S.C. §651 (b)). Current child labor laws demand a higher degree of safety for those under the age of 18 by prohibiting them from engaging in jobs determined to be hazardous by the Secretary of Labor. Furthermore, people generally are more averse to risks that are not under their control (i.e., risks imposed on them) than they are to those over which they believe they have control or which they voluntarily assume (National Research Council, 1989; Slovik, 1987). The committee believes that most young people (and their parents) expect their workplaces to be safe and, therefore, do not voluntarily assume the risk of injury at work. The laws, in combination with the different values placed on voluntary versus involuntary risks, argue for attention to work-related injuries, particularly in cases when changes in the workplace could prevent injury.

Children and adolescents routinely face hazardous working conditions. In spite of being legally prohibited from the most hazardous jobs, significant numbers of teens are still injured on the job each year. Factors that contribute to these injuries are largely determined by where the youngsters work, but the specific characteristics of workplace risks need to be better understood. Attention also should be paid to the roles played by inexperience, age, and developmentally inappropriate work assignments, as well as to factors related to physical and emotional development. Virtually no research has been done on illnesses resulting from occupational exposure during adolescence.

Existing injury surveillance systems contain significant gaps. No single data source captures all occupational injuries. Although CFOI combines data on fatal occupational injuries from multiple sources, no comparable system is available at the federal level for nonfatal work-related injuries.

Surveillance of young people's work-related injuries is contingent on reliable identification of work-relatedness. It is reasonable to assume that occupational injuries suffered by youngsters are less likely to be recognized as work-related than are those suffered by adults. The potential for systematic omission of injured youths from existing occupational injury surveillance systems has not been rigorously evaluated. Ambulatory care data may provide an important complement to conventional occupational injury surveillance datasets, such as workers' compensation and the Survey of Occupational Injuries and Illnesses, and to the ability to examine occupational injuries in relation to other injuries suffered by children and adolescents.

4

Work's Effects on
Children and Adolescents

ADOLESCENT DEVELOPMENT AND
THE ROLE OF WORK

Most people have their first experiences in the labor force during their teenage years. It is important, therefore, to consider how employment contributes to the developmental agenda of adolescence and to examine how experiences in the labor force can aid or hinder young people's emotional, intellectual, and physical development, as well as their socioeconomic attainments in life. To answer these questions requires an understanding of the nature of adolescent development in modern society.

Most experts agree that adolescence occupies a crucial role in contemporary human development for several interrelated reasons. First, adolescence is a period of potentially great malleability, during which experiences in the family, school, and other settings influence the individual's long-term development: To put it most succinctly, the adolescent experience matters for future performance. Second, adolescence is a period of tremendous variability. It is the time when people's life courses begin to diverge in important ways, in part because modern society allows for much diversity and flexibility during those years. Finally, adolescence is an especially important formative period, during which many developmental trajectories become established and increasingly difficult to alter. Together, the malleable, variable, and formative natures of adolescence make it crucial that schools and other institutions that exert influence over youngsters during this period are structured in ways that optimize the youngsters' chances to have healthy and happy adolescences and to become successful adults.

Generally speaking, a major part of development during adolescence revolves around preparation for the family, work, and citizenship roles of adulthood. Success in each of these domains depends, at the most fundamental level, on the development of certain personal competencies (including the capacity for self-reliance and responsible behavior), interpersonal competencies (including the capacity to form and maintain satisfying relationships with others), and social competencies (including the capacity to function as a member of a broader community). Adolescence is the period during which these capabilities both develop and solidify. Work experience, like any other experience, can be evaluated in terms of the degree to which, and the ways in which, it helps young people become personally, interpersonally, and socially mature.

The development of these psychosocial competencies cannot be viewed outside the broader context in which a young person or a cohort of young people comes of age. Contextual circumstances shape society's definitions of personal, interpersonal, and social competence. Thus, the context in which adolescents develop not only establishes the pathways through which maturity is pursued, but dictates the very competencies that define maturity. Because the components of "competent" adulthood in the twenty-first century will differ from what they were a century ago, the preparation today's adolescents need for successful adulthood is vastly different from that needed by their great-great-grandparents.

In essence, the role of work in the young person's transition to adulthood depends not only on the nature of adolescence—on what adolescents need to develop—but also on the nature of adulthood and on what society expects its adult members to be able to do. Regulations and guidelines concerning young people's participation in the labor force therefore require periodic reexamination in light of the changed, and changing, nature of adolescence and the transition to adulthood. In more concrete terms, what is the role of work in the development of personal, interpersonal, and social maturity, given the conditions that define adolescence and adulthood in today's society?

To understand the role of work in the lives of adolescents requires answers to questions about the nature of the work that youngsters perform; the characteristics and conditions of the settings in which they labor; the amount of time they devote to their jobs; and the ways in which experiences at work complement or compete with the other demands of the adolescent years (Finch et al., 1997).

THE NATURE OF WORK BY YOUNG PEOPLE

Special features of working in adolescence need to be taken into account in considering its consequences for development during this phase of life. In comparison with work by adults, work by young people tends to be more discretionary (i.e., not financially essential), part-time rather than full-time, and unstable, as youngsters move in and out of the labor force in response to changes in the needs of employers, labor market conditions, and shifting circumstances in other arenas of their lives. The number of hours spent working and the scheduling of those hours are apt to change frequently. High school students are more available for employment during the summer (Manning, 1990) and vacation periods than during the regular school year and more during the weekends than weekdays. Nevertheless, about 80 percent of all students work for pay during the school year at some time during their high school years.

In addition to these temporal dimensions of work, particular attributes of work experience may assume special importance for youth. Such attributes include, for example, the extent to which employment enables adolescents to apply what they learn in school or presents them with other learning opportunities; the ways in which their earnings are used; the degree of stressfulness of the work; and the quality of the young people's relationships with their supervisors or other adults in the workplace. Today, the types of jobs that most adolescents in the United States hold are disconnected from what is taught in school, do not systematically teach the job skills necessary for advancement, and provide little meaningful interaction with adult supervisors (Greenberger and Steinberg, 1986).

Relatively little systematic research has addressed the quality of young people's jobs. Through the high school years, adolescents move from informal work, such as babysitting, yard work, and shoveling snow, to more formal employment, particularly in fast-food and other retail and service industries, and become more dispersed across job categories. They are also more likely to have supervisory responsibilities and receive more training from their employers as they grow older (Mortimer et al., 1994).

CONSEQUENCES OF WORKING

A challenge associated with almost all research on the consequences of working for young people is that of selection effects. That is, young people who work may be different before they began to work than those who do not work and those who work long hours may be different than those who work fewer hours. For example, adolescents who are not interested in school may choose to work longer hours than those who enjoy school. Other differences among the groups may include their past academic performance, their career goals, their families' incomes, their parents' education levels, their motivation, and a host of other factors that are often not explicitly measured. These differences make it extremely difficult to ascertain whether working itself causes any particular outcome (either positive or negative) or whether those outcomes might have occurred whether or not the young people engaged in work.

Because researchers cannot randomly assign young people to the workplace, the committee relied on a careful review of studies that follow young people over time (longitudinal studies) and that take account of the pre-existing differences among youngsters who engage in various work patterns (statistically controlling for differences). These studies measure the statistical correlation between working and various outcomes, that is, the degree to which the occurrence of certain outcomes varies with different work patterns, in the context of pre-existing differences. Although no direct causal link between work and outcomes can be made from correlational studies, a pattern of consistent findings from studies with good statistical controls may be the best information available. Without random assignment, however, selection effects must be considered as an alternative interpretation of results.

Data from several well-designed, nationally representative longitudinal surveys are used in many of the studies discussed below. These include the National Longitudinal Survey of Youth (NLSY), the National Educational Longitudinal Survey (NELS), High School and Beyond, and the National Youth Survey (see Appendix A for more information about these surveys). Studies that use data from surveys of regional samples and cross-sectional studies (with data from one point in time) are also discussed when they complement the national longitudinal studies and when they cover information not available in the national studies. Examples of cross-sectional studies are Monitoring the Future, which surveys a national sample of high school seniors annually, and first-year data from the National Longitudinal Study of Adolescent Health.[1] Regional studies include the Youth Development Study, which follows a random sample of students who were in the 9th grade in 1988 in St. Paul, Minnesota, and a study by Steinberg and colleagues (1993), which followed a sample of students from nine high schools in Wisconsin and northern California for 1 year. A possible shortcoming in regional studies is that conclusions based on these samples may not be generalizable to the national population. (For a good description of other possible methodological shortcomings in many of the studies discussed below, see Ruhm, 1997:Table 1.)

Research on the effects of working on adolescents has focused on a variety of outcomes, including education, vocation, relationships, personal development, and problem behaviors. Although these studies look at a wide variety of consequences, they tend to treat work rather unidimensionally. Most of the studies examine the effects of work intensity, generally measured by average hours of work per week during the school year. Only a few studies try to take into account variations in work intensity over time. No studies on the consequences of work have considered actual work schedules, such as the hours worked on school days versus nonschool days or start and stop times on school days. These types of details are more difficult to collect, given the variability of young people's work schedules, and they are not available in the datasets used to study work outcomes.

---

[1]Second-year data from the National Longitudinal Study on Adolescent Health have been collected, but analyses of them were not available at the time of this report. As the name of the study implies, it will be a source of longitudinal data.

Educational Outcomes

Young people who combine school and work must meet the requirements of two potentially demanding social roles. As hours of employment increase, adolescents may experience difficulties in juggling the demands of work and school, as well as other activities. Teachers often note that working students are tired in class and do not have time to do homework; in one study, teachers' negative attitudes toward employed students increased with the length of their teaching experience (Bills et al., 1995).

If students are employed, the demands—and rewards—of work may draw them away from school, decreasing their school attendance and increasing the likelihood that they will drop out altogether. This outcome would appear to be much more likely if the hours of work are long. Based on data from the National Education Longitudinal Survey, which followed students who were in 8th grade in 1988, Schoenhals and colleagues (1997) found that the number of hours worked had a statistically positive relationship to absences from school in the 10th grade—after controlling for background and demographic variables, school type, curriculum, prior academic performance, prior work experience, and early school behavior and misbehavior—especially among those who worked more than 30 hours per week. In the High School and Beyond Survey, which tracked a large representative panel of individuals who were high school sophomores in public school in 1980, Chaplin and Hannaway (1996) found that working more than 14 hours per week in the sophomore year (1980) was negatively related to school enrollment 2 and 4 years later, after accounting for demographic, background, family, and school characteristics. In the National Longitudinal Study of Youth, which followed a large representative panel of young people who were between 16 and 19 years old in 1979, Carr and colleagues (1996) found that working more hours per week during high school was associated with lower levels of educational attainment achieved for both males and females by the age of 28 to 31.

The number of weeks worked in high school was also associated with decreased educational attainment for males. These associations remained after controlling for a large number of individual and family differences. Similarly, Mihalic and Elliot (1997) found that working for more than 1 year during high school was associated with lower educational aspirations. Marsh (1991), using data from the High School and Beyond surveys, found that the number of hours worked during the sophomore year of school was significantly and positively related to dropping out of school, even after background variables and sophomore school performance and motivation variables were controlled for: That is, the more hours worked during the sophomore year, the greater the likelihood of dropping out of school. In contrast, using data from the National Longitudinal Survey of Youth, Carr et al. (1996) found no significant influence of hours of work during high school on the probability of completing high school. However, Carr et al. (1996) did not confine their analysis to hours of work during the sophomore year as did Marsh (1991). It is possible that heavy investment in work early in high school has a different effect than work during a student's junior or senior year.

At the same time, however, learning to maintain an appropriate balance between school and work, by limiting work hours so that work does not unduly interfere with educational pursuits, might foster continuance in school. If students limit their work hours, the monetary and other benefits of employment may be sustained without disrupting their roles as students. Furthermore, since most young people who go to college (or pursue other kinds of post-secondary education) support themselves, at least partially, while going to college, learning to balance school and work earlier, while still in high school, could be beneficial with respect to higher educational attainment.

Supporting this line of reasoning, Tienda and Ahituv (1996), using data from the National Longitudinal Survey of Youth, report that students who have worked the previous year are less likely to quit school between the ages of 17 and 19 than are those who did not work. However, the extent to which youngsters remain in school decreased as the average weekly hours of work rose, after controlling for family background, scholastic aptitude, other background and demographic variables, and previous work experience. Similarly, D'Amico's (1984) analysis of data from the same survey showed that employment at low intensity (defined as fewer than 20 hours per week) was associated with lower school dropout rates among 11th graders.

Among boys in the Youth Development Study, one particular pattern of participation in the labor force during high school proved to be especially salutary: nearly continuous employment limited, on average, to 20 hours a week or less. The boys who followed this pattern were found to have undertaken the most months of post-secondary schooling (Mortimer and Johnson, 1998) during the years following high school. Males who worked at higher levels of intensity (more than 20 hours per week on average), as well as those who had more limited work experience (not working at all during high school or working for only short periods), had less postsecondary educational attainment. These differences were not explained by apparent selection factors. A similar pattern was observed among females, but was accounted for by earlier differences in educational motivation and performance.

There may be ethnic, racial, social class, and sex differences in these effects. Steel (1991) analyzed data from the NLSY and found that the generally positive effect of high school employment (at ages 17 and 18) on enrollment in an educational institution 2 years later is conditioned by race, sex, and the time spent working. Among white youth, being employed had a positive effect on enrollment. However, this positive relationship was mitigated by hours of work: for each additional hour worked during high school, future school enrollment dropped. This negative effect was even more pronounced among black youth. Carr and colleagues (1996), also using NLSY data, found that as hours of employment in high school increased, the likelihood of entering college and of completing college were reduced, after taking into account demographic and background variables, family differences, school aptitude, and educational expectations. They found this effect on educational attainment persisted up to a decade after high school completion. Ruhm's (1997) analysis of NLSY data found a similar effect for girls.

In general, this evidence suggests that low-intensity employment may support post-secondary educational outcomes while high-intensity employment may hinder them. These studies consistently find that as hours of work per week during high school increase, decreases are seen in the amount of future education. Although these studies statistically control for many pre-existing differences among students who work at high and low intensity, as noted above, without random assignment of students to various work patterns, it cannot be proved that high-intensity work decreases educational attainment. It is possible that unobserved differences among students are responsible for both their decisions about work intensity and education. Nevertheless, the preponderance of evidence suggests a link between high-intensity work in high school and lowered eventual educational attainment.

Although there is much concern about whether working lowers students' academic performance, the evidence with respect to this outcome is inconsistent. Some well-designed longitudinal studies report negative effects of employment, or hours of work, on grades (Marsh, 1991; Mortimer and Finch, 1986). Others show no significant effects (Mihalic and Elliot, 1997; Mortimer and Johnson, 1998; Mortimer et al., 1996; Schoenhals et al., 1977). Parents also have reported that their children's work has not affected their grades (Phillips and Sandstrom, 1990). Steinberg and colleagues' (1993) longitudinal assessment of change in grade-point average, considered as an outcome of employment, yielded mixed findings. Students who worked at low intensity (defined as 1-20 hours per week) at the outset of the study and increased their hours to more than 20 per week had lower grades at the end of a 1-year interval than students who worked at low intensity and left the work force during this period. Among students who worked more than 20 hours at the outset of the study, those who stopped working increased their level of school engagement. The results of this study cannot be generalized as the sample was not representative, but they do suggest the need for researchers to examine the effects of patterns of work intensity over time.

It is important to note that the dividing point of 20 hours of work per week is not based on research results; rather, most researchers have adopted that number as a reasonable marker between "low-intensity" and "high-intensity" employment. Given an average school week of about 30 hours, students who work 20 hours per week during the school year have the equivalent of a 50-hour work week. Surveys often collect hours worked in 5- or 10-hour groups, precluding researchers from examining hours of work as a continuous variable. Furthermore, the number of hours worked per week does not take account of when those hours are worked, either on what days of the week or what times of the day, both of which may affect the effects of work on school outcomes.

It is plausible to assume that the motivational context and social meanings of employment influence its effects on academic performance. For example, Marsh (1991) and Ruscoe and colleagues (1996) report that employment has a beneficial effect on grades when the workers are using their earnings to save for college. (In the

Youth Development Study, almost one-half of the employed seniors were saving at least part of their earnings for their future educational expenses [Call, 1996a].) If working is associated with higher grades under certain conditions that are under the students' control (such as the saving of earnings for college or the limiting of work's intensity), the effects of employment could well be due to selection. That is, the students' motivation to attend college or their concern about having sufficient time for their school work would likely encourage them to limit their hours of work and would explain any positive associations between paid work and achievement.

It may seem paradoxical that working does not have a more consistent effect on academic performance. Two recent studies report that neither employment status nor work intensity influences the amount of time spent doing homework (Mortimer et al., 1996; Schoenhals et al., 1997). Steinberg and Cauffman (1995) suggest that because the national average for time spent on homework is so low (fewer than 4 hours per week), employment is unlikely to diminish students' already very modest involvement in this activity. Teachers may also lighten homework assignments if they know about their students' work schedules. For the inconsistent findings with respect to work's effect on grades, there is some evidence that employed students may select undemanding courses so as to maintain high grade-point averages despite their jobs (Steinberg and Cauffman, 1995).

Very little attention has been given to the quality of students' jobs (in contrast to the intensity of their work) as a factor influencing their educational performance and attainment. However, Barling and colleagues (1995) report that the amount of time spent doing homework does not decline with hours of work when adolescents report using skills to a great extent in their jobs and having a very clear understanding of their roles as workers. When jobs entail little use of skills or clarity of roles, the amount of time spent studying declines with increases in the number of hours worked. (This cross-sectional study did not enable controls for prior experiences of the students that might have accounted for their having different job types.)

There is some emerging evidence from school-to-work programs that integration of school-based and work-based learning may help to overcome some of the negative effects on educational attainment associated with working while in school. For example, several youth apprenticeship demonstration projects reported that large proportions of participants enrolled in post-secondary education (Kopp and Kazis, with Churchill, no date), a surprising result because the target group had been non-college bound high school students. Some school-to-work sites have also reported this result, along with higher grades and improved post-graduate employment. (For examples, see the National School-to-Work Office Web site: http://www.stw.ed. gov.) These results must be treated with caution because they are usually based on high school seniors' reports of their post-graduation intentions rather than follow-up surveys and because they seldom include control groups or comparison groups, but they do suggest the reasonable hypotheses that youth apprenticeship and other aspects of school-to-work would not reduce the likelihood of high school graduates enrolling in post-secondary education. One report based on post-graduation follow-up interviews indicated that three-fourths of graduates remained enrolled in post-secondary education in the first year after graduation and more then two-thirds remained enrolled 2 years later. It also found rather high levels of career directedness 1 and 2 years after graduation, suggesting that youth apprenticeship can counteract the tendency of youth without college degrees to "flounder" during their first few years in the labor market (Hamilton and Hamilton, 1997).

One of the most carefully designed studies examined youth apprentices in printing in Wisconsin. Orr (1998) found that youth apprentices achieved higher grades, had relatively fewer absences, reported clearer career goals, and reported more hours of employment and higher earnings 6-8 months after graduation. Orr's comparison group were students enrolled in printing courses in conventional vocational education, including a few with cooperative education placements, as well as youth apprentices' classmates who were enrolled in the general course of study (i.e., neither college preparatory nor vocational). In contrast with reports on other youth apprenticeship programs, Wisconsin printing graduates were less likely than comparison graduates to enroll in higher education, largely because nearly all were employed in printing and in the same firm where they received their training.

Vocational Development and Occupational Attainment

Working during high school may have direct short-term influences on occupational and income attainments during the years immediately following high school, as many young people stay with (or rejoin) employers for whom they worked while attending high school; these jobs are often held by students who are simultaneously pursuing post-secondary education (Mortimer and Johnson, 1998). Young workers may also learn job-seeking skills, including where to look or whom to consult for job information, how to complete application forms and other paperwork, and how to conduct themselves at job interviews. Early contacts at work could constitute early "social capital," providing useful information for future job searches. Young people may also obtain, through paid work, some understanding of the job market and their degree of competitiveness and worth in relation to other job applicants. Lowe and Krahn (1992) found that Canadian high school graduates who had worked during high school were less likely to be willing to accept "menial" jobs than were those with no work experience. They also found that employment had a positive effect on an economic literacy test (which covered such topics as diminishing returns, opportunity costs, and demand theory). Greenberger and colleagues (1980) report that adolescent workers are more likely than nonworkers to have personal checking and savings accounts, credit cards, and financial responsibilities.

Working during high school could affect young people's vocational development and success by influencing their work ethics, commitments to employment, and understandings of the routines and requirements of the workplace. Because vocational issues are particularly salient during adolescence, it is plausible to expect that initial work experiences would have a formative influence on the development of work attitudes and habits. The quality of work, as well as the social context of working, may be particularly important for the development of work-related values and attitudes. Adolescents who helped their families economically during the Great Depression by working in part-time jobs developed clear vocational goals and commitment to their careers (Elder, 1974). By contrast, relatively few urban youth today give even a portion of their earnings to help support their families. Steinberg and Cauffman (1995) argue that working, under current circumstances, can lead to cynicism about work, misconduct, and tolerance of unethical practices in the workplace.

The actual job I'm doing is not going to help me, but being around people, dealing with people and their attitudes, that's going to help me.

High school student
Youth panel for the committee

Although no relationship was found between employment status or hours of work and occupational values among students in St. Paul, Minnesota, both intrinsic and extrinsic work values were heightened among those who acquired job skills that were perceived as useful for the future (Mortimer et al., 1996). Perhaps young workers come to view the benefits of working as being within reach and, therefore, increasingly desirable, if they are given opportunities to learn and successfully adapt to the demands of work.

Parents of working youth believe that employment promotes a sense of responsibility, time-management skills, and positive work values (Aronson et al., 1996; Phillips and Sandstrom, 1990). Even though most young workers do not think that they will continue in the same kinds of jobs after they complete their schooling, they may learn behaviors that will prepare them for any future job. They may learn, for example, how to relate to people from diverse backgrounds, including customers, clients, coworkers, and supervisors; to take responsibility and be dependable; to follow employers' directions and rules; to keep track of their schedules (which, for many working youth, change frequently); and to get to work on time. Even so-called marginal jobs require individuals to mobilize some effort, to develop some degree of self-discipline, and to apply themselves to tasks (Snedeker, 1982).

Consistent with these potentially positive consequences for vocational development, a number of studies have reported that paid employment during high school is associated with positive work-related effects on employment after high school, as measured by the acquisition of work after leaving high school, the duration of employment (or unemployment), and income attainment (Freeman and

Wise, 1979; Marsh, 1991; Meyer and Wise, 1982; Mihalic and Elliott, 1997; Mortimer and Finch, 1986; Ruhm, 1995; Ruhm, 1997; Steel, 1991; Stern and Nakata, 1989). In a study of students with and without disabilities in Oregon and Nevada, Benz and colleagues (1997) found that having had two or more work experiences during the last 2 years of high school was positively related to being employed 1 year after high school. Among Canadian young people not attending post-secondary school, those who had worked during high school had more months of full-time employment, but not higher wages, in the second year after leaving high school than those who had not worked during high school (Lowe and Krahn, 1992). Marsh (1991) reports that working while attending high school reduces the risk of unemployment during the 2 years following high school. Steel's (1991) analysis of National Longitudinal Survey of Youth data finds that hours per week of high school employment are positively related to weeks of employment for whites for 2 years following high school; for African Americans and Hispanics, however, the relationships between hours worked and employment after high school were not statistically significant.

Some analysts have expressed concern that the gains by teenagers who were employed during high school may be temporary. Several authors have used the same study, the National Longitudinal Survey of Youth, to try to address this concern. Carr and colleagues (1996) report that the gains persist for as long as a decade following high school. Adjusting statistically for the background factors and educational attainments that were available, employment in high school was shown to have positive effects on employment and wages nearly a dozen years later. Using data from the same study (NLSY), Ruhm (1997) reported that 6-9 years after high school graduation, students who had worked during their senior year had greater economic attainment, including higher earnings, wages, occupational status, and fringe benefits, despite a small decrement in completed schooling that was associated with time on the job. Future economic gains were greater for students who had invested more hours in work. The greatest economic gains were found among students who worked 21 to 24 hours per week during high school; at the same time, decreases in educational attainment were substantial for those who worked more than 20 hours per week (Ruhm, 1997). This analysis controlled for other factors that might explain the findings, specifically socioeconomic status, family environment, and the respondent's ability and motivation toward school. The absence of information on the quality of the work prevented consideration of what could be an important factor in understanding the effects of work.

All of the analyses of the NLSY data have controlled for factors other than hours worked while in school in explaining the persistent benefits of work. Managing these confounding factors in statistical models is complex and the results may be difficult to interpret. Recently, the data from the NLSY were examined by Hotz and colleagues (1998), using econometric modeling to study the effects of working during school on future wages.[2] When they controlled for person-specific unobserved heterogeneity (i.e., potential differences between subjects that were not measured), working during high school had no significant effects on wages at age 27. In fact, in this model, the effects of going to school full-time and not working appeared to have much bigger payoffs in terms of future wages than combining work and school.

Mortimer and Johnson (1998), using data from the St. Paul Youth Development Study, reported that long duration of work in high school was associated with being employed part-time during the 4 years after high school. Part-time employment after high school was, in turn, linked to enrollment in post-secondary education. They found that working more than 20 hours per week during high school predicted entry into full-time employment after high school. Working more than 20 hours per week and having a long duration of work during high school, for males only, was associated with higher earnings 4 years after high school than the earnings of those with less work experience during high school.

Though most research has focused on investment in work, the quality of the early work experience may also be important for occupational outcomes. For example, the use of skills as an adolescent worker predicts success in the job market during the first 3 years after high school graduation (Stern and Nakata, 1989).

---

[2]Based on a framework developed by Cameron and Heckman (1992), which draws on earlier work by Heckman (1982) and Heckman and Singer (1984).

Relationships

The development of interpersonal competencies, including the capacity to form and maintain satisfying relationships, is a primary developmental task during adolescence. However, most nationally representative surveys do not collect information on the quality of young people's relationships with their families and peers. And, except for Monitoring the Future and the National Youth Survey, most of the studies that investigate the effects of work on relationships use local or nonrepresentative samples, making their findings difficult to generalize to U.S. adolescents as a whole. Yet because of the importance of interpersonal relationships during adolescence, the research summarized in this section, though limited, provides useful information about potential effects of teenage work on relationships.

The job sites where adolescents work are often age segregated (Greenberger, 1988). Although young workers have much contact with people of their own ages, relationships with coworkers may be rather superficial, and the conditions of work may interfere with the development of close friendships. Conversely, working may confer status on young workers, improving their peer relationships. Good relationships with coworkers or supervisors may counterbalance difficult peer or family relationships.

Students in the National Youth Survey who worked for a longer duration (during a 1-year period in high school) spent less time with their parents than did other students (Mihalic and Elliot, 1997). Greenberger and colleagues (1980) reported that time spent with parents was less among employed students than among other students and that it diminished as the hours of work increased (see also Greenberger and Steinberg, 1986; Mortimer and Shanahan, 1994). Steinberg and Dornbusch (1991), found that the numbers of hours high school students in California and Wisconsin worked were associated with their spending less time in family activities. There is evidence that youngsters become more independent of their parents when they are employed more intensively during high school (Mortimer and Shanahan, 1994; Shanahan et al., 1991; Steinberg and Dornbusch, 1991; Steinberg et al., 1993), a consequence that parents tend to view as a good thing (Phillips and Sandstrom, 1990). Although such independence may be deleterious when accompanied by insufficient parental monitoring, acquiring independence from parents is a normal developmental step for adolescents.

Because so many young people work and commit so many hours to their jobs, their working may be inconvenient for their families, or worse, may provoke disagreements or conflicts with their parents. For example, adolescents who work may be less available for household chores (Greenberger and Steinberg, 1986); parents of employed adolescents may be called on to do other tasks that they would ordinarily not have to perform (e.g., taking the adolescents to work, transporting the paper carriers by car on rainy days, and so forth). A study using data from the National Survey of Families and Households (see description in Appendix B) provides evidence that disagreements between parents and children increase when the children are employed. Parents of workers, in comparison with parents of nonworkers, reported more disagreement about chores, curfews, smoking, drinking, drug use, money, school, and getting along with the family (Manning, 1990). Bachman and Schulenberg (1993), on the basis of Monitoring the Future data, found that nonworkers reported the fewest arguments with parents. Arguments increased with hours of work to about 20 hours and then decreased (for girls) or assumed an inconsistent pattern (for boys) for more hours of work. In the Youth Development Study, the boys and girls who worked more hours also reported more arguments with parents (Mortimer and Shanahan, 1994).

The evidence regarding the time spent with the family and the frequency of disagreements might suggest that the general quality of relations with parents is impaired when adolescents are employed, but this does not appear to be the case. Greenberger and colleagues (1980) report no significant effects of adolescents' employment status or intensity on the quality of their relations with their families. An analysis of Youth Development Study data yielded the same conclusion (Mortimer and Shanahan, 1994). There was some indication in the latter study, however, that boys who were able to acquire skills on their jobs became closer to their fathers over time; this pattern was not found for girls. Schulenberg and Bachman (1993) also report that learning and using skills on the job were associated with less perceived interference between the job and family life. Thus, difficulties associated with high levels of work intensity were attenuated by high quality work. In contrast, when adolescents were in jobs that they did not perceive as making good use of their talents and skills, as being unconnected to future work, and as the kinds of jobs that people do "only for the money," they were more likely to see the jobs as interfering with other parts of their lives as the intensity of the work increased.

There is some evidence (Call, 1996b) to indicate that positive work conditions can alleviate detrimental effects that the strain in parent-adolescent relationships can have on adolescents' mental health and adjustment. For example, when adolescents reported receiving no support from their supervisors, strain in the parent-child relationships diminished the adolescents' self-esteem, mastery, and well-being. However, when supervisory support was present, such strain had no significant effects on these aspects of the adolescents' mental health. Interestingly, in view of these findings, more than one-third of employed students reported that they were "quite close" or "very close" to their supervisors and that the supervisors were "often" or "always" willing to listen to their problems and help them find solutions.

In evaluating the effects of adolescents' employment on parent-child relationships, it is essential to take the social context and meaning of work into account. Shanahan and colleagues (1996a) compared the associations between adolescents' earnings and parent-child relationships in urban and rural settings. In rural settings, adolescents' earnings promoted more sharing of advice between parents and adolescents, and the adolescents' emotional ties with their parents remained stable or improved. In urban settings, earnings were not linked to these positive outcomes. In rural settings, young people who worked more than 10 hours per week spent more time with their families than those who worked fewer than 10 hours per week (Shanahan et al., 1996b). In urban settings, as hours of work increased, the amount of time spent with families decreased (Mortimer and Shanahan, 1994). Some of the rural effect could be due to young people who live and work with their parents on family farms, but the majority of rural families are not farm families. In this study, 34 percent of the families resided on farms, 12 percent in nonfarm rural areas, and 54 percent in towns with populations of less than 6,500.

The investigators interpret this pattern in terms of ecological differences in the meaning of adolescents' work. "In rural settings, productive activities are more likely to be construed as adult-like behaviors because rural work functions in unique ways to the benefit of families" (Shanahan et al., 1996a:122). In rural settings, work by adolescents is more likely to be a part of the family economic strategy—in fact, adolescents' earnings were four times more likely to be spent in ways that contributed to their families (e.g., giving money to parents, saving for future education, or paying for school fees) in rural settings than in urban settings. Although such uses of earnings were less common in urban settings, such expenditures were positively related to youngsters' relationships with their parents in both settings.

Although orientation to peers is a factor that influences whether adolescents choose to work or not (Mortimer and Johnson, 1998), and there is some indication that employed adolescents are more involved in dating (Bachman and Schulenberg, 1993; Mihalic and Elliot, 1997), there is little evidence that adolescents' work status or the intensity of their work affects their peer relations either positively or negatively. However, good work experiences—those that foster job skills and work involvement—are associated with enhanced closeness of peer relations and belief that work confers status in the peer group. Positive connections between school and work have also been found to foster this belief (Shanahan and Mortimer, 1996). This evidence suggests that when adolescents' work connotes achievement and progress toward adult status, it also encourages a perception that work gives status in the peer group.

Personal Development

Work is among the most central markers of the transition to adulthood: acquiring and successfully maintaining the role of a worker brings economic independence and a major component of adult identity. Because virtually all adolescents, girls as well as boys, expect to work in adulthood, the adult role of worker is likely to be a highly salient component of an adolescent's future possible self (Markus et al., 1990). If part-time jobs signify progress in moving toward that goal, one might expect that they would have positive implications for personal development and mental health. An adolescent who works must juggle the multiple roles of worker, student, friend, and family member. Doing this successfully may give the youngster a general sense of efficacy, as one who can meet the challenges of multiple roles—both now and in the future.

In view of potential benefits of working for personal development, it is not surprising to find widespread approval of employment for youngsters. Many people, including parents of adolescents who work, believe that working during this phase of life promotes responsibility, time-management skills, and self-confidence (Phillips and Sandstrom, 1990). In fact, employed youth describe themselves as more punctual, responsible, and dependable than those who are not employed (Greenberger, 1984).

Along with working students' multiple role responsibilities comes the potential for role conflict, especially as work hours increase. If adolescents are not successful in juggling role demands, the conflicts between work and other roles could undermine their sense of competence. This undesirable outcome would appear to be more likely as work hours increase. Among high school seniors in the Monitoring the Future studies, the young people who were the most satisfied with their lives—after controlling for background factors and educational commitment and success—were those employed 6 to 10 hours per week; they were more satisfied than nonworkers and than those who worked more than 10 hours per week (Bachman and Schulenberg, 1993).

Although it is widely believed that working promotes money management skills, some have questioned whether having relatively large amounts of discretionary income during this phase of life is beneficial. Bachman (1983) warns that early paid work could generate subsequent dissatisfaction with some living standards and lifestyles. Young workers use their earnings largely to purchase things they want but do not necessarily need (Greenberger and Steinberg, 1986; Johnston et al., 1982; Yeatts, 1994).

Furthermore, employment may limit young people's horizons. Greenberger and Steinberg (1986) point out that since work often consumes so much time, adolescents miss out on a critical "moratorium" period to explore alternative identities and interests. According to this argument, employment draws young people away from more developmentally beneficial pursuits.

In an analysis of the effects of working and hours of work on how adolescents use their time, Schoenhals and colleagues (1997) report that the number of hours worked per week had a strong negative association with the time youngsters spent watching television during the 10th grade: that is, as hours of work increased, time spent watching television decreased. If watching television—which entails relatively little challenge, low demand, and usually little educational benefit—is the activity mainly sacrificed by employment, it could account for the null findings regarding the effects of working on the time youngsters spend doing homework (Mortimer and Johnson, 1998; Mortimer et al., 1996; Schoenhals et al., 1997).

However, Bachman and Schulenberg (1993) report that hours of sleep significantly decline as seniors' hours of work increase. The investigators also report that those working longer hours are less likely to eat breakfast. They are also less likely to exercise vigorously if they work up to 25 hours per week, after which exercising increases. Carskadon and colleagues have similarly found a reduction in sleep and increased daytime sleepiness among high school students who work; the effects increase as the numbers of hours worked increase (Carskadon, 1990; Carskadon et al., 1989).

Because the quality of adult work has been found to have substantial consequences for adult psychological functioning (Baker and Green, 1991; Kohn et al., 1983; Mortimer et al., 1986), some researchers have studied whether adolescent psychological functioning is similarly responsive to the quality of work. Young workers may be exposed to job-related stressors, especially if they are required to take on adult responsibilities when their coping skills are not yet adequate (Greenberger, 1988). Moreover, combining school and work may not be easy; adolescents generally perceive it as stressful, and increasingly so, as they progress through high school (Mortimer et al., 1994). This is especially the case for those boys who work nearly continuously, at high levels of intensity, during high school (Mortimer and Johnson, 1998). In an analysis of data from the first year of the National Longitudinal Study on Adolescent Health, Resnick and colleagues (1997) found that working more than 20 hours per week during the school year was associated with emotional distress (defined as physical or emotional symptoms of distress as reported by the young people themselves or by their parents).

There is evidence that the quality of youngsters' work does, in fact, significantly affect their mental health. In the Youth Development Study, opportunities for advancement and compatibility between school and work for boys and good pay for girls promoted a sense of self-efficacy over time (Finch et al., 1991). Boys' sense of efficacy increased when their supervisors included them in discussions about work tasks and did not subject them to close supervision; girls' sense of efficacy increased when they were provided with early opportunities at work to be helpful to others (Call, 1996a; Call et al., 1995). Among males, job stressors (e.g., time pressure, overload) and early decision-making autonomy on the job heightened their distress, while the acquisition of useful skills diminished their depressed moods (Shanahan, 1992; Shanahan et al., 1991). Among females, work stress and responsibility for things outside their control were related to an increase in depressed moods (Shanahan et al., 1991) and a decrease in efficacy (Finch et al., 1991). There is further evidence from the Youth Development Study that the quality of work during high school has continued implications for personal outcomes (e.g., for modes of coping with problems at work, well-being, and depressed mood) 4 years following high school.

Moreover, the quality of the work experience may alter the effects of work hours. That is, when the work is of high quality, the potential negative effects of working long hours on personal development may be buffered. Thus, in a cross-sectional study of 10th-through 12th-grade urban white Canadians, hours worked was positively associated with self-esteem when autonomy and role clarity were high (Barling et al., 1995). Senior participants in the Monitoring the Future studies whose jobs offered them opportunities to use their skills and taught them new skills reported higher rates of satisfaction with life and hope for the future than did other participants (Schulenberg and Bachman, 1993). Those whose jobs were relevant to their future pursuits were less susceptible to difficulties related to longer work hours. In contrast, among those who saw little relationship between present and future jobs, an increase in work intensity was associated with decrements in health and well-being. Thus, work of low quality may interact with long hours to produce negative effects on personal development. For example, Shanahan (1992) reported that work stress and lack of supervision increased depressed moods among boys who worked more than the median number of hours in the 10th and 12th grades.

Problem Behaviors

It is in the set of activities that are generally referred to as "problem behaviors" that studies find the clearest indications of deleterious influences of teenage employment. The preponderance of evidence, ranging from national longitudinal studies to cross-sectional studies employing representative sampling designs, has found higher rates of problem behaviors, such as alcohol and other drug use and minor delinquency, among young people who work—particularly among those who work at high intensity—in comparison with their nonworking peers. These findings persist even after statistically controlling for other correlates of problem behaviors. As noted above, because these studies have been conducted in natural settings, they do not lend themselves to experimental designs. Therefore, definitive conclusions that high-intensity work causes behavior problems among youth cannot be made. However, given the consistency in findings across varying youth populations and settings, it seems very likely that high-intensity work does contribute to problem behaviors among young people.

In comparison with young people who do not work, employed students are more likely to engage in deviant behavior and school misconduct (Greenberger and Steinberg, 1986; Steinberg and Dornbusch, 1991; Tanner and Krahn, 1991; Wright et al., 1997). Using National Youth Survey data, Wofford (1988) found that minor delinquency is greater for adolescents working full-time than for those working part-time and greater for those working part-time than for those not working at all. However, adolescents who do not work at all tend to commit the more serious offenses (e.g., aggravated assault or theft of an item valued more than $50) (Wofford, 1988).

For males, long work hours have also been linked to theft and trouble with the police, as well as to aggressive behavior, especially for those working more than 30 hours per week (Bachman and Schulenberg, 1993). These researchers used data from Monitoring the Future and statistically controlled for the effects of region, urbanicity, parents' education, race, high school grade-point average, 4-year-college plans, and high school curriculum. Higher intensity workers (i.e., those working longer hours) were also more likely to be victims of aggression and theft, but most of the incidents occurred in or near schools (Bachman and Schulenberg, 1993). Wright et al. (1997) found that high work intensity increased the likelihood of delinquent involvement among males who were already at risk for delinquent behavior: That is, the more hours such high-risk adolescent males worked, the more likely they were to engage in delinquent behavior. Hours of work had no direct effect on likelihood of delinquent involvement among females or low-risk males. The researchers analyzed the relationship between work intensity and delinquency using the 1988 National Survey of Families and Households, a cross-sectional, nationally representative sample of 13,079 individuals within 9,643 households. The respondents in this study were the parents of the adolescents.[3]

Adolescents who work more than 20 hours per week have been found to be prone to using cigarettes, alcohol, and illegal drugs (marijuana, cocaine) (Bachman and Schulenberg, 1993; Greenberger and Steinberg, 1986; Mihalic and Elliott, 1997; Mortimer et al., 1996; Resnick et al., 1997; Schulenberg and Bachman, 1993; Steinberg and Dornbusch, 1991). Students in St. Paul, Minnesota, who worked more than 20 hours per week engaged in more alcohol use than their classmates each year during high school (Mortimer et al., 1996). In fact, the link between intensive work and substance use is one of the strongest findings in this area, manifest even when the data are subjected to extensive statistical controls for background variables and pre-existing differences in substance use between the groups. For example, Mortimer and colleagues (1996) found that hours worked during high school were associated with alcohol use, an association that held after statistical control for frequency of past alcohol use, sex, parental socioeconomic status, race, family composition, and nativity. Mihalic and Elliott (1997), in studying the short-term effects of work hours on the use of alcohol, marijuana, and other drugs among 11- to 17-year-olds from 1976 through 1980, statistically controlled for sex, age, parental socioeconomic status, place of residence (urban/suburban, rural), ethnicity, and prior drug and alcohol use (at first interview): They found that employment had an effect on marijuana and alcohol use above and beyond any preemployment differences.

Greenberger and Steinberg (1986) and Bachman and Schulenberg

---

[3]In this study (Wright et al., 1997), the researchers developed a measure that categorized youths by risk for delinquency, based on research findings in criminology. Risk factors assessed in this study were parental criminality, parental role rejection, family mobility, household size, self-control, parent-child conflict, family income, a nonintact marriage, and low school commitment. Each factor was dichotomized at the median to show presence or absence of risk. Youths with four or more risk factors present were considered high risk.

(1993) have suggested that employment is sometimes one component of a syndrome of "pseudomaturity" or "precocious development," including such adult behaviors as drinking and smoking and earlier (Mihalic and Elliott, 1997) or more frequent (Bachman and Schulenberg, 1993) dating. Working adolescents may come to think of themselves as adults, given access to adult-like job responsibilities and economic independence. Relationships with older coworkers could introduce adolescents prematurely to more ostensibly adult ways of handling stress or spending leisure time. (Tanner and Krahn [1991] report evidence that having delinquent friends acts as an intervening variable between working as an adolescent and committing illegal acts.) Employment appears to foster behaviors by teens that may signify adult status and identity but that pose problems when they are engaged in by youth (or engaged in excessively by adults).

Although working long hours is associated with increased substance use and other problem behaviors, very little research has examined whether the quality of the work experience directly affects these outcomes or alters the effects of employment. Steinberg and Cauffman (1995) pointed out that adolescents' use of drugs and alcohol was linked to work stressors in a sample of high school students in California (Greenberger and Steinberg, 1986). Based on data from Monitoring the Future, Schulenberg and Bachman (1993) found that skill utilization at work was associated with decreased cigarette and marijuana use for adolescents generally and in decreased alcohol use for females. Moreover, adolescents who described their jobs as not requiring the use of their skills, as being unconnected to the future, and as being "the kind of work that people do just for the money" used cigarettes more frequently as the intensity of their work increased. Work intensity was found to be less consequential for young people who described their jobs as relevant to their futures.

MINORITY AND DISADVANTAGED YOUTH

Two high school students working side by side in the same establishment may have very different work experiences. The job may represent a short-term means of earning spending money for the college-bound middle-class student, but it may be the beginning of a lifetime of episodic employment in low-wage jobs for a disadvantaged student. For this reason, the issues regarding work for disadvantaged populations deserve special attention.

Poor and minority children and youth need all of the same protections from hazardous work that advantaged children and youth need. In addition, they have some distinctive needs:

• access to the benefits of employment;
• protection from discrimination, which may block them from getting better jobs and may affect their health and safety while working; and
• protection from the hazards of employment in the underground economy (which are beyond the reach of child labor laws).

Studies consistently find that poor and minority youth are less likely to be employed than are middle-income white youth (Ahituv et al., 1994; Carr et al., 1996; Keithly and Deseran, 1995; Lewin-Epstein, 1981; Tienda and Ahituv, 1996); thus, they are less likely to experience either the developmental advantages or the disadvantages of employment during childhood and adolescence. For example, the Current Population Survey (March, 1995) reports that by the age of 17, 82.8 percent of whites have had job experience, compared with 79.1 percent of Hispanics and 69.5 percent of African Americans. On the basis of U.S. 1980 and 1990 census data, O'Regan and Quigley (1996) present evidence that the spatial isolation of minority and poor households decreases employment opportunities. This means that disadvantaged children and adolescents are less frequently exposed to work and, therefore, to work-related threats to their health and safety, but they also receive fewer benefits of employment. Poor youngsters are more likely to need income to help provide for their own or their families' needs. Furthermore, they need added opportunities to develop their human capital if they are to overcome the barriers of poverty and discrimination. Keithly and Deseran (1995) examined the relationships between youth labor force participation and individual, family, and local labor market factors, using 1980 public-use census data. They found that the likelihood of adolescent employment increased with family income up to $54,999 in 1980 dollars, when employment levels dropped. They concluded (Keithly and Deseran, 1995:486):

Contrary to theories that suggest that economic need propels youths into the labor force, factors such as lower household income and parents not working substantially *decrease* the odds of youth participation in the labor force.

A recent book makes a compelling case, based on research conducted in high-performance firms, that employability in the current and future labor force is increasingly determined by a combination of basic academic knowledge and "soft skills," defined as "the ability to work in groups and to make effective oral and written presentations" (Murnane and Levy, 1996:9). A similar combination of academic and behavioral skills was identified by the Secretary's Commission on Achieving Necessary Skills (SCANS)(1991) (see Box 4-1). These insights into what makes people employable are helpful, especially in contrast to the assumption—which underlies much vocational education and training—that employability is determined primarily by the possession of specific work skills. Job-specific skills remain critical in many fields, but they are both more easily learned and more quickly outmoded than are the new basic skills: To succeed at work today, most people need to acquire knowledge, skills, attitudes, and behaviors that are quintessential middle-class virtues.

The new basic skills and most of the skills identified by SCANS are the qualities that many youngsters acquire from attending good schools; from having strong families; from participating in church, scouts, 4-H, and other community organizations; and from engaging in a disciplined manner in such activities as sports, music, and dance. Summer and after-school work experience can also contribute to the new basic skills. Having fewer opportunities for such activities, many poor and minority youngsters experience difficulty finding and keeping jobs, even if they can overcome discriminatory practices and their geographic isolation from many jobs. For example, they may be unaccustomed to schedules and supervision and may lack customer-relations skills. In some cases, they may have developed competing competencies (Walther, 1976): For example, they may have found a highly aggressive interpersonal style that is accepted in their neighborhood, but such a style is unlikely to impress job interviewers. The speech, dress, and manners that serve young people well in their homes and neighborhoods may disqualify them from desirable jobs. Thus, obtaining work experience may be more important for disadvantaged youth than for relatively advantaged youth. But that work experience must be of high quality to have the

---

BOX 4-1
THE SECRETARY OF LABOR'S COMMISSION ON ACHIEVING NECESSARY SKILLS

The Secretary's Commission on Achieving Necessary Skills (SCANS) (1991) produced a list of goals and objectives of what employees need to be considered effective workers. SCANS proposed a set of five competencies workers should have.

Workplace Competencies

- **Resources**—They know how to allocate time, money, materials, space, and staff.
- **Interpersonal skills**—They can work on teams, teach others, serve customers, lead, negotiate, and work well with people from culturally diverse backgrounds.
- **Information**—They can acquire and evaluate data, organize and maintain files, interpret and communicate, and use computers to process information.
- **Systems**—They understand social, organizational, and technological systems; they can monitor and correct performance; and they can design or improve systems.
- **Technology**—They can select equipment and tools, apply technology to specific tasks, and maintain and troubleshoot equipment.

In addition, SCANS recommended three foundation skills and personal qualities that are needed for solid job performance.

Foundation Skills

- **Basic Skills**—reading, writing, arithmetic and mathematics, speaking, and listening.
- **Thinking Skills**—the ability to learn, to reason, to think creatively, to make decisions, and to solve problems.
- **Personal Qualities**—individual responsibility, self-esteem and self-management, sociability, and integrity.

---

desired effect. Because of the neighborhoods they tend to live in, those who are employed are likely to work in small firms and on a casual basis, arrangements that give them less protection in their jobs. It is especially critical that disadvantaged youth have opportunities to take leadership positions, not only to serve as subordinates (Hamilton and Claus, 1981). Poor, urban adolescents are also more likely than their middle-class counterparts to earn money illegally in the underground economy (e.g., from theft, drug sales, prostitution) (Wilson, 1987, 1996)—which is more dangerous than legal employment—although this phenomenon cannot be traced in national surveys.

Although good employment experiences may be particularly beneficial for disadvantaged youngsters, working may sometimes lead them away from school. For those who are initially less interested or involved in school or whose poor performance in school threatens their self-esteem, working may present an alternative that may become more attractive than maintaining the student role. Tienda and Ahituv (1996), using data from the NLSY, show that an increase in work effort (average weekly hours of work) at 18 years of age has a negative effect on the probability of college enrollment, especially among youth whose mothers did not complete high school. In the High School and Beyond study, only high-risk youth (defined by below-average socioeconomic status, low test scores, and low parental monitoring) were less likely to complete high school if they worked very long hours (more than 29 hours per week in their sophomore year). However, at-risk youth who worked 15 hours or more during their sophomore year in high school also had higher earnings 10 years later (Chaplin and Hannaway, 1996).

CONCLUSIONS

Whether working has positive or negative consequences for young people is a complex question. Employment is such a multifaceted phenomenon that many factors must be considered, including the broader contexts in which youth work (e.g., urban or rural), the intensity of their work, and the quality of their work experience. Moreover, there are many potential outcomes of employment, some positive and some negative.

The conclusions that can be drawn from the scientific literature are limited by the fact that all the studies involve correlational rather than experimental studies. However, researchers will certainly never be able to randomly assign young people to various work conditions, in order to conclusively show whether or not work causes certain outcomes. Well-designed correlational studies with good statistical controls for pre-existing differences among students who work at different intensities, such as those reviewed in this chapter, provide the best evidence that is likely ever to be available on the consequences of work during high school.

In several studies using NLSY data, long hours of work during high school, particularly during the senior year, have been associated with higher wages and steadier employment for up to 10 years after high school. These apparent economic advantages are accompanied by some decrease in overall educational attainment. If there are long-term economic advantages to working while in school, studies of people beyond their late 20s will have to be conducted. Ruhm (1997) speculates that the strong positive correlation between senior year employment and measures of job status 10 years later make it likely that this economic advantage will persist. Chaplin and Hannaway (1996) also suggest that the earnings advantage may persist for at-risk youngsters.

Of concern, however, is that the apparent short-term economic advantages of work experiences during high school are associated with some decrease in overall educational attainment. And, overall educational attainment has been found to be a strong predictor of long-term economic well-being (Angrist and Krueger, 1991; Bureau of the Census, 1993; DiPrete and McManus, 1996). It is possible that students who complete college, particularly those who pursue advanced degrees, could take more than 10 years after high school graduation to reap the economic rewards of their schooling. It will be important to study what happens to these groups of young people as they reach their peak earning years in their 40s and 50s, to ascertain if the benefits of high school employment persist or are overshadowed by reduced educational attainment. In fact, a recent study using econometric modeling techniques (Hotz et al., 1998) found that, once unmeasured differences between subjects were accounted for, the economic advantages to working while in high school disappeared: Students who went to school full-time without working had a much bigger wage advantage at age 27 than those who combined school and work.

Looking at the developmental consequences of employment for youth provides substantial evidence that working long hours is not good for them. Many studies show that high-intensity work while in school—generally defined as more than 20 hours per week during the school year—can be deleterious. Long hours of work are associated with increased likelihood that youngsters will engage in problem behaviors, including substance use and minor deviance. Long hours of work also are associated with diminished good health habits (e.g., sleep, exercise, and eating breakfast) and decreased time young people spend with their families. Moreover, as noted above, a high level of work during adolescence has been found to be associated with decreased eventual educational attainment. But, employment that is limited in intensity (generally defined as 20 hours per week or less) during high school has been found to promote postsecondary educational attainment. Even those researchers who find economic benefits associated with long hours of work during high school conclude that only light to moderate work should be encouraged (see, for example, Ruhm, 1997:770). Thus, overall, there is considerable evidence that high-intensity work can be deleterious, but that low- to moderate-intensity work can be beneficial.

The scientific literature does not allow a precise determination of the number of hours that constitute "too much" work for young people. Most studies have defined high-intensity work as more than 20 hours per week while school is in session, either for fairly arbitrary reasons or because of how data have been collected. Some studies have found negative outcomes beginning at 15 hours of work per week, and some found positive outcomes for more than 20 hours of work per week.

Most studies have focused on the hours that young people work, but there is reason to believe that the quality of work is also important for adolescents' development. Dimensions of work quality, including skill utilization and learning, relations with supervisors, and job-related stressors, have been found to have wide-ranging consequences for personal and vocational development, as well as for adolescents' relationships with parents and peers.

In conclusion, the scientific evidence raises fundamental questions about the intensity of work currently permitted for young people as well as the quality of the jobs that are available to them. Good jobs may be particularly important for poor youth, who are less able than middle-class adolescents to find part-time employment and more likely to be employed in low-skilled, hazardous jobs.

5

Agriculture

Agriculture holds a special place among industries in the United States. It is often treated differently than other industries under federal and state laws and regulations. The child labor laws applied to agriculture are less restrictive than those applied to nonagricultural industries, despite that fact that agriculture is one of the most hazardous industries in the country (see Chapter 6). Children working on their parents' farms are exempt from many legal protections: They are allowed to perform even those tasks designated as hazardous, which is not the case in nonagricultural work, where children are prohibited from hazardous jobs even if working in their parents' businesses.[1] Farms are also exempted from many health and safety standards under the Occupational Health and Safety Act. In fact, congressional riders to the annual appropriations bill prohibit the Occupational Health and Safety Administration (OSHA) from spending any money to "prescribe, issue, administer, or enforce any standard, rule, regulation, or order" under the act on farms that do not maintain temporary labor camps and that have ten or fewer employees (U.S. Departments of Labor, Health and Human Services, and

---

[1]In this chapter, the terms *agriculture* and *farm* are used interchangeably and in the broadest sense, which may include commercial farms, family farms, ranches, nurseries, and other establishments.

Education, and Related Agencies Appropriations Act, 1998, HR 2264, 105th Congress; this same language appears annually in the appropriations bill). In addition, farms are among the few workplaces that also serve as homes to many children and adolescents, which can make it difficult to distinguish work-related agricultural injuries from nonwork-related injuries.

Today, rapid changes are occurring in agriculture in the United States and around the world. The globalization of trade, advances in biotechnology, and such engineering feats as the leveling of land with sophisticated laser equipment, are resulting in an industrialization of agriculture and a notion that farms are becoming firms (Department of Agricultural Economics, 1995). These changes affect not only the types of tasks and equipment used on farms, but also the numbers and sizes of farms. Since 1940, the numbers of farms and farmworkers in the United States have been decreasing; see Figure 5-1. At the same time, the average size of farms has increased. In 1960 there were 3.96 million farms averaging 297 acres each; by 1996 the number of farms had dropped to 2.06 million, and their

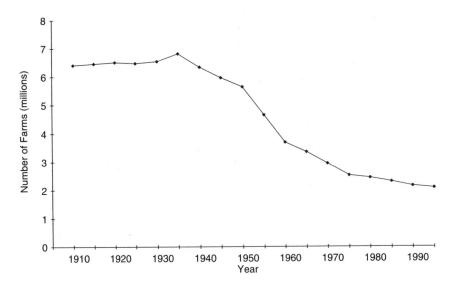

FIGURE 5-1 Number of U.S. farms, 1910 to 1995.
SOURCE: Data from National Agricultural Statistics Service. Available at http://www.usda.gov.nass/graphics/data/fl_frmwk.txt.

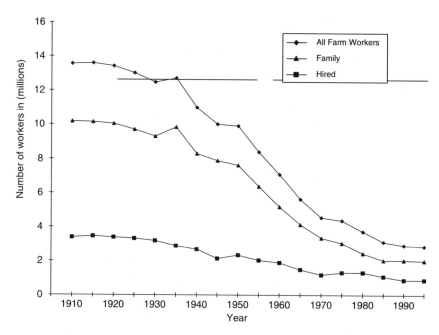

FIGURE 5-2 U.S. farmworkers by type, 1910 to 1995.
SOURCE: Data from National Agricultural Statistics Service. Available at http://
www.usda.gov/nass/graphics/data/fl_frmwk.txt.

average size had grown to 469 acres (Olenchock and Young, 1997a;
U.S. Department of Agriculture, 1997). This change has also affected the prevalence of family farms and family labor. In 1940,
75.6 percent of all workers on farms were family members, defined
by the U.S. Department of Agriculture as self-employed or unpaid
family workers. This percentage had declined to 69.4 percent by
1995; see Figure 5-2. The results of changing farms and demographics of workers may yield new types of agricultural diseases and injuries (Olenchock and Young, 1997b), such as chemical and biological exposures, resulting in new acute syndromes or chronic
conditions.

As the average size of farms continues to increase and more
workers are hired, there will likely be fewer children and adolescents
of the owners working on farms. However, there may be a subsequent increase in the number of adolescents hired as farmworkers
and in the number of farmworkers' children who are working alongside their parents in the fields. The results of the National Agricul-

tural Workers Survey indicate a trend towards an increased percentage of hired farmworkers who are between 14 and 17 years old: This age group now makes up 7 percent of all hired farmworkers working on crops (U.S. General Accounting Office, 1998). The Bureau of Census's Current Population Report indicates that there were 923,000 children younger than 15 years and 346,000 children between the ages of 15 and 19 residing on U.S. farms and ranches in 1991 (Dacquel and Dahmann, 1993). There are no data on the number or proportion of children and adolescents residing on farms who are directly involved with agriculture as paid or unpaid workers. Nor are there good data on how many children of paid farmworkers work with their parents in the field.

Three somewhat distinct groups of young people work on farms: children living and working on their parents' farms, adolescents who are hired to work on farms not owned or operated by their parents and whose parents are not so employed, and children who accompany their migrant farmworker parents. No data adequately documents the numbers of any of these groups. In 1996 about 300,000 young people between the ages of 15 and 17 worked in agriculture according to Current Population Survey data (U.S. General Accounting Office, 1998). About 75 percent of them were paid farmworkers, 15 percent were self-employed, and 10 percent were unpaid family workers. From National Agricultural Workers Survey data for 1993-1996, it is estimated that there were an average each year of 128,500 hired agricultural workers between the ages of 14 and 17 (U.S. General Accounting Office, 1998). Almost one-half of those 14- to 17-year-olds were living on their own, away from their parents (Mines et al., 1997).

The Current Population Survey, which is a household sample, may be likely to miss populations who do not have a stable residence, such as migrant agricultural workers. The National Agricultural Workers Survey includes only hired farmworkers 14 years of age or older; self-employed and unpaid family farm workers are excluded. Therefore, both of these surveys are likely to undercount the actual number of children and adolescents working in agriculture (Arroyo and Kurre, 1997; U.S. General Accounting Office, 1998). There is anecdotal evidence of very young children, usually children of migrant farmworkers, working in the fields but they are not counted in any systematic way, making it difficult to estimate the extent of agricultural work by children under the age of 14.

I'm 9 years old and I've been working in the fields with my parents since I was 4. We work hard, sometimes over 10 hours a day. We cut paprika with shears and stoop over to bag onions. We pick nuts and tap garlic.

Testimony before the Forum on
Federal Study on Child Labor
March 23, 1998, San Francisco, California

Whether young people are working on their parents' farms, are hired to work on the farms of others, or are accompanying their migrant farmworker parents, many of the hazards they face are similar. Analysts of child labor issues in agriculture often differentiate between family farm children and migrant farmworker children. Although this distinction may be useful for selected purposes, it is misleading in suggesting that there are exclusive categories of children who work in agriculture. In reality, there is a spectrum of variables with a range of conditions that affect the health and safety of all child laborers in agriculture. For example, any child working in agriculture could incur a traumatic injury or chronic disease. Conditions external to the work itself, such as poverty, education, and public policy may have a far stronger effect on children's well-being, but these conditions affect individuals in different ways. For example, migrant farmworker children are more likely to be living in poor conditions than nonmigrant children. Because it is so difficult to distinguish among the different groups of young farmworkers in either the employment or injury data, this chapter deals with the agricultural setting in general. When a particular group may be more affected by a specific hazard, it is noted. This chapter details some of the unique features of agriculture as a work setting, the types of risks young people encounter on farms, the injuries they suffer, and the barriers to regulating child labor on farms.

UNIQUE FEATURES OF AGRICULTURE

Life-Style and Family Farms

Since colonial times, farming has been held in high regard in the United States. The continent was unsettled territory, and the primary occupation of the new settlers was farming. English traditions exerted strong influences on colonial life and agriculture: The new immigrants brought with them notions of private property, a market system, and such farming tools as plows, hoes, and harvesters. They planted wheat and vegetables from European seeds and borrowed corn and tobacco seeds from the Indians. Because land was plentiful, various domesticated animals, such as sheep, swine, cattle, and horses, were left to graze unsupervised in nearby forests. However, although the pattern in Europe was often for the farmers to live in central villages with their land holdings on the outskirts, in colonial America they lived on their individual farmsteads. This settlement pattern encouraged a reliance on family labor, plus a strong sense of independence, individualism, and personal freedom. What the colonists wanted to avoid at all costs was the feudal land tenure system where workers on farms were not the land owners. Thus, through the years, the United States has protected an almost unlimited right to buy and sell real estate, including farm land, and the freedom to work the land as owners choose (Wilkening and Gilbert, 1987).

The strong belief in "agrarianism" reached a peak in the nineteenth century. Farming was considered the most legitimate and beneficial of occupations, farmers the most moral and patriotic of citizens (Danbom, 1997). But even today, Americans believe that most farmers are the ideal citizens: They work for themselves, they control the production decisions, they are fiercely independent, and they express their opinions in the political process of voting. From focus groups with family farmers, most believe that the heritage they have gained from their great-grandparents has been passed down through the generations, along with the land; they yearn to continue their farming lineage to their children and grandchildren, even when economic times are difficult. Thus, farm families expect their children to learn the business, help with the chores from an early age, and "shadow" the same-sex parent in their farm duties. The lifestyle on many family farms maintains traditions of years past. Daily routines are directed by the farm operator (usually the father) and

TABLE 5-1 U.S. Farm Resident Population
and Average Acres per Farm, 1850-1995

Year	Farm Population (as percent of U.S. total)	Average Acreage per Farm
1850	68.1	203
1860	n/a	199
1870	50.5	153
1880	43.8	134
1890	42.3	137
1900	41.9	147
1910	34.9	139
1920	30.1	149
1930	24.9	157
1940	23.2	175
1950	15.3	216
1960	8.7	297
1970	4.8	373
1980	2.1[a]	426[b]
1990	1.9[a]	461[b]
1995	n/a	469[c]

[a]Data from Dacquel and Dahmann (1993:Table A).
[b]Data from Bureau of the Census (1992:Table 1077).
[c]Data from Rasmussen (1997).

SOURCE: For 1850-1970, data from Bureau of the Census (1970).

are dominated by production needs, weather, and economic factors. Family participation plays a central role in preserving stability. The work and recreation activities of adults and children receive social support through public and privately sponsored programs, such as 4-H, Future Farmers of America, Cooperative Extension Service training, and rural churches.

However, over the past 150 years, there has been a remarkable decrease in the farm population and an increase in the average size of farms in acres (see Table 5-1). In 1780 and the revolutionary years, almost 95 percent of men reported being farmers; by 1880, the percentage had dropped just under 50 percent; today, less than 2 percent report farming as an occupation (Mills, 1995). What is remarkable is that this ever smaller number of farms and farmers has increased production, keeping up with the food and fiber demands of a growing population and producing a sizable excess for export. This dramatic change is attributable to three factors: (1) mechanization—the replacement of human and animal labor with capital investments; (2) specialization—the move from varied products of smaller farms to monoculture, or the output of only one product (such as strawberries, wheat, apples) on much larger farms; and (3) technological advances, including herbicides that replace hand weeding, fertilizers that permit growing the same crop on the same land year after year, and genetic manipulations that produce blemish-free fruit or slow-ripening tomatoes so that they can be transported long distances, and animal husbandry that uses artificial insemination to produce animals with desirable traits.

The growth of large-scale, intensive, often irrigation-based agriculture is matched by the decline of the small- or medium-size farms. The survival of smaller farms often depends on farmers or their family members taking an off-farm job in order to ensure the economic survival of the farm. Farmers with smaller farms also seek specialty niches, such as special fruits and vegetables, aimed at urban markets. These products are more labor intensive and are not as prone to mechanization.

While the number of farm workers has declined, including both hired and family workers, there has been a steady increase in immigrant labor pools employed in agriculture. Fitchen (1995:252) comments:

> . . . contrary to earlier forecasts, growers have not moved toward mechanization, but toward "Mexicanization" [a term coined by Palerm, 1991] . . . in such crops as strawberries, apples, pears, broccoli and asparagus, and specialty nursery plants.

Especially in California and other Western states, thousands of Mexican Americans and Mexican nationals are filling the seasonal labor needs of intensive hand labor needed during the planting, weeding, and harvesting, especially in fruit and vegetable monocropping. Florida and the Eastern seaboard states also attract immigrant workers, many of whom are from Haiti and other West Indian nations, as well as from Mexico and other Central American countries.

What do these changes imply for the numbers of children working in agriculture in the future? The answer is mixed: With the decline in the numbers of family farms, fewer farm children will be working on their parents' farms, but it is anticipated that there will be larger numbers of children of migrant farm laborers involved in agriculture. For the latter children, many are likely to be underage children traveling with and helping their parents during their search for temporary work.

Home and Work-Site Issues

Unlike most occupational settings, agriculture often has unclear distinctions between the home and the workplace. The majority of farms are contiguous with the families' residences and have few outside (i.e., nonfamily) employees. The nature of production agriculture may require work at any time of the day, every day of the year. Thus, the separation between obligations to attend to work and to children can rarely be made by adults who raise their families on farms.

The proximity of the worksite to the home facilitates having young people assist with planned or unscheduled work on the farm. Their easy availability to participate in work makes it difficult to distinguish when children are working rather than doing family chores or being present at the workplace. Often, the unpredictable nature of farming (e.g., the difficult delivery of a newborn calf) may place a young worker in a situation for which there is insufficient training and preparation. Agricultural injuries to children also may occur when they are bystanders to work (Stueland et al., 1996). Youngsters may be playing in or around large vehicles, moving machinery, and large animals. This makes it difficult to distinguish agricultural work-related injuries to children and adolescents from those not related to work.

Children who work in the fields are also exposed to numerous hazards. Many of these hazards are particularly germane to young migrant farmworkers, who work in the fields alongside their parents—a pattern that began at the turn of the century. At that time, many farms in the Northeast and on the Atlantic coast could not compete with the large, mechanized wheat and grain farms that were opening in the Midwest; many of the old farms switched to growing fruits and vegetables for the burgeoning urban markets. Because these were seasonal markets, the farms needed large numbers of workers for fairly short periods of time. Children were often included in this labor pool. At first, immigrants and their children were brought in by truckloads from the cities. For example, Italian immigrants worked on New Jersey cranberry farms:

> Since children and women can work efficiently in berry picking and vegetable cultivation, Italians made the family "the working unit,". . . There are women and children in swarms[;] old, young and middle-aged are found in every field (The Dillingham Commission, 1911, quoted in Hahamovitch, 1997:31).

When workers began to request better wages, the growers preferred to use displaced African American plantation workers from the South. Most of these workers brought their children along because there was no place to leave them, and they could assist their parents in picking berries and weeding the fields. The only groups who did not bring their children were the foreign workers contracted for by the U.S. government. This included workers from Jamaica, Haiti, and other places in the Caribbean. The formal contracts called for specific numbers of males or females, and children were not included.

The use of migrant seasonal workers was not limited to the East Coast. In the early 1900s, midwestern farms first attracted migrant seasonal workers from such cities as Chicago, Milwaukee, and Detroit (Slesinger and Muirragui, 1981). California farmers met their early need for farmworkers through waves of immigrants: Chinese in the 1880s, Japanese in the early 1900s, Mexicans and Filipinos after World War I, and Mexicans again during World War II (Martin, 1988:5). After World War II, cities offered good wages and steady work in the factories, which not only reduced the pool of available farmworkers, but also prompted rural workers to move to the city. Urged by the agricultural industry to relieve the resulting shortage by importing workers, the federal government stepped in. One well-known example was the Labor Importation Program (Bracero Program), which permitted Mexican nationals to seek agricultural work in the United States from 1941 to 1964. Since that time, even without a program, there has been a steady influx of workers from Mexico and other Latin American countries into the agricultural fields of the United States. Many of these migrant workers bring their families with them, and their children continue to be brought to the fields to work. Data from the National Agricultural Workers Survey indicate that 28 percent of hired farmworkers have children living with them and 13 percent of those children are reported to be working in the fields (U.S. General Accounting Office, 1998).

Reasons for Children's Work in Agriculture

From the perspective of the parents whose children work in agriculture, there are numerous reasons for the practice. Hired farm laborers, including migrant and seasonal workers, often include children and adolescents in family work teams. Economic need, the availability of jobs for people with limited command of the English language, and the fact that little training is necessary may make working in agriculture an attractive choice for many people.

On family farms, the reasons for children's participation in hazardous work was recently reported in a study of Wisconsin farm fathers (Lee et al., 1997). Fathers were asked about selected factors that influenced their decision to allow young children to drive tractors, ride on tractors, and be near the hind (kicking) legs of dairy cows. These high-risk activities were very common practices, and the fathers believed strongly that they were justified because they would help children gain farm experience, develop a strong work ethic, spend time with other family members (during farm work), build self-confidence, and save work time and money for their fathers.

Economic necessity is the main reason migrant children work in the fields. Most migrant farmworkers do not earn enough to raise their families out of poverty (Davis, 1997). A national survey conducted between 1989 and 1991 estimated that about 57 percent of migrant farmworkers and 73 percent of migrant children under the age of 14 live in poverty (Gabbard et al., 1994). Added hands in the field mean more productivity for migrant families when they are paid on a piece-work basis.

Common payroll practices work to the detriment of children, among others, in farmworkers' families. Frequently, the earnings of whole families are listed in payroll records under the name of the male head of household. This practice keeps children and other family members from earning the minimum wage or receiving credit toward Social Security, unemployment compensation, or workers' compensation benefits. By appearing to have fewer workers on their payrolls, some employers are able to completely avoid coverage under the Fair Labor Standards Act, because omitting all but the heads of households on their payroll lists may reduce the number of "man days" of labor in a calendar quarter to below the 500-man-day threshold that triggers coverage by the act (29 U.S.C. §213(a)). Although there are no reliable data on how many children of migrant farmworkers actually work in the fields, farmworker advocates and enforcement officials report that the single greatest problem facing children working in agriculture is children working under their parents' payroll numbers (U.S. General Accounting Office, 1998).

INJURIES TO CHILDREN AND ADOLESCENTS IN AGRICULTURE

As for other industrial sectors, there are no reliable annual U.S. statistics regarding fatal and nonfatal occupational injuries and disease in agriculture because there is no national surveillance system for agricultural workers. In addition to the general limitations of the data that are available (see Chapters 2 and 3) for both adult and young agricultural workers, in agriculture there are the added difficulties of differentiating bystanders from workers; inconsistencies in the definitions of work, farm, and child; and the lack of a universal classification scheme for coding agricultural injuries.

The estimates that have been made are based on adaptations of sources such as the National Electronic Injury Surveillance System (NEISS) of the Consumer Product Safety Commission and state fatality reports. A recent report suggests that an average of 104 individuals younger than 19 die in farm-related incidents every year, which is an annual rate of 8.0 deaths per 100,000 population (Rivara, 1997). Because the source of these estimates does not permit distinguishing deaths unrelated to work from those deaths associated with active labor on farms, the true rate of agricultural work-related childhood fatalities is unknown. There is evidence, however, that most of these fatalities are work-related because children 10 and older—who are more likely than younger children to be working—had substantially higher fatality rates than those in younger age groups. Furthermore, males, who are traditionally assigned more hazardous jobs on farms, had fatality rates that were 2.4 times greater rate than those of females, with the highest fatality rates occurring in the adolescent years.

Further evidence of the importance of agriculture's role in work-related fatalities among children and adolescents comes from the Census of Fatal Occupational Injuries, which shows 108 deaths of children younger than 18 in agriculture for the years 1992 through 1995. Although only about 8 percent of all young workers are employed in agriculture, 40 percent of the work-related deaths of children and adolescents under the age of 18 during that period occurred in agriculture (Derstine, 1996).

A 1993 report from the National Institute for Occupational Safety and Health estimated that children aged 10 and older suffered nearly 13,000 agricultural work-related injuries that resulted in lost worktime (Myers, 1995). Of these injuries, nearly two-thirds occurred during the months of June, July, and August, when children would typically be out of school and available to work. It is estimated that each year more than 100,000 children suffer preventable injuries associated with agriculture (T. Miller, 1995); this figure includes children who are residents, visitors to farms, and active laborers.

HAZARDS FACED BY CHILDREN IN AGRICULTURE

Studies regarding children's work in agriculture reveal a variety of specific tasks and chores performed by children, beginning at very young ages (Aherin and Todd, 1989; Hawk et al., 1991; Tevis and Finck, 1989). Children's work on farms ranges from gathering eggs by the age of 5 to operating a pickup truck before the age of 11 (Tevis, 1994). Males perform nearly all tasks at a younger age than females. Some work is relatively low risk (e.g., carrying a feed bucket), but many tasks carry the risk of serious injury (e.g., feeding pigs, hauling manure, applying pesticides). Children who are working in the fields may be near or in the way of machinery, including tractors and trucks; they may fall off ladders while picking fruit; they may get dizzy from dehydration because they do not have access to drinking water. Studies show that the most common agents of minor injury to children are animals and falls, while the most common agents of serious injury are tractors and moving machinery (Purschwitz, 1990; Rivara, 1997; Stallones and Gunderson, 1994).

Other conditions that pose risks to children are poor sanitary facilities, inadequate housing, long hours in the fields, and heavy lifting and carrying of produce. Furthermore, there is concern for both the acute and long-term effects that might result from workers' being exposed to pesticides and other agricultural chemicals, beginning at young ages.

Pesticides[2]

Pesticides that are used extensively in U.S. agriculture include such compounds as insecticides, herbicides, defoliants, molluscicides, nematocides, algicides, and acaricides (Shaver and Tong, 1991). Pesticides may be absorbed into the body through the skin, by inhalation, and by ingestion. Agricultural workers can experience exposure through these routes in a variety of ways. In addition to the exposure that occurs during the processes of diluting, mixing, and applying the substances, workers can be exposed to drifting chemicals from cropdusting, and can come into contact with residues during harvesting, weeding, and pruning and while eating in the field. Water may become contaminated and then be used for drinking, bathing, and cooking. Particularly hazardous are labor-intensive crops, such as fruits and vegetables, which are extensively treated with pesticides.

Pesticides have been associated with a number of delayed health effects, such as chronic dermatitis, fatigue, headaches, sleep disturbances, anxiety, memory problems, and different kinds of cancers, birth defects, sterility, blood disorders, and abnormalities in liver and kidney function, chronic neurotoxicity, and adverse reproductive consequences (Moses, 1989; Sharp et al., 1986; Wasserstrom and Wiles, 1985). Estimates of the occurrence of pesticide-related illnesses are difficult to make because underreporting is likely: Many migrant farmworkers who might be affected never see physicians or are never properly diagnosed; if the workers do seek medical attention, the health-care professionals may be unfamiliar with the symptoms of pesticide-related illnesses, and farmworkers may not know the names of the pesticides being used. Although relatively new regulations require workers to be informed if a field is to be sprayed, there is no information as to how well the warning procedure is being followed. In addition, there is relatively little information on the effects on children and adolescents of exposure to pesticides and whether they should stay out of sprayed fields longer than adults.

---

[2]This section relies heavily on Mobed et al. (1992).

Between 1985 and 1992, the Environmental Protection Agency reported more than 750 cases of reported exposure to pesticides involving youngsters under 18. The data on which these figures are based have been shown to have numerous weaknesses, such as limited coverage, underreporting of exposures, and lack of key data (U.S. General Accounting Office, 1993); therefore, the number of reported cases is likely to be an undercount of actual exposures.

Although several reviews have addressed the association of cancer and pesticide exposure among farmers and permanent farm help (Council on Scientific Affairs, 1988; Zahm and Blair, 1993; Zahm et al., 1997), few population-based studies have been published about the effects of pesticides and virtually none have focused on young workers. In California, three projects—a case study of a childhood cancer cluster (California Department of Health Services, 1988), a hospital record-based study of birth defects (Schwartz and LoGerfo, 1988), and a health survey (Mines and Kearney, 1982)—examined some of the effects. The investigations suggest that chronic health problems increase as a result of exposure to pesticides, but the studies have been limited in size and scope, and no clear conclusions have been reached regarding the magnitude of pesticide-related effects, particularly for children.

Poor Field Sanitation

A lack of clean drinking water, hand-washing facilities, and toilets presents another hazard to agricultural workers. This lack of sanitary facilities contributes to a spread of parasites. Rates of parasitic infections among migrant farmworkers have been found to be much higher than rates among the general population (Occupational Safety and Health Administration, 1987). A lack of water to wash and an absence of toilets in the field may result in infections, dermatitis, parasites, urinary tract infections, respiratory illnesses, eye disease, and other illnesses (Occupational Safety and Health Administration, 1987).

Long Hours and Strenuous Labor

Fatigue has been associated with increased risk of injury on the job (M. Miller, 1995; Rosa, 1995). Children's work in agriculture may include assisting with daily chores (such as milking cows) or periodic work (such as baling hay), which often involves early morning or late evening work, or both, in addition to standard work hours or school attendance. Adolescents may be particularly susceptible to fatigue due to physiological changes that cause them to require more sleep (Carskadon, 1990, 1997; Carskadon et al., 1980; see Chapter 4). Fatigue or drowsiness associated with extended work hours may lead to poor judgment in performing duties, including the temptation to take dangerous shortcuts. Agricultural work is strenuous physical work—such as lifting heavy loads, working in awkward positions, and constantly repeating actions—that has been linked to musculoskeletal trauma (Bernard, 1997). How these activities may differentially affect children and adolescents has yet to be examined. Strenuous physical labor may be compounded by the effects of high temperatures in the fields, making agricultural workers subject to heat-related illnesses and injuries (U.S. Environmental Protection Agency, 1993). It is known that young children are more vulnerable to heat-related illnesses than adults; however, whether older children and adolescents are also more vulnerable than adults is not known (Arroyo and Kurre, 1997).

Threats to the Well-Being of Migrant Farmworker Children

In addition to being exposed to the risks from agricultural work that all young workers on farms may experience, migrant farmworker children experience additional risks, including living under adverse housing and sanitary conditions and having problems related to the children's inability to obtain consistent and good education. Because of moving on a seasonal basis, changing schools, missing the beginnings or ends of semesters, and possibly having difficulties with English as a second language, these children are candidates for dropping out of school before obtaining their high-school diplomas. They are also less likely to learn the skills that could lead to careers other than farm work as their primary occupation as adults. Migrant farmworker adolescents often lack their families' supervision. The National Agricultural Workers Survey found that 47 percent of farmworkers below the age of 18 do not live with their parents; 80 percent of farmworker teens born outside the United States live away from their parents (Mines et al., 1997).

REGULATION OF AGRICULTURE

The various labor laws and regulations that apply to children are discussed in detail in Chapter 6. Because of the many exemptions and exclusions that apply uniquely to children working in agriculture, however, information relevant to those children from the Fair Labor Standards Act (FLSA) and the Occupational Safety and Health Act is also discussed here.

Fair Labor Standards Act

Box 5-1 lists the current rules and regulations regarding hours and hazardous conditions that apply to children working in agriculture. Farmworkers were initially excluded from protection under the Fair Labor Standards Act of 1938. A 1974 amendment set a minimum of age 12 as the legal limit for children to participate in farm work, but exemptions were granted for 10- and 11-year-olds. In all other industries, children must reach the age of 14 before they can legally work. The list of hazardous conditions from which children under 16 are prohibited is also listed in Box 5-1. These conditions ban children from the most likely sources of nonfatal and fatal injuries: operating machinery and handling breeding animals. Despite the fact that operating tractors under 20 horsepower and handling nonbreeding animals present serious hazards to children, they are legally permitted (Purschwitz, 1990). None of the FLSA rules and regulations applies to children working on their parents' farms.

Occupational Safety and Health Act

Box 5-2 summarizes the regulations that pertain to agriculture under the Occupational Safety and Health Act. It must be noted, however, that regulations are enforced only on establishments with 11 or more employees, which covers only about 5 percent of agricultural establishments in the United States. This does not mean that smaller farms ignore these regulations; indeed, many do abide by most basic safety rules and provide protective equipment. However, the Occupational Safety and Health Administration is prohibited by Congress from enforcing any of its regulations on small farms (see Chapter 6 for further details).

BOX 5-1 Fair Labor Standards Act

All children working on their parents' farm are exempt from limits on hours of work and hazardous conditions. For other children working in agriculture:

Hours

- Individuals over the age of 15 may perform any job, hazardous or not, for unlimited hours.
- Children aged 14 and 15 may perform any nonhazardous farm job outside of school hours.
- Children aged 12 and 13 may work outside school hours in nonhazardous jobs, either with their parents' consent or on the same farm as their parents.
- Children under the age of 12 may perform nonhazardous jobs outside of school hours with their parents' consent on farms not covered by minimum-wage requirements.
- Children aged 10 and 11 may be employed to hand-harvest short-season crops outside of school hours, under special waivers.

For other children under 16 working in agriculture, they are prohibited from:

Hazardous Conditions

- Operating tractors with horsepower greater than 20 power take off.
- Operating corn pickers, cotton pickers, grain combines, hay mowers, forage harvesters, hay balers, potato diggers, mobile pea viners, feed grinders, crop dryers, forage blowers, auger conveyors, nongravity-type self-unloading wagons or trailers, power post-hole diggers, power post drivers, or nonwalking type rotary tillers.
- Operating trenchers or earth-moving equipment, fork lifts, potato combines, or power-driven saws.
- Handling breeding animals, sows with suckling pigs, cows with newborn calves.
- Felling, bucking, skidding, loading, or unloading timber with a butt diameter of more than 6 inches.
- Using ladders or scaffolds more than 20 feet high.
- Driving a bus, truck, or car while transporting passengers, or riding as a passenger or helper on a tractor.
- Working inside fruit, forage, or grain storage units, silos, or manure pits.
- Exposure to agricultural chemicals classified as Category I or II of toxicity.
- Working with explosives.
- Being exposed to anhydrous ammonia.

BOX 5-2
Occupational Safety and Health Act Regulations

Farms and ranches are exempt from Occupational Safety and Health Act regulations if they employ 10 or fewer employees and do not have labor camps. About 95 percent of farms in the United States are therefore exempt.

Larger farms must abide by the regulations specific to agriculture:

• roll-over protection for tractors;
• safety guards on farm field equipment, farmstead equipment, and cotton gins; and
• provision of drinking water, toilets, and handwashing facilities in the fields (field sanitation).

Large farms must also abide by a limited number of standards that apply to all industries. These standards apply to the following:

• temporary labor camps;
• storage and handling of anhydrous ammonia;
• logging operations;
• slow-moving vehicles;
• cadmium; and
• retention of Department of Transportation markings, placards, and labels.

See Chapter 6 for further details.

The original Occupational Safety and Health Act was passed in 1970, but it took 17 years for the Occupational Safety and Health Administration to pass requirements pertaining to standards for sanitary facilities in agricultural fields. That is, only in 1987 were regulations established to require a supply of drinking water, portable toilets, and water to wash hands in the fields of the larger farms.

BARRIERS TO REGULATION OF AGRICULTURE

Interventions protecting children from agricultural hazards generate philosophical debate over issues germane to parenting, public policy, and agricultural economics (Aherin et al., 1992; Kelsey, 1991, 1994; Kelsey et al., 1994; Mull, 1994). Since the 1970s, an idealized view of farmers and farm work has led politicians to permit distancing of agriculture from the occupational safety movement (Kelsey, 1994). Major farm organizations oppose federal inspections or investigations on small farms (American Farm Bureau Federation, 1998). At the same time, child safety advocates strongly endorse the adoption of public policy measures to safeguard children, because of the demonstrated success of such measures in reducing injuries in other arenas (American Academy of Pediatrics, 1988; Finney et al., 1993; Pless and Arsenault, 1987).

In the majority of farm operations, farm owner-operators are responsible for seeking information on appropriate safety standards and for purchasing machinery equipped with safety features. Farm owner-operators are also responsible for maintaining safety in the operation of equipment, in the structures, and in the entire work environment, while monitoring the presence, training, and participation of others in the farm work. These responsibilities may prove daunting, both in terms of financial and time investments, to owners of small farms.

Under the Fair Labor Standards Act and the Occupational Safety and Health Act, legal exemptions limit federal or state authority over hours of work, salary, and occupational safety standards related to youngsters involved in farm work. Farm owner-operators who employ young workers other than members of their immediate families are required to abide by child labor laws and hazardous work orders for their nonexempt workers. They are exempt from abiding by these laws when they employ their own children. Evidence to date suggests that public policy regarding agriculture currently bestows very limited protection for children (Landrigan et al., 1994).

CONCLUSIONS

Agriculture remains one of the most hazardous occupations in the United States, and as many as one-third of the individuals who suffer farm-related injuries are children. Numerous studies have reported acute, traumatic injuries suffered by children who work with farm machinery, livestock, or tractors. Far fewer studies have reported on the chronic effects of farm work—such as those associated with extended work hours, adverse weather conditions, repetitive work methods, and exposures to bacteria, viruses, and pesticides and other compounds—on young people.

As with many types of employment, working on farms may yield positive outcomes for children. In some cases, they are eager to participate in farm work, knowing they may have the opportunity to acquire increasing work responsibility and, possibly, farm ownership in the future. Improved self-confidence, self-esteem, and work skills are attributes often detected in young people engaged in some aspects of farm work. At the same time, the lack of legal protections for many aspects of farm work by children and adolescents raises questions about the negative aspects of such work. Ideally, agriculture should provide safe, appropriate opportunities for young people to develop meaningful skills and attributes that increase their likelihood of succeeding in the adult labor market.

6

Laws, Regulations, and Training

The hours of work and types of jobs that children and adolescents may perform are regulated at both the state and federal levels by a variety of agencies. In general, businesses involved in interstate commerce are subject to federal laws. Businesses not subject to federal regulation may be covered under state laws, which often differ from each other and from federal laws.

The principal federal law that addresses the protection of children at work is the Fair Labor Standards Act (FLSA). This act allows for the regulation of the hours and types of work performed by individuals under the age of 16 so that their employment "is confined to periods which will not interfere with their schooling and to conditions which will not interfere with their health and well-being" (29 U.S.C. §203 (1)). The FLSA does not authorize the regulation of the hours worked by 16- and 17-year-olds, but it does permit the Secretary of Labor to specify certain jobs as hazardous and prohibit 16- and 17-year-olds from working in those jobs. Not all working children are covered by the federal child labor provisions. The FLSA applies only to businesses that are engaged in interstate commerce and have annual gross income in excess of $500,000. According to the Department of Labor, 6.5 million workplaces with 110 million employees are subject to FLSA; there are no data on how many of these employees are children or adolescents.

At the state level, child labor regulations and levels of protection vary widely. Children are protected differently depending on whether they work in agricultural or nonagricultural jobs, in the public or private sector, and in small or big businesses. The laws and rules of most states provide less protection for children than do the federal laws and rules, although a few states provide more protection.

Whether child labor laws are applicable to children and adolescents working in certain new federal programs is unclear. The School-to-Work Opportunities Act, for example, requires only that students receive broad instruction, to the extent practicable during the work-based component of the program, on all aspects of the industry in which they are working (20 U.S.C. §6113 (a)(5)); there is no specific requirement that the school-based portion of the curriculum address health and safety issues, including training in on-the-job hazards.

Although not specifically aimed at children, other laws and programs are also relevant for children and adolescents who work. Most important among these is the Occupational Safety and Health Act, passed in 1970, which addresses the safety and health of all workers. Some aspects of the Federal Insecticide, Fungicide, and Rodenticide Act are relevant to children's and adolescents' exposure to pesticides. Workers' compensation laws also affect youngsters' work experiences and protection.

This chapter first reviews the laws and regulations that apply to children and adolescents in the workplace and discusses issues related to the enforcement and effectiveness of the laws and regulations. The chapter then discusses health and safety training efforts.

LAWS AND REGULATIONS PERTAINING TO CHILD LABOR

Fair Labor Standards Act

The Fair Labor Standards Act of 1938, as amended (29 U.S.C. Chapter 8 §201 et seq.), provides for the health and welfare of working people and authorizes the U.S. Department of Labor to establish special rules for the protection of children. These rules, issued by the Employment Standards Administration, set limits on the hours and times that children under the age of 16 may work; describe—in documents called hazardous orders—specific work that cannot be performed by children under the age of 18 in nonagricultural jobs and under the age of 16 in agricultural jobs; and establish minimum ages for various types of work. The act prohibits "oppressive child labor in commerce," which it defines as work that may be detrimental to children's health or well-being. Another stated purpose is to ensure that the employment of 14- and 15-year-olds does not interfere with their schooling. In general, these standards represent an all-or-nothing approach; regulations prohibit some types of employment for children but ignore the conditions of work for youngsters in permissible jobs.

By statute, different employment standards apply to children employed in nonagricultural work and those engaged in agricultural work (29 U.S.C. §213 (c); see also, 29 C.F.R. 570 (C)(3)). Hours of work and hazardous orders, even for the same hazard, vary significantly under each set of standards.

Few standards in the FLSA apply to all children and adolescents at work. Although the basic minimum age for employment is 14 in nonagricultural occupations (except for those declared hazardous by the Secretary of Labor), there are various exemptions. Minors younger than 14 may work for their parents (except in mining, manufacturing, or the jobs declared hazardous by the Secretary of Labor). They may also be employed in movie, radio, or theatrical businesses and to deliver newspapers.

Children working in agriculture are covered under different, less protective standards than are those working in other industries. Children of any age can be employed in any job on a farm owned or operated by their parents. Those who are 12 or 13 may perform any nonhazardous farm job outside of school hours, either with their parents' consent or on the same farm as their parents. A 1977 amendment to the FLSA allows the Department of Labor to grant special waivers for the employment of children aged 10 and 11 to hand-harvest certain seasonal crops outside of school hours, although no such waivers have been granted by the department since 1986.[1]

---

[1]As a result of a 1980 decision by the U.S. Court of Appeals for the District of Columbia (National Association of Farmworker Organizations et al., v. Marshall, 202 U.S. App. DC 317; 628 F.2d 604), the department has been enjoined from issuing these special waivers if any pesticides have been used on the crops to be harvested.

Hours and Times of Work

The standards that apply to agricultural and nonagricultural work differ significantly with respect to the hours of work allowable for children and adolescents. For nonagricultural jobs, the FLSA limits the number of hours and the times of day at which work can begin and end for those under the age of 16; youth over the age of 16 are allowed to work unlimited numbers of hours. Most of the specific requirements regarding permissible hours of work for non-agricultural jobs do not apply to agricultural work. The exception is work during school hours. No one under the age of 16 may work during school hours except on a farm owned and operated by the child's parents. As noted above, children working on their parents' farms are completely exempted from coverage under the FLSA: Regardless of age, they may perform any job—whether hazardous or not—with no time restrictions. The general standards for permissible hours of work and starting and stopping times in nonagricultural work are shown in Box 6-1. The permissible age for work, jobs, hours, and start and stop times in agricultural jobs are shown in Box 6-2.

Despite federal rules, much is left to the states, which can and often do adopt less stringent standards, particularly regarding hours of work. For example, a number of states allow 14- and 15-year-olds to work more than 40 hours per week while school is in session (National Consumers League, 1992). In the absence of federal regulations limiting the maximum hours of work for 16- and 17-year-olds, some states have adopted their own varying standards, while many states follow the federal lead and have no standards for the hours 16- and 17-year-olds are allowed to work. A few states, such as Washington and New York, have adopted child labor standards that are more stringent than federal protections. For example, New York uses the federal standards for 14- and 15-year-olds, but it also imposes slightly less restrictive hour and time of work limitations on 16- and 17-year-olds. Washington's child labor law is stricter than the federal standard for all adolescents, limiting 14- and 15-year-olds to 16 hours of work per week and 16- and 17-year-olds to 20 hours of work per week while school is in session. State laws are summarized in Table 6-1 (at the end of this chapter). When both federal and state laws are applicable, the FLSA requires that the more stringent law be followed.

BOX 6-1
Fair Labor Standards Act Restrictions on Hours Worked
in Nonagricultural Jobs

• Individuals aged 18 or older may perform any job, whether hazardous or not, for unlimited hours, in accordance with minimum wage and overtime requirements.

• Children aged 16 or 17 may perform any nonhazardous job for unlimited hours.

• Children aged 14 or 15 may work outside school hours in various nonmanufacturing, nonmining, nonhazardous jobs up to:

  • 3 hours on a school day;
  • 18 hours in a school week;
  • 8 hours on a nonschool day; and
  • 40 hours in a nonschool week.

• Children aged 14 or 15 may work only between the hours of 7 a.m. and 7 p.m., except from June 1 through Labor Day, when evening hours are extended to 9 p.m.

Federal law does not authorize the Department of Labor to regulate the maximum permissible hours for 16- and 17-year-olds, largely for historical reasons: The FLSA was passed in 1938, when many 16- and 17-year-olds were working full-time and not attending school (Greenberger and Steinberg, 1986; Kett, 1977). Now, the vast majority of adolescents are still in school. In 1990, 93 percent of 16-year-olds and 88 percent of 17-year-olds were in school.[2]

It has been suggested that some 16- and 17-year-old students might drop out of school if their work hours are limited. Although this committee did not thoroughly review the literature on dropping out of school, it appears that multiple factors, many of which precede entry into the work force, may lead youngsters to drop out of school (Steinberg, 1996). Young people who drop out of school do not necessarily enter the work force: Based on 1990 census data, 73

---

[2]School enrollment figures are from an analysis of 1990 census data performed by National Research Council staff.

BOX 6-2
Fair Labor Standards Act Rules for Hours Worked in Agricultural Jobs

• Children aged 16 and older may perform any job, hazardous or not, for unlimited hours.

• Children aged 14 or 15 may perform any nonhazardous farm job outside of school hours.

• Children aged 12 or 13 may work outside school hours in nonhazardous jobs, either with parents' consent or on the same farm as parents.

• Children under the age of 12 may perform nonhazardous jobs outside of school hours with their parents' consent on farms not covered by minimum-wage requirements.

• Children aged 10 or 11 may be employed to hand-harvest short-season crops outside of school hours, under special waivers. [Note: A court injunction currently blocks the issuing of these waivers if any pesticides have been used on the crops.]

• Minors of any age may be employed by their parents at any time in any job on a farm owned or operated by their parents.

percent of 16-year-olds and 65 percent of 17-year-olds who are not in school are not working, either.[3]

It has also been suggested that limiting the hours of work may make it more difficult for teens to find jobs. Often, when employment of a particular group is made more difficult or more costly for employers, the employment level of that group declines. However, the experience in Washington state suggests that this may not necessarily be the case for young people. In 1992, Washington state changed its child labor laws to impose a 20-hour per week, 4-hour per day limitation on 16- and 17-year-olds during the school year. The Washington state law also prohibits 16- and 17-year-olds from working past 10:00 p.m. on a night preceding a schoolday. A 1994 study by the Washington state Department of Labor and Industries (Department of Labor and Industries, 1994) found no decrease in the number of jobs available to minors following the new law. Only 15 percent of employers reported negative effects from the change.

---

[3]Committee analysis of 1990 census data.

Hazardous Occupation Orders

The FLSA allows the Secretary of Labor to designate, by means of documents called hazardous occupation orders (usually referred to as hazardous orders), specific agricultural and nonagricultural employment as hazardous or particularly detrimental to minors' health or well-being. Anyone under the age of 18 is prohibited from working in nonagricultural industries and occupations named in a hazardous order; in agriculture, hazardous orders apply to youth under the age of 16.

There are currently 17 federal hazardous orders for nonagricultural occupations and 11 for agriculture (29 C.F.R. 570 (E)). These orders are predominantly related to physical hazards, such as using power tools, operating power-driven machinery, engaging in mining, working with explosives, and driving vehicles with passengers; see Boxes 6-3 and 6-4.

The hazardous orders were issued decades ago and have rarely been updated to reflect contemporary work. Some of the restrictions have become irrelevant. At the same time, youngsters in today's workplaces encounter hazards that did not exist, were not recognized, or were not performed by minors when the standards were written. For example, the orders do not address a range of well-recognized occupational health hazards, such as exposures to regulated carcinogens and reproductive toxins, or musculoskeletal risks that may pose different, and possibly higher, risks to young workers (see Chapter 3 for a discussion of the susceptibility of children and adolescents). Few states regulate young people's exposure to biohazards, carcinogens, reproductive toxins, toxic sensitizers, and substances that cause irreversible damage to certain organs. (See Washington state law for an example of a state that does regulate these exposures; WAC 296-125-030.)

The process for updating the federal hazardous orders has been controlled, since 1993, by the Administrative Procedures Act (5 U.S.C. §553). This act requires that a notice of proposed rulemaking be published in the Federal Register; that interested persons be given the opportunity to submit written data, views, or arguments; and that, after consideration of relevant matters, the final rule be published at least 30 days before its effective date. In 1994 the Department of Labor issued an advance notice of proposed rulemaking on child labor regulations, orders, and statements of inter-

---

BOX 6-3
Nonagricultural Jobs Prohibited by Hazardous Orders

Seventeen hazardous nonfarm jobs, as determined by the Secretary of Labor, are prohibited for youngsters under the age of 18. Generally, they may not work at jobs that involve:

1. manufacturing or storing explosives
2. driving a motor vehicle and being an outside helper on a motor vehicle
3. coal mining
4. logging and sawmilling
5. power-driven wood-working machines*
6. exposure to radioactive substances and to ionizing radiation
7. power-driven hoisting apparatus
8. power-driven metal-forming, punching, and shearing machines*
9. mining, other than coal mining
10. slaughtering, or meat packing, processing, or rendering (including power-driven meat slicing machines)*
11. power-driven bakery machines
12. power-driven paper-products machines*
13. manufacturing brick, tile, and related products
14. power-driven circular saws, band saws, and guillotine shears*
15. wrecking, demolition, and ship-breaking operations
16. roofing operations*
17. excavation operations*

---

*Limited exemptions are provided for apprentices and student-learners under specified standards.

SOURCE: U.S. Department of Labor (1990:3).

---

pretation (59 Fed. Reg. 25167 [1994]) and sought the views of the public on any changes it considered necessary in child labor regulations. NIOSH, based on research on jobs that pose hazards to children and adolescents, made a number of recommendations about needed changes in the hazardous orders in its comments to advanced notice of proposed rulemaking (National Institute for Occupational Safety and Health, 1994). As of September 1998, the proposed rule had yet to be issued.

BOX 6-4
Agricultural Jobs Prohibited by Hazardous Orders

Eleven hazardous farm jobs, as determined by the Secretary of Labor, are out of bounds for teens below the age of 16. Children and adolescents working for their parents are exempt from these prohibitions. Generally, those under age 16 may not work at jobs that involve:

1. Operating a tractor of over 20 power-take-off horsepower, or connecting or disconnecting an implement or any of its parts to or from such a tractor*†

2. Operating or assisting to operate any of the following machines: corn picker, cotton picker, grain combine, hay mower, forage harvester, hay baler, potato digger, mobile pea viner, feed grinder, crop dryer, forage blower, auger conveyor, unloading mechanism of a nongravity-type self-unloading wagon or trailer, power post-hole digger, power post driver, or nonwalking type rotary tiler*†

3. Operating or assisting to operate any of the following machines: trencher or earth moving equipment, fork lift, potato combine, or power-driven circular, band, or chain saw*

4. Working on a farm in a yard, pen, or stall occupied by bull, boar, or stud horse maintained for breeding purposes; sow with suckling pigs, or cow with newborn calf (with umbilical cord present)*

5. Felling, bucking, skidding, loading, or unloading timber with butt diameter of more than 6 inches*

6. Working from a ladder or scaffold at a height of over 20 feet*

7. Driving a bus, truck, or car while transporting passengers, or riding as a passenger or helper on a tractor

8. Working inside the following: a fruit, forage, or grain storage unit designed to retain an oxygen deficient or toxic atmosphere; an upright silo within 2 weeks after silage has been added or when a top loading device is in operating position; a manure pit; or a horizontal silo while operating a tractor for packing purposes

9. Handling or applying pesticides and other agricultural chemicals classified as Category I or II of toxicity by FIFRA

10. Handling or using a blasting agent, including but not limited to, dynamite, black powder, sensitized ammonium nitrate, blasting caps, and primer cords

11. Transporting, transferring, or applying anhydrous ammonia

---

*Limited exemptions are provided for student learners
†Limited exemptions are provided for participants in 4-H training program or vocational agricultural training program

Hazardous orders can also be changed by legislation. For example, Hazardous Order No. 12 was eased in 1996 by Public Law 104-174 to allow youngsters aged 16 or older to load certain scrap-paper balers and paper-box compactors, although they still are not allowed to operate or unload them. Legislative (or administrative changes) may not necessarily take into account current knowledge about hazards for adolescents. For example, despite evidence that one of the most common causes of death for children and adolescents in occupational settings is motor-vehicle incidents (Castillo et al., 1994), a bill was introduced in the 105th Congress to relax the current restrictions on the use of motor-vehicles by young workers. This bill (H.R. 2327) would substantially revise Hazardous Order No. 2, which prohibits all occupational driving by individuals under the age of 18 except on "an occasional and incidental basis" and would allow youths between the ages of 16 and 18 to drive as many as 50 miles from their places of employment so long as the time spent driving did not exceed one-third of the workday or 20 percent of the work week.

There are hazardous orders for specific types of work, but there is none that address the need to protect youths in generic ways. Youngsters working with hazardous materials or equipment may be at risk without supervision. The potential for violent assault in jobs that involve the exchange of money is another hazard that face today's young workers. There are many tragic examples of assaults on adolescents, particularly in retail and fast-food establishments. Although some states attempt to regulate this problem by limiting the late hours youths may work, assaults and hold-ups happen throughout the day.

In addition to these general problems, the hazardous orders for children in agriculture raise further concerns. Despite the fact that agriculture is among the most dangerous occupations in the United States, 16-year-olds are permitted to engage in work on farms that they would have to be 18-years-old to perform anywhere else. The current safety-based orders have not been updated to reflect new and emerging technologies, work practices, and actual exposures to health and safety hazards in agricultural workplaces where youngsters are employed. The risks are even greater for children who work on farms owned or operated by their parents because no child labor provisions apply to such children, although hazardous orders do apply to nonagricultural family-owned and -operated businesses.

Work Permits

Regulations promulgated under the FLSA encourage employers to obtain federal or state certificates of age from minors to protect the employers "from unwitting violation of the minimum age standards" (29 C.F.R. 570.5) These certificates must include, at a minimum, the names and addresses of the minors and their parents or guardians; places and dates of birth of the minors (including the evidence on which this information was based); the minors' sex; the names, addresses, and industries of the employers; and the occupations of the minors. Forty-one states and the District of Columbia issue certificates, often called work permits, that meet the requirements of the Department of Labor (29 C.F.R. 570.9-570.10).

The requirements and contents of the work permits vary considerably among states. Generally, schools issue the permits to students, rather than to employers. The vast majority of state and local education authorities have not provided the local issuers with training about child labor or health and safety laws, nor have they used the data that could be gathered when issuing permits for intervention, enforcement, training, or educational purposes (Beyer, 1997). Furthermore, the permit systems have not been evaluated to determine whether the issuance of work permits successfully limits youngsters to workplaces that are age-appropriate and free of prohibited employment risks.

The Fair Labor Standards Act specifically allows states to establish additional requirements for the issuance of work permits. For example, six states (Alabama, California, Massachusetts, Nebraska, Oklahoma, and Washington) require youngsters to be regularly attending school if state law so requires before work permits will be issued; two states (New Hampshire and North Dakota) require students to have satisfactory academic levels before they can receive certificates; and six states (Alabama, Indiana, Maine, Michigan, New Hampshire, and New York) allow schools to revoke permits if the schools find that the youngsters' school work has become unsatisfactory. Many, but not all, states take advantage of the permit process to help inform adolescents of the child labor laws by offering a pamphlet that explains the restrictions on young workers' hours and occupations (31 states) or by listing such restrictions on the permit application forms or permits themselves (27 states).[4]

---

[4]Information about state work permits comes from an informal survey of child labor em-

The state of Washington uses the work permit process to assist its enforcement of the hour and industry restrictions and to protect children and adolescents from conditions that could be detrimental to their health, safety, or welfare. In Washington, not only must minors obtain parent/school authorization forms, but the employers who hire them are also required to obtain work permits from the Department of Labor and Industries. These employer permits, which may include restrictions on minor employees' working conditions, must be posted and can be revoked at any time if the employers violate any conditions of the permit (WAC 296-125-020). Oregon has recently changed its permit process so that teens no longer are required to get work permits, but employers of young people must reapply annually to be certified as youth employers (National School-to-Work Office, no date).

Occupational Safety and Health Administration Rules

The Occupational Safety and Health Act (29 U.S.C. Chapter 15 §651 et seq.), passed in 1970, requires that employers provide work and places of employment that comply with specific safety and health standards and are free from other recognized hazards that may cause serious physical harm. Although children and adolescents are entitled to the same protections as adults, they receive no additional protection, with one exception: The regulations concerning exposure to ionizing radiation for individuals under 18 years of age are 10 percent of the permissible level of exposure for adults (29 C.F.R. 1910.1096 (b)(3)). The act specifies that state regulations (adopted by state occupational safety and health programs) must be at least as protective as federal rules; occasionally, they are more protective. The act is administered by the Occupational Safety and Health Administration (OSHA).

There are two major problems with the current rules as they apply to protecting working children and adolescents. First, the OSHA's standards have not been written or reviewed with regard to special risks for children. A National Research Council (1993) re-

---

ployment practices conducted in the summer of 1991 by the staff of the U.S. Senate Subcommittee on Labor. The results of the survey are available from the Child Labor Coalition of the National Consumers League, Washington, D.C.

port, *Pesticides in the Diets of Infants and Children,* documented the specific bases for children's heightened vulnerability to certain toxic substances: (1) disproportionately heavy exposures (occupational and environmental); (2) rapid growth and development that can be easily disrupted; and (3) more time to develop chronic diseases triggered by early exposures. According to current research, the areas of greatest concern for children are their exposure to carcinogens, reproductive toxins, endocrine disrupters, and musculoskeletal hazards (see Chapter 3).

Second, most of the OSHA's standards do not apply to agricultural workplaces (29 C.F.R 1910). These exemptions include most basic safety rules (e.g., protection against electrocution and unguarded machinery) and specific standards for regulated carcinogens, reproductive toxins, neurotoxins, endocrine disrupters, and biohazards, as well as more generic standards for informing workers about hazards, personal protective equipment, access to medical and exposure records, and whistle-blower protection. Thus, agricultural workers may be exposed to the same hazards as nonagricultural workers but enjoy none of the protection of the Occupational Health and Safety Act. An example of the disparate protection is that workers who are manufacturing a pesticide, such as ethylene dibromide, are fully covered by the act's extensive standards regarding regulated carcinogens, but workers applying this pesticide or handling treated crops are entitled only to the lesser protections of the Federal Insecticide, Fungicide, and Rodenticide Act (administered by the U.S. Environmental Protection Agency). Furthermore, congressional riders to annual appropriations bills prohibit the enforcement of all OSHA standards on farms that have 10 or fewer employees and do not have labor camps.[5] Inasmuch as most farms (nearly 95 percent) have 10 or fewer employees (Bureau of the Census, 1994), few children working in agricultural jobs are protected by the Occupational Safety and Health Act.

Although states may be more protective than the federal government, few have enacted standards to protect agricultural workers. A notable exception is the state of Washington, which has extended to agriculture the full range of health and safety protections currently

---

[5]Departments of Labor, Health and Human Services, and Education, and Related Agencies Appropriations Act, 1998, H.R. 2264, 105th Congress; this same language appears annually in the appropriations bill.

in place for general industry and construction (WAC 296-307). Texas, facing litigation in 1987, enacted right-to-know legislation for agricultural workers, who had been excluded from the state's hazard communication standard for all workers (which regulates what information about hazardous materials must be provided to workers).

Other Federal Laws and Initiatives

The Federal Insecticide, Fungicide, and Rodenticide Act and the Related Protection Standards

The Federal Insecticide, Fungicide, and Rodenticide Act (FIFRA) (7 U.S.C. §136), administered by the Environmental Protection Agency (EPA), regulates the registration and use of pesticides, including the protection of agricultural workers who may be exposed to pesticides and their residues. This act requires the EPA to protect against any unreasonable adverse effects to humans or the environment, which includes balancing the costs and benefits of the use of all pesticides (7 U.S.C. §136 (bb)). This approach markedly differs from that of the Occupational Safety and Health Act, which has no cost-benefit requirement in setting standards to protect the health and safety of nonagricultural workers.

The EPA's Worker Protection Standards regulations (40 C.F.R. 170), which were promulgated in 1992 and fully implemented in 1996, cover employees who handle agricultural pesticides and those who cultivate and harvest plants on farms or in greenhouses, nurseries, or forests. These regulations are intended to eliminate or reduce the exposure to pesticides; mitigate the exposures that occur; and inform employees about pesticide hazards. The regulations include provisions regarding the use of personal protective equipment for those working directly with pesticides, the setting of re-entry times before which workers must avoid treated areas, the notification of workers about areas that have been treated, and the training of employees in basic pesticide-safety measures.

FIFRA and its implementing regulations have the same standards for children as for adults. As discussed in Chapter 3, there is evidence that young children have increased susceptibility to pesticides, but little is known about the differential effects of pesticides on older children and adolescents. To date, the EPA has not reevaluated pesticide standards to take into account special risks to young workers. As noted above, the FLSA hazardous orders do prohibit anyone younger than 16 from working with Toxic Category I and II pesticides, but children as young as 10 are allowed to hand-harvest crops, under certain conditions, which potentially exposes them to pesticides.

Although many current laws and regulations do not take children's susceptibilities into account, a notable exception is the Food Quality Protection Act of 1996, which requires the EPA to explicitly determine the safety for children of allowed pesticide residues on food. Although this act enforces protection of young children as consumers, it does not address the special risks of pesticides to children and adolescents who work with pesticides or treated crops.

Executive Order on the Protection of Children

Identifying the need for special attention to environmental health and safety risks to children, President Clinton in 1997 issued Executive Order 13045 to protect children from environmental health and safety risks. The order calls on each federal agency to:

- make it a high priority to identify and assess environmental health and safety risks that may disproportionately affect children; and
- ensure that its policies, programs, activities, and standards address disproportionate risks to children that result from environmental health risks or safety risks.

The Executive Order also established the Task Force on Environmental Health Risks and Safety Risks to Children to recommend federal strategies for children's environmental health and safety. These strategies are to consider:

- statements of principles, general policy, and targeted annual priorities to guide the federal approach to achieving the goals of this order;
- a coordinated research agenda for the federal government;
- recommendations for appropriate partnerships among federal,

state, local, and tribal governments and the private, academic, and nonprofit sectors;

• proposals to enhance public outreach and communication to assist families in evaluating risks to children and in making informed consumer choices; and

• identification of high-priority initiatives that the federal government has undertaken or will undertake in advancing the protection of children's environmental health and safety.

The task force, which is led jointly by the Secretary of Health and Human Services and the Administrator of the Environmental Protection Agency, is also to report biennially on "research, data, or other information that would enhance our ability to understand, analyze, and respond to environmental health risks and safety risks to children" and, if needed, to suggest new legislation to protect children. Following the issuance of the Executive Order, EPA and the Department of Health and Human Services announced plans to jointly establish research centers on environmental threats to children's health, and EPA also established an Office of Children's Health Protection to direct this regulatory and research effort. However, this important initiative may not necessarily address the health and safety risks associated with child labor unless children are defined to include adolescents. In addition, attention has not yet focused on the environmental health risks children and adolescents face as workers.

WORKERS' COMPENSATION

Workers' compensation provides no-fault insurance for occupational injuries and illnesses. Each state has its own workers' compensation law, with varying coverage requirements and benefit levels. Private employers are required to have workers' compensation insurance in 47 states, although waivers are available in 24 of those states; coverage is elective in New Jersey, Texas, and for all but "extrahazardous" occupations in Wyoming (U.S. Department of Labor, no date: Table 1).[6] Workers employed in interstate com-

---

[6]Workers' compensation information is available electronically at http://www.dol.gov/dol/esa/public/regs/statutes/owcp/stwclaw [1997, September 19].

merce and federal employees are covered under the Federal Employment Compensation Act. As with the Fair Labor Standards Act and the Occupational Safety and Health Act, most state workers' compensation laws treat agricultural workers differently; only 12 states provide coverage of agricultural workers similar to that of other workers (U.S. Department of Labor, no date: Table 3).[7]

Workers' compensation reaches more workers and occupies the attention of more employers than do all other occupational safety and health programs put together. Its objectives extend to both social insurance and the improvement of working conditions. As a social insurance program, it assumes the cost of medical expenses associated with occupational injuries and illnesses, and it replaces a portion of workers' lost income. As a safety and health program, it has the potential to provide incentives for employers to improve working conditions or otherwise reduce the burden of claims. State workers' compensation agencies also provide a range of services that include voluntary consultations for employers, return-to-work assistance for workers, dispute resolution, and other measures designed to make program costs less onerous. Although the effectiveness of workers' compensation, in this country and elsewhere, has been studied extensively, no research has focused on the needs of young workers. The system may well underserve this population because benefits are related to the loss of income rather than the loss of schooling and because children and adolescents underuse the system. In addition, many state workers' compensation laws limit the legal remedies available for the occupational injury or death of anyone under the age of 18 (National Institute for Occupational Safety and Health, 1997).

Indemnity Principle

The underlying principle in workers' compensation indemnity is that the primary financial hardships experienced by victims of injury and illness are their medical costs and their loss of income. States employ formulas to determine the fraction of this lost income that the system will replace, generally two-thirds, up to a statutory maxi-

---

[7]The 12 states are Arizona, California, Colorado, Connecticut, Hawaii, Idaho, Massachusetts, Montana, New Hampshire, New Jersey, Ohio, and Oregon.

mum. For young workers still in school, however, the most important cost of work-related injuries or illnesses may not be their lost wages but the disruption of their educations—missed classes, lower grades, and other education-related adverse outcomes. In addition, young workers have a longer time over which to suffer from disabilities or illnesses that result from early work-related incidents. A few states do provide double indemnity compensation for young workers who are injured while child labor laws were being violated.

Utilization

Evidence points to general underutilization of workers' compensation. Several studies (Cone et al., 1991; Leigh et al., 1996; Stout and Bell, 1991) have found that between 30 percent and 60 percent of work-related fatalities are not represented in workers' compensation records. In a study of nonfatal work-related injuries to adolescents, Parker and colleagues (1994) found that 67 percent of the eligible injuries were not reported to workers' compensation. Several factors may account for workers' failure to file legitimate claims: lack of understanding of their rights to compensation; fear of retaliation; pressure from their employers; or their own desire to be team players. ("Experience-rated" methods allow firms to pay workers' compensation premiums based in part on their claims history, providing incentives for employers to minimize the number of claims.)

These factors may play an even greater role for teenagers. Young workers are still finding their place in the adult world and may be more susceptible to pressure not to file claims. They also have less knowledge of this complex system and their rights under it and fewer resources for pursuing their claims, if they are covered at all. Young workers' low usage of workers' compensation remedies reflects the larger problem that key regulatory systems for workers rely to a great extent on the initiative of those workers directly affected. That workers may not take the initiative in the face of many workplace pressures is always a concern, but the concern is greater when inequalities of age and experience are factors as well.

ENFORCEMENT OF CHILD LABOR LAWS AND REGULATIONS

Fair Labor Standards Act

The Wage and Hour Division of the Department of Labor is responsible for overseeing the rules and regulations pertaining to FLSA, including those related to child labor. The act is enforced by means of inspections of workplaces. Inspections can be conducted in response to complaints: Anyone can file a complaint on his or her own behalf or on behalf of someone else, alleging the violation of FLSA requirements. In addition, the Wage and Hour Division has a program of targeted inspections and a program of directed inspections. Targeted inspections focus on specific industries (for example, retail establishments) or types of employment sites (for example, shopping malls) for a specified length of time. These inspections usually cover all aspects of the FLSA, but in some cases are targeted to a specific section of the law, such as child labor regulations. Directed inspections focus more narrowly on segments of an industry or parts of the act. The number of inspectors available for enforcement varies, depending on the department's annual budget, but it is relatively small. As of the end of fiscal 1997 (September 30), the Wage and Hour Division had 942 inspectors, a 20 percent increase over the number of inspectors at the end of fiscal 1996.[8] These inspectors are responsible for overseeing all the businesses covered by the FLSA.

In fiscal 1996, the Department of Labor found 7,873 young people working in 1,820 establishments in violation of child labor laws and regulations; in fiscal 1997, there were 5,270 young people working in 1,141 establishments in violation of child labor laws and regulations.[9] The number of violations varies a great deal by year, depending on the industries that are targeted for investigation. For example, in the late 1980s, the department targeted retail and fast-food establishments, industries that employ large numbers of adoles-

---

[8]Information on the inspection process at the Wage and Hour Division is based on discussions with Art Kerschner, Jr., and William Fern of the Wage and Hour Division, U.S. Department of Labor.

[9]Personal communication from Art Kerschner, Jr., Wage and Hour Division, U.S. Department of Labor.

cents. More than 10,000 violations were found that year—nearly three times as many violations as had been found in the previous year.[10] In 1995, agriculture and construction were targeted, and the number of violations found decreased dramatically, because few children and adolescents are employed in construction and regulations are more lenient for agriculture. In 1990, the Department of Labor conducted four strike-force enforcement sweeps looking specifically for child labor violations. A total of 9,542 inspections were conducted nationwide and 27,634 children were found to be employed illegally (i.e., in violation of FLSA regulations) (U.S. General Accounting Office, 1991). As is discussed in more detail in Chapter 3, studies have found that a sizable number of serious injuries are suffered by children and adolescents employed illegally, particularly when they are employed in violation of hazardous orders (U.S. General Accounting Office, 1991).

For businesses that are covered by the FLSA, a civil penalty of not more than $10,000 may be assessed for each *minor* employed in violation of any part of the child labor regulations. In addition, as of 1994, fines of up to $10,000 for each *violation* that leads to the serious injury or death of a minor covered by the FLSA have been allowed.[11] (That is, multiple violations could be associated with the work of one child and each violation is subject to a fine.)

The many small companies that do not satisfy the minimum threshold for coverage under FLSA are covered under state laws, which are enforced by state agencies. The enforcement of state child labor laws varies throughout the nation, in terms of number of staff, number and extent of inspections, and assessed and collected penalties. The number of compliance officers or inspectors at the state level is also limited. Only three states reported having more than 50 compliance officers responsible for enforcing all adult and child labor laws (National Consumers League, 1993). Various surveys have documented widespread inconsistencies not only in child labor standards (hours of work, age of work, updating lists of hazardous occupations), but also in enforcement. A 1993 survey by the Child

---

[10]Personal communication from Art Kerschner, Jr., Wage and Hour Division, U.S. Department of Labor.

[11]All civil monetary penalties are reassessed every 4 years. It is likely that the child labor violation penalty will be increased to $11,000 sometime in 1998 (personal communication from Art Kerschner, Jr., Wage and Hour Division, Department of Labor).

Labor Coalition of the National Consumers League reported that the total amounts collected by the states in penalties for child labor violations in 1992 ranged from $0 to $150,000, with a majority of states collecting nothing. For those that did collect at least one fine, the minimum civil penalty for a single child labor violation ranged from $5 to $150, and the maximum ranged from $50 to $10,000. Very few states even permit fines as high as $10,000. States' standards for and enforcement of criminal penalties for child labor violations also vary dramatically.

Occupational Safety and Health Act

Standards set by OSHA under the Occupational Safety and Health Act do not specifically target young workers or their employers in its standards-setting or enforcement activities. OSHA uses targeted inspections to achieve compliance; inspections are also performed after workers complain of violations and after accidents or deaths. The agency delegates enforcement to state agencies with approved occupational safety and health programs, which must be at least as effective as the federal OSHA standards. As of August 1997, 23 states had such plans.[12]

Exacerbating the problem of limited resources for enforcing child labor laws and regulations is the equally limited authority of each of the relevant agencies to cite employers for violations that are not within their jurisdiction. For example, compliance officers from the Department of Labor's Wage and Hour Division may not cite obvious violations of OSHA's health and safety standards. The Wage and Hour Division can refer violations to OSHA, and vice versa, under an existing agreement between the agencies; however, no records are kept of how many referrals are made or of the disposition of the referrals, so the effectiveness of interagency referral is difficult to study. Violations by companies that do not satisfy the minimum threshold for coverage by the Fair Labor Standards Act are referred to the states' labor departments, which might or might

---

[12]The 23 states are Alaska, Arizona, California, Connecticut, Hawaii, Indiana, Iowa, Kentucky, Maryland, Michigan, Minnesota, Nevada, New Mexico, New York, North Carolina, Oregon, South Carolina, Tennessee, Utah, Vermont, Virginia, Washington, and Wyoming.

not follow up on potential violations and hazards. Children often fall through these jurisdictional cracks.

Effectiveness of Regulation

One of the principal means for achieving occupational safety and health goals is government regulation of employers (Weeks, 1991). To what extent and under what circumstances do laws and regulations improve the health and safety of workers in general and children and adolescents in particular? The answer to these questions depends on the extent to which laws and regulations actually deter the behavior they were created to deter (i.e., the extent to which employers comply with the laws and regulations) and whether deterring violations actually improves workers' health and safety.

The basic assumption of the deterrence model of regulatory enforcement is that an agency with clear regulations and an extensive ability to detect and severely punish noncompliance can achieve a high degree of compliance with the law (Gray and Scholz, 1993). However, these ideal enforcement conditions seldom exist. Regulations are often complex, and agencies have limited resources for enforcement. Furthermore, studies have found that, compared with the costs of compliance, the threat of enforcement plays a minor role in corporate responses to health and safety issues (Bartel and Thomas, 1985; Sigler and Murphy, 1988). Gray and Scholtz (1993) speculate that inspections with monetary penalties increase managers' attention to potential safety hazards, thereby helping to reduce injuries. More telling, inspections triggered by complaints were found to reduce injuries regardless of whether penalties were imposed or not (Scholz and Gray, 1997).

The Mine Safety and Health Administration (MSHA) is an example of an agency that has successfully reduced health and safety hazards through regulatory enforcement. Following the passage of the Coal Mine Health and Safety Act of 1969, there was a sharp and sustained decrease in the fatality rate per hours worked and per ton of coal mined. Productivity in coal mining decreased for approximately 10 years after the act was implemented but then improved steadily (Weeks, 1991). Although there is evidence of OSHA'S effectiveness, there is little evidence that its regulations have affected occupational injury rates in the United States to the same extent that MSHA has affected underground mine fatality rates (Mintz, 1984;

Stewart, 1979; Weeks, 1991). The level of MSHA enforcement in underground mining is far higher than the level of OSHA enforcement in other industries. Each mine is inspected four times annually, and there were 2,735 inspectors for approximately 100,000 miners in 1989, compared with 2,404 OSHA inspectors for 85,000,000 workers in other industries.

OSHA's targeted inspection programs have proved effective at reducing workers' compensation claims for work injuries. For example, a targeted inspection program in Washington state's construction industry in 1991-1992, focused on enforcing a protection standard to prevent falls, resulted in a decrease of claims for injuries due to falls from 1.78 to 1.39 per 100 full-time employees in the group of targeted contractors, which was significantly different from any change in the claims rate among other construction contractors (Nelson et al., 1997). In general, better surveillance of occupational injuries and illnesses is necessary for OSHA to effectively and efficiently target inspections.

Enforcement of child labor laws under FLSA appears to suffer from too few inspectors to visit work sites, but there have not been any evaluations of the effectiveness of the FLSA rules with respect to how well they protect working youth.

TRAINING AND OTHER EFFORTS TO EDUCATE YOUNG WORKERS

Government enforcement of child labor laws and regulations is important, but it is insufficient to ensure that the work performed by children and adolescents is safe and nonexploitative. Indeed, the primary function of laws and regulations may be to define correct practices rather than to force compliance. Therefore, education is a necessary complement to enforcement. Education about the employment of children and adolescents has several purposes. Informing young people, parents, educators, employers, and others about child labor laws and regulations is one purpose. Training them to prevent work-related illness and injury and to respond appropriately to workplace hazards is another. Education can also contribute to improving the quality of youngsters' work experiences, minimizing the harmful consequences and maximizing the benefits.

A number of efforts now under way around the country are trying to make youngster's work experiences safe and healthful. The efforts primarily focus on education and training. Such programs include providing occupational health and safety training to adolescents, educating children and their parents about child labor laws, and educating parents about the age-appropriateness of tasks. Educational efforts about child labor laws and age-appropriate tasks also target employers. Other efforts, notably school-to-work programs, focus on making adolescents' work experiences useful, meaningful, and integrated with their school work. Because such programs have not yet been rigorously evaluated, little can be said about their effectiveness. This report would not be complete, however, without some discussion of the efforts to improve the quality of work for children and adolescents.

Lack of awareness of health and safety issues relevant to working children and adolescents—both by the young workers themselves and by adults—has been recognized by a number of organizations as a significant obstacle to preventing injury and illness on the job. The American Academy of Pediatrics, the American Public Health Association, and the National Institute for Occupational Safety and Health have called for better training and education on issues related to the health and safety of adolescent workers.

Health and safety education for workers has been recognized as an important component of preventing work-related illnesses and injuries (Keyserling, 1995; Komaki et al., 1980; Maples et al., 1982; Office of Technology Assessment, 1985; Wallerstein, 1992; Wallerstein and Weinger, 1992; Zohar et al., 1980). Recent studies indicate, however, that working teens may not be receiving adequate health and safety training on the job. In a survey of 14- to 16-year-olds who had been injured while working, 54 percent reported having received no instruction on how to avoid injuries or how to work safely with the equipment they used (Knight et al., 1995). General surveys of working youth find similar results, with about half of surveyed young workers reporting no health and safety training (Bowling et al., 1998; Runyan et al., 1997).

Not only are children and adolescents not receiving health and safety information, but adults involved with children—parents, teachers, health-care providers, staff members of community organizations—often lack the information necessary to promote the health and safety of youngsters in the workplace. For example, both state and federal regulators report that employers' ignorance of child labor laws is common.[13] A recent survey of health care providers who treat adolescents found that over three-quarters of them were unfamiliar with the child labor laws pertaining to prohibited jobs and hours.[14]

Efforts to educate the public about potential hazards to young workers have been mounted by federal and state government agencies. For example, in May 1995 the National Institute for Occupational Safety and Health (NIOSH) issued an alert on preventing deaths and injuries of working adolescents. The alert described child labor laws and potential hazards for young workers and provided suggestions for employers, parents, educators, and adolescents. A tear-off flyer, meant to be posted and distributed to workers, summarized the information. The U.S. Department of Labor created a web site in 1997 to provide information to adolescents about such topics as safety on the job, child labor laws, and the minimum wage.[15] State agencies also produce flyers and posters aimed at publicizing child labor laws and tips for being safe on the job.

School-to-Work Opportunities Act

The purpose of the School-to-Work Opportunities Act of 1994 (20 U.S.C. §6101-6251) is to strengthen positive interactions between school and work. The Act calls for the creation of school-to-work systems containing three core elements: school-based learning, work-based learning, and connecting activities. School-based learning is classroom instruction and curricula that integrates high academic standards with career awareness, career exploration, and occupational skill standards established by employers and employees. Work-based learning "means that work places become active learning environments by engaging employers as partners with educators in providing opportunities for all students to participate in high-quality work experiences" (U.S. Departments of Education and Labor, 1996:8). Connecting activities, which are meant to ensure that

---

[13]Personal communication from Art Kerschner, Jr., Wage and Hour Division, U.S. Department of Labor and from Joan Parker, Massachusetts Attorney General's Office.

[14]Data from C. Mudgal, Massachusetts Department of Public Health; unpublished tabulations.

[15]The U.S. Department of Labor, Wage and Hour Division Youth Page can be found at http://www.dol.gov/dol/esa/public/youth/home.htm.

school and workplace activities are integrated, include matching students with employers, establishing school mentors to act as liaisons with employers, providing technical assistance to schools and employers, and linking participants with community services.

Rather than establishing federal programs, the act provides venture capital to states and communities to encourage them to redirect other resources (state and local education taxes and other federal funds) toward the act's purposes. By the fall of 1997, 37 states and 137 communities had received implementation grants. Data from the first 17 states to receive grants indicate that $1 in private funds was raised for each $2 in federal funding. Consistent with its modest funding, the act also eschews strict guidelines, fostering instead a diverse array of approaches at state and local levels.

The School-to-Work Opportunities Act originated in concerns arising in the late 1980s about a growing gap between what adolescents learn in school and what employers expect of new workers. Despite employers' need for workers with good academic skills (especially reading, verbal communication, math, and problem solving), studies of high school students find that they see little connection between school and life outside of school, are bored in school, and therefore, put little effort into school (Steinberg et al., 1996). Accounts of German apprenticeship posed a contrast to this separation between school and work and to the American pattern of delayed career entry among youth who do not graduate from college (Hamilton, 1990). In the early 1990s several foundations and the Department of Labor began funding youth apprenticeship demonstration programs and other precursors of the school-to-work initiative (Olson, 1997).

School-to-work differs significantly from conventional vocational education, though it incorporates some of its features. Although many secondary vocational education programs provide a direct route into productive careers, teaching occupational skills that enable graduates to perform related work, the benefits are confined to a relatively small proportion of graduates who take a coherent sequence of vocational courses and then find related employment after graduation. Many more vocational graduates take too few courses to gain real skills or they enter the work force in unrelated fields. (For a brief review of research on vocational education, see Stern et al., 1994.) Too many secondary vocational programs are disconnected from contemporary work skills and labor markets and are undemanding academically, providing no advantage in subsequent employment. The better vocational programs emphasize preparation for both employment and post-secondary education. This emphasis, often under the banner of "tech prep" (parallel to college prep), has been supported by the Carl D. Perkins Vocational and Applied Technology Education Act (20 U.S.C. §2301 et seq.), which is the conduit for federal funding of vocational education. High Schools That Work, one of the most ambitious and successful school reform networks, combines high academic standards with effective vocational education (Bottoms and Sharpe, no date; see especially Chapters 6-7). Both tech prep and the integration of vocational education with high academic standards are envisioned as components of a comprehensive school-to-work system.

Cooperative education is one well-established practice in vocational education, and it is identified as a type of work-based learning in the School-to-Work Opportunities Act. Like youth apprenticeship, it uses work experience to teach employment-related knowledge and skills in connection with relevant school classes. Unlike a formal apprenticeship, it does not teach a common set of competencies and, as a result, does not yield a portable credential. Vocational graduates who have had cooperative education and subsequently work for their training employer achieve higher earnings than their classmates, but that advantage does not carry over to other workplaces (Stern and Stevens, 1992), presumably because they receive no credentials. One intriguing result of research on cooperative education is that it appears to provide all of the benefits of work experience discussed in Chapter 4 with fewer negative consequences (Stern et al., 1997).

The effects of the School-to-Work Opportunities Act cannot yet be assessed with any certainty. First, the initiative is too young to have generated activities that are well enough established to warrant formal evaluation. Second, generalization is impeded by the legislation's encouragement of variety in state and local implementation (see U.S. Department of Labor, 1997). Mathematica Policy Research, Inc., is conducting a national study of School-to-Work implementation, but its report has not been released. The best indication of future effects comes from evaluations of pre-1994 demonstration projects. For example, several youth apprenticeship demonstration projects reported that large proportions of participants enrolled in post-secondary education (Kopp et al., no date), a surprising result because the target group was "non-college" youth. Some school-to-work sites have also reported this result, along with higher grades and improved post-graduate employment. (For examples, see the National School-to-Work Office Web site: www.stw.ed.gov.)

The School-to-Work Opportunities Act, which is overseen jointly by the Departments of Education and Labor, pays only minimal attention to child labor laws and health and safety standards in the program's training components and in the requirements for states' programs. In the work-based experience, students are required to receive "broad instruction, to the extent practicable, in all aspects of the industry" (20 U.S.C. §6113 (a)(5)), including health and safety issues. However there are no specific requirements that such issues be included in the school-based portion. The act does not allow the waiver of any child labor laws for program participants.

Demonstration Projects

In an effort to disseminate information about child labor and safety issues and to promote positive action on the part of young workers, NIOSH is funding three community health education demonstration projects with evaluation components. Projects target a variety of audiences, including parents, employers, educators, health-care providers, government officials, organizations that work with youngsters, and young people themselves. Surveys to collect baseline information about students' knowledge and attitudes have been administered in each of the three communities (Brockton, Massachusetts; Oakland, California; and south central Los Angeles, California). Focus groups with employers and parents have been conducted. Advisory committees, with representatives from each of the target populations, have been established in each community. The schools and organizations that work with youngsters are serving as bases for educating adolescents. In Brockton, occupational health and safety education has been integrated into the school-to-work system. The project has also trained teen peer educators to provide occupational health and safety workshops to youngsters outside of the school setting. In Oakland, occupational health and safety learning activities have been integrated into the curriculum in core academic subject areas. In addition, a school-based peer-education program has been established. In south central Los Angeles, a 3-week education and career planning class now incorporates occupational health and safety, and several community events have been held for parents, educators, and other community members. Materials for parents have been prepared and disseminated, and a brochure for health-care providers is being developed. Employers' outreach activities include workshops for city job program staff, a mentor training program developed for employers participating in the school-to-work program, and a joint labor-management occupational safety and health training program for restaurants. Initial evaluations of the Los Angeles program have shown changes in students' knowledge and attitudes about health and safety (Baker, 1997).

For the first time I learned there were safety and rights for teens at work.

Student in Los Angeles Young Worker
Community Health Education Program

Safety Education Efforts in Agriculture

The past decade has seen a notable increase in the number of grassroots educational efforts, such as community-based safety campaigns, farm-safety day camps, and classroom presentations, which have been supported through funds from the private sector and NIOSH. Unfortunately, few of these programs have been subjected to comprehensive evaluation, and their effects on injury rates is unknown (Aherin et al., 1992; Murphy et al., 1996; National Committee for Childhood Agricultural Injury Prevention, 1996). Several studies have suggested that safety education has little or no effect on minimizing injuries associated with agriculture (Aherin et al., 1992; Shutske, 1994), and that engineering and environmental modifications may provide greater protection than education for young workers in agriculture (Aherin et al., 1992).

Currently, a myriad of educational programs target adults and children in an effort to prevent childhood agricultural injuries (Purschwitz, 1990; Shutske, 1994). Education and training are occurring through formal programs such as 4-H, FFA (formerly referred to as Future Farmers of America), and vocational training; the programs are sponsored in large part by public funding (U.S. Department of Agriculture's Cooperative Extension Service and the U.S. Department of Education).

The National Committee for Childhood Agricultural Injury Prevention, through a consensus development process, identified specific steps to minimize agricultural injuries among children (see Chapter 5). Among the recommended steps were a variety of educational initiatives ranging from a national public-education campaign to the incorporation of agricultural health and safety curricula in classrooms from kindergarten through high school. The committee also called for the rigorous evaluation of educational materials and methods.

Although education is a key part of preventing workplace injuries and illnesses, it cannot solve the problem alone. A comprehensive prevention strategy will require education, engineering modifications, and the rigorous enforcement of both child labor laws and health and safety laws. Also needed is increased research, based on sound scientific principles, to identify successful approaches to intervention.

CONCLUSIONS

Current regulations and standards do not reflect the changes in technology, industries, and hazards that children and adolescents encounter in contemporary workplaces in the United States. Nor do these standards adequately protect children and adolescents, who are more vulnerable than adults to certain health and safety hazards on the job. Child labor standards have not kept up with contemporary research on the psychosocial, health, and safety implications of work and school for teenagers.

Connecting education more closely with work is a promising strategy for improving the health, safety, and quality of young people's work experiences. Instruction in health and safety at both the school and the workplace and attention to reducing hazards in the workplace should become a larger part of vocational education, school-to-work, and related initiatives that try to strengthen connections between education and employment.

Everyone with a role in the employment of young workers needs more and better knowledge and the ability to use it effectively. They need to have: (1) knowledge about the basic legal issues (e.g., regulations that limit the number of hours minors may work); (2) access to information and advice about specific concerns (e.g., how to respond to a boss who assigns illegal hours); (3) access to relevant information at "teachable moments" (e.g., after an injury); and (4) training in how to reduce risks and what to do when faced with unsafe or unlawful situations. Information is fundamental, but education and training are also needed to enable people to take appropriate action. Information and education needs vary among different audiences (teenagers, parents, employers) and will need to be targeted to them.

TABLE 6-1
SELECTED STATE CHILD LABOR STANDARDS FOR
NONFARM EMPLOYMENT (AS OF JANUARY 1, 1996)

TABLE 6-1 Selected State Child Labor Standards for Nonfarm
Employment (as of January 1, 1996)[a]

| State | Under 16 Years Old | | | | | | |
| | Maximum Hours/Day | | Maximum Hours/Week | | Maximum Days/Week | | |
	School Day	Non-School Day	School Week	Non-School Week	School Week	Non-School Week	Prohibited Work Hours
Alabama	3	8	18	40	6	6	7 pm (9 pm during the summer vacation) to 7 am
Alaska	9[b]	—	23	—	6	6	9 pm to 5 am
Arizona	3	8	18	40	—	—	9:30 pm (11 pm before non-school day) to 6 am; 7 pm to 6 am in door-to-door sales or deliveries
Arkansas	8	8	48	48	6	6	7 pm (9 pm before non-school day) to 6 am
California	3	8	18	40	6	6	7 pm (9 pm June 1 thru Labor Day) to 7 am
Colorado	6	8	40	40	—	—	9:30 pm to 5 am before school day

16 and 17 Years Old

Maximum Hours/Day		Maximum Hours/Week		Maximum Days/Week		
School Day	Non-School Day	School Week	Non-School Week	School Week	Non-School Week	Prohibited Work Hours
—	—	—	—	—	—	10 pm before school days to 5 am, if enrolled in school
—	—	—	—	6	6	—
—	—	—	—	—	—	—
10	10	54	54	6	6	11 pm before school day to 6 am
4	8	28[c]	48	6	6	10 pm (12:30 am before non-school day) to 5 am
8	8	40	40	—	—	—

Table continues on next page

TABLE 6-1 Continued

State	Under 16 Years Old						
	Maximum Hours/Day		Maximum Hours/Week		Maximum Days/Week		
	School Day	Non-School Day	School Week	Non-School Week	School Week	Non-School Week	Prohibited Work Hours
Connecticut	9[d]	9[d]	48	48	—[d]	—[d]	10 pm (midnight before non-school day in supermarkets) to 6 am
Delaware	4[c]	8	18[c]	40	6	6	7 pm (9 pm June 1 thru Labor Day) to 7 am
Florida	3[e]	8	15	40	6	6	7 pm before school day (9 pm during holidays and summer vacations) to 7 am on school day
Georgia	4	8	40	40	—	—	9 pm to 6 am
Hawaii	10[b]	8	40	40	6	6	7 pm to 7 am (9 pm to 6 am June 1 through day before Labor Day
Idaho	9	9	54	54	—	—	9 pm to 6 am

16 and 17 Years Old

Maximum Hours/Day		Maximum Hours/Week		Maximum Days/Week		
School Day	Non-School Day	School Week	Non-School Week	School Week	Non-School Week	Prohibited Work Hours
9[d]	9[d]	48	48	—[d]	—[d]	10 pm (midnight before non-school day in supermarkets) to 6 am; 11 pm (midnight if before non-school day or not attending school) to 6 am in restaurants or as ushers in nonprofit theater
12[b]	12	—	—	—	—	8 hrs of non-work, non-school time required in each 24-hour day
8	—	30	—	6	—	11 pm to 6:30 am before school day
—	—	—	—	—	—	
—	—	—	—	—	—	
—	—	—	—	—	—	

Table continues on next page

TABLE 6-1 Continued

State	Under 16 Years Old						
	Maximum Hours/Day		Maximum Hours/Week		Maximum Days/Week		
	School Day	Non-School Day	School Week	Non-School Week	School Week	Non-School Week	Prohibited Work Hours
Illinois	3*f*	8	24	48	6	6	7 pm (9 pm June 1 through Labor Day) to 7 am
Indiana	3	8	18	40	—	—	7 pm (9 pm June 1 through Labor Day) to 7 am
Iowa	4	8	28	40	—	—	7 pm (9 pm June 1 through Labor Day) to 7 am
Kansas	8	8	40	40	—	—	10 pm before school day to 7 am
Kentucky	3	8	18	40	—	—	7 pm (9 pm June 1 through Labor Day) to 7 am
Louisiana	3	8	18	40	6	6	7 pm (9 pm June 1 through Labor Day) to 7 am

16 and 17 Years Old

Maximum Hours/Day		Maximum Hours/Week		Maximum Days/Week		
School Day	Non-School Day	School Week	Non-School Week	School Week	Non-School Week	Prohibited Work Hours
—	—	—	—	—	—	—
8*g*	9*h*	40*g*	48*h*	6*g*	—	10 pm (midnight before non-school day with written parental permission) to 6 am for minors of 16 enrolled in school; 11:30 pm to 6 am before school day for minors of 17 enrolled in grades 9 through 12
—	—	—	—	—	—	—
—	—	—	—	—	—	—
6*g*	8*g,i*	40*g*	—	6	—	11:30 pm (1 am on Friday and Saturday) to 6:30 am when school in session
—	—	—	—	—	—	—

Table continues on next page

TABLE 6-1 Continued

| State | Under 16 Years Old | | | | | | |
| | Maximum Hours/Day | | Maximum Hours/Week | | Maximum Days/Week | | |
	School Day	Non-School Day	School Week	Non-School Week	School Week	Non-School Week	Prohibited Work Hours
Maine	3	8	18	40	6	6	7 pm (9 pm during summer vacation) to 7 am
Maryland	4^c	8	23^c	40	—	—	8 pm (9 pm Memorial Day through Labor Day) to 7 am
Massachusetts'	8	8	48	48	6	6	7 pm (9 pm July 1 through Labor Day) to 6:30 am
Michigan	—	10	48^b	48	6	6	9 pm to 7 am
Minnesota	8	8	40	40	—	—	9 pm to 7 am
Mississippi	8^m	8^m	44^m	44^m	—	—	7 pm to 6 am^m
Missouri	3	8	40	40	6	6	7 pm (9 pm June 1 through Labor Day) to 7 am

16 and 17 Years Old

Maximum Hours/Day		Maximum Hours/Week		Maximum Days/Week		
School Day	Non-School Day	School Week	Non-School Week	School Week	Non-School Week	Prohibited Work Hours
$4^{g,j}$	10	$20^{g,k}$	50	6	6	10 pm (12 am before non-school day) to 7 am (5 am before non-school day)^g
12^b	—	—	—	—	—	8 hours of non-work, non-school time required in each 24-hour day
9	9	48	48	6	6	10 pm (midnight in restaurants on Friday, Saturday, and vacation) to 6 am
10	10	48^b	48	6	6	10:30 pm to 6 am, if attending school; 11:30 pm to 6 am if not attending school
—	—	—	—	—	—	11 pm to 5 am before school day (11:30 pm to 4:30 am with written parental permission)
—	—	—	—	—	—	—
—	—	—	—	—	—	

Table continues on next page

TABLE 6-1 Continued

| | Under 16 Years Old | | | | | | |
| | Maximum Hours/Day | | Maximum Hours/Week | | Maximum Days/Week | | |
State	School Day	Non-School Day	School Week	Non-School Week	School Week	Non-School Week	Prohibited Work Hours
Montana	3	8	18^n	40	—	—	7 pm (9 pm during periods outside school year) to 7 am
Nebraska	8	8	48	48	—	—	8 pm to 6 am (under 14); 10 pm to 6 am, for 14- and 15-year-olds
Nevada	8	8	48	48	—	—	—
New Hampshire	3^g	8^g	23^g	48^g	—	—	9 pm to 7 am
New Jersey	3	8°	18	40	6	6	7 pm (9 pm during summer vacation with parental permission) to 7 am
New Mexico^p	8	8	44	44	—	—	9 pm to 7 am
New York	3	8	18^n	40	6	6	7 pm (9 pm June 21 through Labor Day) to 7 am

16 and 17 Years Old

Maximum Hours/Day		Maximum Hours/Week		Maximum Days/Week		
School Day	Non-School Day	School Week	Non-School Week	School Week	Non-School Week	Prohibited Work Hours
—	—	—	—	—	—	—
—	—	—	—	—	—	—
—	—	—	—	—	—	—
—	—	30^g	48^g	6^g	6^g	
8	8°	40	40	6	6	11 pm to 6 am during school term, with specified variations
—	—	—	—	—	—	—
$4^{g,q}$	8	28^g	48	6	6	10 pm (midnight before school day with written permission from both parent and school) to 6 am while school in session; midnight to 6 am while school not in session

Table continues on next page

TABLE 6-1 Continued

	Under 16 Years Old						
	Maximum Hours/Day		Maximum Hours/Week		Maximum Days/Week		
State	School Day	Non-School Day	School Week	Non-School Week	School Week	Non-School Week	Prohibited Work Hours
North Carolina	3	8	18^n	40	—	—	7 pm (9 pm during summer vacation) to 7 am
North Dakota	3^r	8	18^r	40	6	6	7 pm (9 pm June 1 through Labor Day) to 7 am
Ohio	3	8	18	40	—	—	7 pm (9 pm June 1 to September 1 and during school holidays of 5 school days or more) to 7 am; 7 pm to 7 am in door-to-door sales
Oklahoma	3^s	8	18	40	—	—	7 pm (9 pm June 1 through Labor Day) to 7 am; 9 pm before non-school days if employer not covered by FLSA

16 and 17 Years Old

Maximum Hours/Day		Maximum Hours/Week		Maximum Days/Week		
School Day	Non-School Day	School Week	Non-School Week	School Week	Non-School Week	Prohibited Work Hours
—	—	—	—	—	—	11 pm to 5 am before school day while school in session. Not applicable with written permission from parents and school
8	8	48	48	6	6	—
—	—	—	—	—	—	11 pm before school day to 7 am (6 am if not employed after 8 pm previous night);[g] 8 pm to 7 am for door-to-door sales
—	—	—	—	—	—	—

Table continues on next page

TABLE 6-1 Continued

State	Under 16 Years Old						
	Maximum Hours/Day		Maximum Hours/Week		Maximum Days/Week		
	School Day	Non-School Day	School Week	Non-School Week	School Week	Non-School Week	Prohibited Work Hours
Oregon	3^n	8	18^n	40	—	—	7 pm (9 pm June 1 through Labor Day) to 7 am
Pennsylvania	4^c	8	26^c	44	6	6	7 pm (10 pm during vacation from June to Labor Day) to 7 am
Rhode Island	8	8	40	40	—	—	7 pm (9 pm during school vacation) to 6 am
South Carolina	3	8	18	40	—	—	7 pm (9 pm June I through Labor Day) to 7 am
South Dakota	4	8	20	40	—	—	After 10 pm before school day
Tennessee	3	8	18	40	—	—	7 pm to 7 am (9 pm to 6 am before non-school days)

16 and 17 Years Old

Maximum Hours/Day		Maximum Hours/Week		Maximum Days/Week		
School Day	Non-School Day	School Week	Non-School Week	School Week	Non-School Week	Prohibited Work Hours
—	—	44	44	—	—	—
8	8	28[g]	44	6	6	11 pm (midnight before non-school day) to 6 am[g]
9	—	48	—	—	—	11:30 pm (1:30 am before non-school day) to 6 am, if regularly attending school
—	—	—	—	—	—	—
—	—	—	—	—	—	—
—	—	—	—	—	—	10 pm to 6 am (Sunday-Thursday before school days) (midnight with parental permission up to 3 nights a week)

Table continues on next page

TABLE 6-1 Continued

State	Under 16 Years Old						
	Maximum Hours/Day		Maximum Hours/Week		Maximum Days/Week		
	School Day	Non-School Day	School Week	Non-School Week	School Week	Non-School Week	Prohibited Work Hours
Texas	8	8	48	48	—	—	10 pm (midnight before non-school day or in summer if not enrolled in summer school) to 5 am
Utah	4	8	40	40	—	—	9:30 pm to 5 am before school day
Vermont	8	8	48	48	6	6	7 pm to 6 am
Virginia	3	8	18	40	—	—	7 pm (9 pm, June 1 through Labor Day) to 7 am
Washington	3^t	8	18	40	6	6	7 pm (9 pm Friday and Saturday when school is not in session) to 7 am
West Virginia	8	8	40	40	6	6	8 pm to 5 am

16 and 17 Years Old

Maximum Hours/Day		Maximum Hours/Week		Maximum Days/Week		
School Day	Non-School Day	School Week	Non-School Week	School Week	Non-School Week	Prohibited Work Hours
—	—	—	—	—	—	—
—	—	—	—	—	—	—
9	9	50	50	—	—	—
—	—	—	—	—	—	—
4^{t,u}	8	20^{u}	48	6	6	10 pm Sunday-Thursday (midnight Friday and Saturday and when school is not in session) to 7 am (5 am when school is not in session); 9 pm to 7 am in door-to-door sales
—	—	—	—	—	—	—

Table continues on next page

TABLE 6-1 Continued

| | Under 16 Years Old | | | | | | |
| | Maximum Hours/Day | | Maximum Hours/Week | | Maximum Days/Week | | |
State	School Day	Non-School Day	School Week	Non-School Week	School Week	Non-School Week	Prohibited Work Hours
Wisconsin	4^t	8	8^c	40	6	6	8 pm (11 pm before non-school day) to 7 am
Wyoming	8	8	56	56	—	—	10 pm (midnight before non-school day and for minors not enrolled in school) to 5 am

[a]State hours limitations on a schoolday and in a schoolweek usually apply only to those enrolled in school. Several states exempt high school graduates from the hours and/ or nightwork or other provisions, or have less restrictive provisions for minors participating in various school-work programs. Separate nightwork standards in messenger service and street trades are common, but are not displayed in table.

[b]Combined hours of work and school.

[c]More hours are permitted when school is in session less than 5 days.

[d]Connecticut: For under 16 if working in stores or agriculture, the limit is 8 hours per day and 6 days per week; for 16- and 17-year olds if working in stores, the limit is 8 hours per day and 6 days per week. Overtime is permitted in some industries for both age groups.

[e]Florida: For under 16, maximum hours 3 when followed by a school day, except if enrolled in vocational program.

[f]Illinois: Eight hours are permitted on both Saturday and Sunday if minor does not work outside school hours more than 6 consecutive days in a week and total hours worked outside school does not exceed 24.

[g]Limits apply only to those enrolled in school.

[h]For minors enrolled in school, these hours require written parental permission

[i]8 hours allowed on Saturday and Sunday if attending school.

[j]8 hours allowed before nonschool day.

[k]28 hours a week allowed in weeks with multiple days of school closure.

[l]Massachusetts: Under 14, limited to 4 hours per day, 24 hours per week in farm work.

16 and 17 Years Old

Maximum Hours/Day		Maximum Hours/Week		Maximum Days/Week		
School Day	Non-School Day	School Week	Non-School Week	School Week	Non-School Week	Prohibited Work Hours
5^t	$—^v$	26^c	50	6	6	11 pm (12:30 am before non-school day) to 7 am (5 am on non-school day during school week)^v
—	—	—	—	—	—	Midnight to 5 am (for females only)

^{m}In factory, mill, cannery or workshop.

^{n}Students of 14 and 15 enrolled in approved work experience and career exploration programs may work during school hours up to 3 hours on a school day and 23 hours in a school week.

^{o}New Jersey: 10-hour day, 6-day week allowed in agriculture.

^{p}New Mexico: Limits apply only to those under 14.

^{q}8 hours on Friday, Saturday, Sunday, or holiday.

^{r}North Dakota: School day/week hours apply only if child is not exempted from school attendance.

^{s}Oklahoma: 8 hours allowed on school days before nonschool day if employer not covered by FLSA.

^{t}8 hours on Friday, Saturday, and Sunday.

^{u}Washington: 16- and 17-year olds allowed to work 6 hours per school day and 28 hours per school week with special variance agreed to by parent, employer, school, and student.

^{v}Wisconsin has no limit during non-school week on a daily hour or nightwork for 16- and 17-year olds. However, they must be paid time and one half for work in excess of 10 hours per day or 40 hours per week, whichever is greater. Also, 8 hours rest is required between end of work and start of work the next day, and any work between 12:30 a.m and 5 am must be directly supervised by an adult.

SOURCE: Data from Division of External Affairs, Wage and Hour Division, Employment Standards Administration, U.S. Department of Labor.

7

Conclusions and Recommendations

The majority of adolescents in the United States work. The benefits of work include increased self-esteem, responsibility, and autonomy, as well as income, the primary reason most adolescents work. Working during high school may also be associated with increased employment and higher wages as long as 10 years after high school. But there are adverse consequences associated with work, too. Children and adolescents have high rates of work-related injuries. In addition, for adolescents, working long hours during the school year is associated with alcohol, tobacco, and drug use; minor delinquency; lack of adequate sleep and exercise; increased rates of dropping out of high school; and decreased overall educational attainment. For the most part, children and adolescents, their parents, and many of the other adults in their lives are unaware of the adverse consequences of work.

The Committee on the Health and Safety Implications of Child Labor was established to examine how working affects the health and safety of young people and to provide recommendations on how adverse consequences can be prevented. To address its charge, the committee undertook several tasks: reviewing the available data on the extent to which children and adolescents in the United States work; reviewing the available data on their work-related injuries and illnesses; and reviewing the research on work's positive and negative effects on young people. Chapters 1-6 of this report provide a description of the sources of data on the extent of work and of work-related injuries, illnesses, and fatalities among children and adolescents, as well as the limitations of those data; a summary of the research on the consequences of working; and a review of the laws and regulations that govern child labor.

After reviewing the data and literature and examining the U.S. laws and regulations on labor by children and adolescents, the committee agreed on a number of principles that guided their formulation of recommendations. These principles are based on a developmental framework, which recognizes that the needs and abilities of children and adolescents differ from those of adults. The tasks in which children and adolescents engage must be commensurate with their physical, cognitive, emotional, and social abilities. These principles, which represent the judgment and values of the committee, form the basis for ensuring that the work performed by children and adolescents will be safe and healthful and will not compromise their physical, cognitive, emotional, and social development.

Guiding Principle 1: Education and development are of primary importance during the formative years of childhood and adolescence. Although work can contribute to these goals, it should never be undertaken in ways that compromise education or development.

Guiding Principle 2: The vulnerable, formative, and malleable nature of childhood and adolescence requires a higher standard of protection for young workers than that accorded to adult workers.

Guiding Principle 3: All businesses assume certain social obligations when they hire employees. Businesses that employ young workers assume a higher level of social obligation, which should be reflected in the expectations of society as well as in explicit public policy.

Guiding Principle 4: Everyone under 18 years of age has the right to be protected from hazardous work, excessive work hours, and unsafe or unhealthy work environments, regardless of the size of the enterprise in which he or she is employed, his or her relationship to the employer, or the sector of the economy in which the enterprise operates.

With these principles in mind, the committee's recommendations are designed to protect young people in the workplace through education and through updated, enhanced, and adequately enforced laws and regulations. Educational efforts target the behavior of individuals—young people and their parents, employers, teachers, and mentors. While such efforts are an indispensable part of any public policies to protect the health and safety of children, experience in injury prevention has found that legal remedies often result in more rapid and larger changes in occupational safety and health than reliance on individual behavioral change alone (see Chapter 6). The conditions under which minors can work are already limited by regulation. The committee's recommendations address the need for revision or elaboration of those existing limitations. Because such efforts require adequate data, the committee also recommends improved data and surveillance systems and more general research.

SURVEILLANCE SYSTEMS

Young workers' occupational injuries, illnesses, and exposures to hazardous substances are preventable if proper public health actions are taken. Surveillance systems that provide information about where and how youngsters are injured or made ill while working is essential for both targeting and evaluating prevention efforts. Over the past decade, government agencies have substantially improved the surveillance of illnesses and injuries sustained by adult workers; more recent surveillance initiatives have begun to provide information regarding young workers, at least with respect to their work-related injuries. These activities, however, are limited and poorly coordinated. As yet, the principal federal occupational illness and injury surveillance systems have not been evaluated to assess the extent to which they may systematically omit young workers or subgroups of young workers. The lack of specific attention to the need for data regarding issues related to the protection of young workers as a special population has often meant that even existing data concerning relevant age groups are unavailable to the public.

There are few state-based surveillance systems of nonfatal work-related injuries that combine data from multiple sources and allow for important links to intervention programs in the workplace. The field of injury surveillance is expanding, and new opportunities to integrate the surveillance of work-related injuries into more general injury surveillance systems need to be actively pursued. The conventional injury surveillance datasets, such as workers' compensation and the Department of Labor's Survey of Occupational Injuries and Illnesses, need to be supplemented by data from broader resources, such as ambulatory care data, which captures a much greater range of the work-related injuries sustained by the general population. Almost completely lacking is information about the health hazards to which young workers are exposed: Very little information is currently available, and the committee could not identify any surveillance focus on such hazards.

Recommendation: The National Institute for Occupational Safety and Health, in collaboration with the Bureau of Labor Statistics and other relevant federal and state agencies, should develop and implement a comprehensive plan for monitoring the work-related injuries and illnesses sustained by workers under the age of 18 and for monitoring the hazards to which these young workers are exposed. Additional resources should be allocated to the appropriate agencies to implement the components of such a plan that are not currently funded.

The committee has identified a number of surveillance activities that should be priorities for consideration as this planning effort proceeds.

• The National Institute for Occupational Safety and Health (NIOSH) should explore paying specific attention to young workers when conducting hazard surveillance. For example, NIOSH should explore the feasibility and utility of collecting and routinely reporting how many workers are under the age of 18 and what percentage of the work force they represent whenever it assesses exposures to health hazards. (This would apply both to workplaces in which health hazards are evaluated and to those surveyed in the National Occupational Exposure Survey.) Special studies to assess exposure to health hazards among certain populations of young workers, such as young migrant workers' exposure to pesticides, should also be undertaken.

• NIOSH should collaborate with the National Center for Injury Prevention and Control at the Centers for Disease Control and Prevention, the National Center for Health Statistics, and other relevant agencies to enhance the collection of data on the work relatedness of injuries and illnesses. Particular attention should be directed to existing ambulatory care surveillance systems, such as the National Ambulatory Care Survey; the relationship of work to injuries sustained by youngsters should be specifically included as new state-level systems are developed using emergency department data.

• The Fatality Assessment and Control Evaluation program of NIOSH should consider including young people's work-related fatalities on its list of fatalities targeted for in-depth investigations. If full field investigations of all incidents are not feasible, NIOSH should, at least, develop a supplement to its basic data collection instrument to gather key information pertinent to working youngsters.

• State-based surveillance activities, particularly those supported by NIOSH, should be expanded to allow for combining all the sources of data on nonfatal injuries and illnesses sustained by young workers and to develop appropriate links of surveillance so that relevant data collection is designed to support local intervention efforts.

• The Bureau of Labor Statistics should routinely publish tabulations of the available data from the Survey of Occupational Injuries and Illnesses and the Census of Fatal Occupational Injuries (CFOI) for individuals under the age of 18, by separate and appropriate age categories.

• Existing data systems, including the Census of Fatal Occupational Injuries, the National Traumatic Occupational Fatality Surveillance System, the Survey of Occupational Injuries and Illnesses, and the National Electronic Injury Surveillance System, should be evaluated to assess the extent to which they capture and generate representative data on work-related injuries sustained by youngsters.

• The Bureau of Labor Statistics, with the assistance of the Wage and Hour Division, should include information on violations of federal child labor laws in the CFOI database for fatal incidents involving individuals under the age of 18. Such information is important to evaluate the adequacy of hazardous order regulations and compliance with those regulations.

• Targeted periodic surveillance efforts should be undertaken to identify the work-related injuries and illnesses sustained by particularly vulnerable subgroups of young workers, such as young migrant farmworkers, young immigrants, poor youngsters, and minority youngsters.

• Education efforts should be targeted to health care providers who work with children and adolescents to develop professionals who routinely collect essential information about work histories and who routinely provide anticipatory guidance to adolescents about work-related health issues. Because the surveillance of occupational injuries and illnesses is contingent on the recognition that some health problems are related to hazards in the workplace, adequate training of health care providers is essential. In the United States, however, occupational health training for providers is generally extremely limited. Moreover, those specialists who provide other health services specifically to children and adolescents receive no training regarding health and safety for working youngsters. Even in the standard prevention counseling guidelines for young people, occupational safety and health issues are not mentioned.

• All federal agencies that collect data on the occupational injuries and illnesses sustained by youngsters should improve efforts to disseminate this information to state and local public health practitioners who are responsible for injury control and adolescent health.

• A surveillance component should be developed so that schools with work-based learning programs can track and investigate injuries sustained by students in job placements.

DATA

Taken together, federal data sources and national and local survey research provide a fair amount of information about teenagers who have jobs, where they work, and how much they work. However, definitions and nomenclature often vary from source to source, making it difficult to compare information, and little information is available about the extent of work by those under the age of 15. Nor is there much information on subpopulations of young people, such as those who are disabled, poor, or members of minority groups. Information on the quality of the work in which young people engage is also lacking. Finally, there are very little data on children and adolescents who are illegally employed, either in violation of child labor laws or in illicit activities.

The Current Population Survey only asks about work performed by those aged 15 and older, although research and anecdotal evidence suggest that many children and adolescents hold their first jobs at ages much younger than 15. Under the Fair Labor Standards Act (FLSA), many jobs are legal for 14-year-olds; in agriculture, children as young as 10 can legally perform some jobs. In order to understand the work experiences of young people, information on the numbers of children and young adolescents who work and the types of jobs they hold is vital. Good employment data are also necessary to establish information about injury rates.

The information on all adolescents needs to be reported in ways that are useful to researchers and policy makers. Aggregating information into broad groups, such as 15- to 24-year- olds or 16- to 19-year-olds, obscures important differences that may exist at crucial developmental and legal periods.

Information on the numbers of hours worked per job would allow better assessment of workers' exposures to workplace hazards and more accurate calculation of injury rates. These data are particularly important for groups of workers who are not full-time employees, such as children and adolescents. Calculating injury rates by using injuries per employee underestimates the actual extent of exposure for part-time workers. Information on the numbers of hours worked allows for the calculation of injury rates using denominator units, such as full-time-employee equivalents, that account for the actual amounts of exposure to hazards. The Current Population Survey collects information on the hours individuals have worked in the previous week on all their jobs: For those with more than one job, this aggregation does not allow for the calculation of industry-specific injury rates.

> **Recommendation: The Bureau of Labor Statistics should routinely collect and report data on the employment of young people aged 14 and older. Such data should be reported by informative age groupings, by school status (e.g., school year or summer and in-school or not-in-school), and by hours worked per job. For the decennial census, the Bureau of the Census should collect and report similar data on employment for young workers.**

Little information on very young workers and on the employment of special populations of youth is available. In large, national surveys, such as the Current Population Survey, it is difficult to get a sufficiently large sample of these populations for accurate analyses. Therefore, specially targeted studies are needed for particular subgroups of children and adolescents.

Little data exist on the illegal employment of children. Estimates based on violations of child labor laws often combine hour violations and hazardous-order violations. These estimates depend on known violations, which vary from year to year because of such factors as the number of inspectors available and the industries targeted for inspection. Furthermore, these estimates are unlikely to include children and adolescents employed in sweatshops or in other illegal activities.

Recommendation: The Bureau of Labor Statistics should periodically conduct special studies to document the employment of children under the age of 14 and of special populations of children and adolescents, such as minorities, immigrants, migrant farmworkers, and those who are poor or disabled. Also needed are periodic studies of children and adolescents who are illegally employed.

The bureau's sampling methodology is designed to provide reliable estimates of employment at a national level, but the size of the sample often limits the detail with which reliable state-specific estimates can be made. Yet enforcement of child labor laws and occupational safety and health regulations is frequently done at the state level. State-specific estimates of employment in those industries and jobs where youths predominantly work are necessary not only for determining reliable rates of injury or illness, but also for targeting state-based inspections of compliance with child labor laws and sites for workplace-based educational efforts.

Recommendation: The Bureau of Labor Statistics should develop methods to generate reliable estimates of youth employment at the state level.

Many agencies, including the National Center for Health Statistics, the Bureau of Labor Statistics, the National Institute for Occupational Safety and Health, the National Center for Education Statistics, the Bureau of Justice Statistics, and the Occupational Safety and Health Administration collect much information on children and adolescents. The information includes the work experiences of youngsters, but there is no standard for what information is gathered or for how it is reported. Standard definitions and nomenclature are needed to make the various sources of information more complementary. Immediately needed are appropriate definitions for the following:

• Work status: When surveying about young workers, it is important to collect information on jobs that are informal or unpaid, short-term or seasonal, during the summer or during the school year, and so forth. Although all agencies need not collect the same information on all work by youngsters, a common rubric or scheme is needed if information collected by different agencies is to be effectively combined or compared.

• Age groups: Current reporting of data by groups, such as "under 20" or "15-to-24," ignore critical social and behavioral changes that occur during adolescence, as well as the dividing age that legally defines minors (under the age of 18). More appropriate age groupings are essential for addressing issues related to child labor.

• Hours of work: Categories should be standardized so that developmentally appropriate levels of investment in employment can be monitored. For example, hours worked per week might be reported in 5-hour increments. It is especially important to be able to discern the frequency at which minors work at different intensities in examining the consequences of work.

> **Recommendation: Federal agencies that collect data related to work by children and adolescents should establish standardized nomenclature and definitions for such variables as work status, age groups, and hours of work. Those agencies that collect data for health, education, and development purposes should also collect data on the employment of youngsters in their surveys.**

EDUCATION

The health and safety hazards that face children and adolescents in the workplace and the protections to which they are entitled under the law are little known or understood by the children and adolescents themselves, by their parents, or by other adults who are in positions to give them guidance. The committee proposes several plans to begin to remedy this lack of knowledge and to promote understanding of the conditions that allow or promote safe and meaningful work experiences for children and adolescents.

Information and Training

A number of efforts are currently under way around the country to provide information and training related to making workplaces safe and healthy environments for young people. It was beyond the scope of the current study to adequately assess the most appropriate mechanisms for providing such training. Undoubtedly, a variety of mechanisms are needed, depending on whether the target audiences are young people themselves; or their parents, teachers, employers, health care providers, or community leaders. The federal government could play a key role in advancing information in this area by supporting a series of demonstration projects to test the feasibility and effectiveness of various approaches to information and education about health and safety issues related to the employment of young people. Examples of the types of approaches that could be tested include the following:

• Regional resource centers could be funded to provide technical assistance to schools, employers, and local government agencies regarding the health and safety of young workers. The activities of such centers might include conducting qualitative research to identify the gaps in information; developing and disseminating appropriate materials on health, safety, and well-being to various key audiences, including health care professionals, educators, parents, and employers; developing educational curricula for teaching children and adolescents about workplace health and safety; facilitating the adoption of curricula in schools and work-based learning programs; and facilitating collaboration among government agencies at the state and local levels to develop programs and policies to enhance the health and safety of young workers.

• Mechanisms could be developed to help young workers who have encountered hazardous or otherwise unacceptable working conditions to understand their rights and to take appropriate action. Regional resource centers are one possible source of assistance; linking youngsters with organizations that have narrower responsibilities is another.

• Community-based approaches, involving partnerships among young workers, their parents, their employers, their schools, health care providers, community organizations, and others, have the potential to provide comprehensive and coordinated services and to identify young people's employment as an issue in which the entire community has a stake. NIOSH is currently funding three such demonstration projects. An evaluation of the effectiveness of these projects should improve our understanding about how best to focus a community's attention on the health and safety needs of young workers.

NIOSH or an agency of the Department of Labor would be a logical lead agency to coordinate educational and training activities and demonstration programs. If provided adequate resources, such a lead agency would be able to collaborate with other agencies in an initiative to assemble the required blend of expertise in both content about child labor health and safety issues, in effective presentation and dissemination of information, and in training. Agencies collaborating with NIOSH and the Department of Labor should include, at a minimum, the Department of Education, the National School-to-Work Office, the Bureau of Maternal and Child Health of the Department of Health and Human Services, and the CDC's Center for Injury Prevention and Control. These federal agencies should provide information, materials, and technical assistance to state and local agencies, including state departments of education and labor and local school systems.

> **Recommendation: A national initiative should be undertaken to develop and provide information and training to reduce the risks and enhance the benefits associated with youth employment. Adequate resources should be allocated to an agency to lead this effort.**

Occupational Health and Safety in School-to-Work Programs

The purpose of the School-to-Work Opportunities Act of 1994 was to leverage other resources to foster partnerships, at the state and local levels, that would build systems to support the transition of adolescents from school into lifelong careers. The act will terminate in October 2001. Because state and local resources and other federal resources (e.g., the Elementary and Secondary Education Act, the Carl D. Perkins Vocational and Applied Technology Education Act, and the Job Training Partnership Act) would have to be redirected to maintain these efforts after that time, it is important to evaluate current school-to-work programs. An evaluation of the School-to-Work Opportunities Act is under way, but it is unclear whether the evaluation will adequately assess the presence and effectiveness of health and safety training or the safety of work placements under the act. Those program aspects that are found to be successful in connecting school and work and in providing appropriate health and safety training to young people deserve to be continued. There may be a need for a continuing federal role to disseminate information about effective programs.

Recommendation: The Departments of Education and Labor, in their evaluation of the School-to-Work Opportunities Act, should make certain that the evaluation includes comprehensive assessment of the success of different programs in conveying appropriate and effective workplace health and safety information and training. Those practices found to be effective should be continued after the School-to-Work Opportunities Act expires.

Commendable Workplaces for Youth

The committee believes that regulations and enforcement need to be strengthened for the protection of the health and safety of young workers. The committee also believes that commending those who are providing healthy, safe, and beneficial workplaces for young people is important. The committee envisions the establishment of a seal of approval for such workplaces, based on nationally developed criteria, but administered at the local level.

A coalition of leaders from government, industry, labor, education, health, youth groups, and others who have stakes in youth employment, as well as young people and their parents, would develop the criteria for identifying workplaces that are beneficial to youth. Once the criteria and methods for implementing them have been developed at the national level, recognition would be granted locally. Local coalitions with comparable membership would publicly recognize those workplaces that meet the criteria. In addition, all workplaces where young people receive publicly supported education and training (e.g., internships, cooperative education, youth apprenticeship, and placements subsidized by the Job Training Partnership Act and other federal funds) could be required to meet the criteria, with participation by other employers on a voluntary basis.

Identifying commendable workplaces would have several beneficial effects. Publicly identifying employers who maintain developmentally appropriate healthy working conditions would convey critical information to youth, parents, and educators. It would encourage all employers to improve conditions for young workers, not only as a matter of image and public relations, but also because the most desirable young workers would seek to work in the workplaces identified as commendable. The criteria for being designated as a commendable workplace for young workers might include the following:

- adhering to all child labor laws and regulations;
- maintaining a safe and healthy workplace;
- providing information to young workers about industry-specific and workplace-specific safety risks, employees' rights (e.g., when and how to lodge complaints), protective practices, and pertinent child labor laws and regulations;
- providing adequate training (regarding such things as handling equipment and following workplace procedures, including emergency procedures) for young workers at the inception of employment and whenever major new tasks are assumed;
- allowing for visitation and inspection by school personnel, parents, or other interested parties;
- providing special training for supervisors of youth employees;
- recognizing that education is young workers' highest priority and, therefore, paying attention to their school performances; and
- providing opportunities for young workers to learn and use new knowledge and skills, including technical, social, and personal skills.

Financial support for the establishment of such criteria might come from a combination of government agencies, foundations, non-profit community groups, and business organizations. Implementation and maintenance of the recognition system might be supported by fees paid by employers.

> **Recommendation:** The Secretary of Labor should convene a prestigious group representing all affected parties to develop criteria for designating "commendable workplaces for youth." These criteria would be used by local groups to identify which employers would earn the designation and to determine which employers are eligible to employ young people in publicly supported school-related programs.

PROTECTIVE MEASURES

The regulatory standards developed decades ago to protect youth from hazardous work, excessive hours, and unsafe or unhealthy work environments do not reflect contemporary work hazards and the important changes in rates of school attendance and youth employment, particularly among 16- and 17-year-olds. Youth are currently subject to different standards depending on whether they work in the public or private sector, in small or big businesses, in different industries, and in businesses covered by state or federal laws. In particular, child labor and occupational health and safety standards for youngsters working in agriculture are far less protective than for all other industries, even with regard to the same hazards and the risks posed by long work hours.

Hours of Work

Current federal standards limit work during school weeks to 18 hours for youth under age 16. The Department of Labor is not authorized by law to establish restrictions on working hours for 16- and 17-year-olds. As the vast majority of 16- and 17-year-olds are still attending school, the historical reasons that justified the exemption of youngsters 16 and older from the hour limitations are no longer applicable. Furthermore, many studies have shown that long hours of work while in school can have adverse consequences. Although the definition of the term *long* differs across studies, most studies have used 20 hours per week (while school is in session) as the dividing line between "low-intensity" and "high-intensity" work. As noted above and detailed in Chapter 4, high-intensity work is associated with unhealthy and problem behaviors, including substance use and minor deviance, insufficient sleep and exercise, and limited time spent with families. Moreover, high-intensity work during adolescence has been found to be associated with decreased eventual educational attainment.

In contrast to these negative consequences, some other studies have found positive results associated with moderate- to high-intensity work during high school. The results include increased employment and higher earnings for as long as 10 years after students leave high school. While conclusions about positive benefits have been questioned in some analyses (one study found that the apparent increase in earnings disappeared after carefully controlling for unobserved differences among groups of students and that it was the students who did not work at all during high school who had the highest earnings a decade later), the findings suggest that attention will need to be given to how to specify the circumstances under which the benefits outweigh the negative consequences of high-intensity work by adolescents.

On balance, in the judgment of the committee, the scientific evidence supports increased restrictions on the intensity of work by children and adolescents. In keeping with its guiding principles and the research evidence, the committee believes that limiting the hours of work for most 16- and 17-year-olds during the school year is essential to their healthy development. Because of limits in the evidence, however, one cannot specify precisely at what intensity of work the negative consequences outweigh the benefits. Following the majority of the evidence to date, and the conventional cutoff used in many studies, the committee strongly supports a limit of 20 hours of work per week during the school year for adolescents under most circumstances.

The committee acknowledges that care will have to be taken in setting an upper limit in number of work hours for 16- and 17-year-olds. Some circumstances may warrant exemptions from the limitations on work hours during school, such as for adolescents in extreme financial need or for emancipated minors. There may also be special circumstances, related to an individual student or to the quality of the work (e.g., high-quality school-to-work placements), under which high-intensity work may be determined to have fewer negative consequences than benefits.

It has been suggested that there may be some students who might drop out of school if their work hours are limited. The committee did not thoroughly review the literature on dropping out of school, but multiple factors, many of which precede entry into the work force, may lead youngsters to drop out of school. Dropping out of school has also been linked to the labor market, with dropout rates declining as unemployment rates rise. Clearly, the issue of dropouts deserves further investigation and, as standards are implemented, this is a question that should be monitored closely.

As with any policy change, other unintended consequences may occur, as well. For example, restrictions on the hours that adolescents can work might reduce their employment opportunities. Often, when employment of a particular group is made more difficult or costly for the employer, the employment level for that group declines, but the experience in Washington state suggests that this may not necessarily be the case for young people (see Chapter 6). After Washington imposed stricter limits on work by 16- and 17-year-olds, there was no decrease in the number of jobs available for adolescents.

One method to arrive at the appropriate restrictions would be for the Department of Labor to establish an expert advisory committee charged with recommending what specific limits should be placed on allowable work hours for youngsters aged 16 and 17 and what, if any, exceptions to these limits should be permitted. In addition to the number of hours worked per week, the advisory committee should also investigate whether hours per day and start and stop times of work, particularly on school nights, should be included in the regulation.

Recommendation: The Department of Labor should be authorized by Congress to adopt a standard limiting the weekly maximum number of hours of work for 16- and 17-year-olds during the school year. This standard should be based on the extensive research about the adverse effects of high-intensity work while school is in session.

Currently, children and adolescents working in agriculture are permitted to work many more hours and at younger ages than those who work in nonagricultural workplaces. Yet, the negative consequences of long hours of work are equally serious for youngsters working in agriculture as for those working in other industries.

Recommendation: The current distinction in federal child labor restrictions on the total maximum weekly hours youngsters are allowed to work in agricultural and nonagricultural industries should be eliminated in favor of the more stringent nonagricultural restrictions.

Hazardous Work

Many existing hazardous orders, which restrict the types of jobs those under 18 (under 16 in agriculture) may perform, refer to machinery and processes that are no longer used, and they fail to address the full range of health and safety hazards and technologies in the contemporary workplaces in which youngsters are now employed. None of the current hazardous orders takes into account the special risks to young workers caused by exposure to carcinogens, biohazards, reproductive toxins, and ergonomic hazards, the health effects of which may not be evident until adulthood.

Changes in hazardous orders should be based on research and data on jobs that pose hazards to children and adolescents. NIOSH performs and reviews this research and is in a position to evaluate hazardous occupations for young people, although it may need additional resources to perform thorough evaluations. The institute has already made a number of research-based recommendations about needed changes in hazardous orders in its 1994 comments to the Department of Labor. The reviews and updates should be performed on a periodic basis to ensure that the hazardous orders remain up to date.

Recommendation: The Department of Labor should undertake periodic reviews of its hazardous orders in order to eliminate outdated orders, strengthen inadequate orders, and develop additional orders to address new and emerging technologies and working conditions. Changes to the hazardous orders should be based on periodic reviews by the National Institute for Occupational Safety and Health of current workplace hazards and the adequacy of existing hazardous orders to address them.

All working children and adolescents should be equally protected from similar hazardous occupational conditions, including those caused by chemical exposures or dangerous machines, regardless of the types of industry or the workers' relationships to their employers. The current distinction between agricultural and nonagricultural industries is frequently artificial. The committee's review determined that activities and machinery are often similar in both settings. For example, tractors are used in both agricultural and nonagricultural industries, and construction activities occur on farms. Activities that are hazardous for those under the age of 18 in nonagricultural settings are equally hazardous in agricultural settings, yet current regulations do not protect 16- and 17-year-olds on farms from performing hazardous tasks, nor do they protect youngsters of any age on their parents' farms. The only appropriate justification for a lower minimum age for performing hazardous work would be demonstrably lower risks in the industry, but this is not the case for work in agriculture: agriculture is one of the most dangerous industries in the country.

Recommendation: The current distinctions between hazardous orders in agricultural and nonagricultural industries should be eliminated. Furthermore, the minimum age of 18 should apply for all hazardous occupations, regardless of whether the adolescent is working in an agricultural or nonagricultural job, and whether the minor is employed by a stranger or by a parent or other person standing in for the parent.

Minimum Levels of Protection

State regulations vary widely on the maximum weekly hours that are permitted for minors under the age of 16. Although some states have enacted regulations that are consistent with the Fair Labor Standards Act regulations, 16 states allow minors to work more than the federal maximum. For example, Wyoming allows minors to work as many as 56 hours per week, Idaho allows 54 hours per week, and a number of other states allow 48 hours per week. For businesses that do not meet the threshold for coverage under the FLSA, the less protective standards apply in those states.

A few states regulate the maximum permissible hours of work

per week for 16- and 17-year-olds, and these rules also vary, ranging from 20 to 50 hours per week.

States' hazardous orders also differ with regard to coverage and interpretation from the FLSA hazardous orders. Although some states have incorporated the federal standards, other states have adopted their own definitions, as in the case of operating power-driven machinery. Consistent with the principle of equal protection for all children, the committee believes that federal hour limitations and hazardous orders should be considered the minimum safe requirements for working children and adolescents. States should be free to have more stringent regulations, but not less stringent ones.

Recommendation: All state regulations for minors' working hours and hazardous orders should be at least as protective as federal child labor rules.

Under current law, young workers in agriculture are not entitled to the same health and safety protection as in those other industries. Only a few Occupational Safety and Health Administration standards apply to agriculture. Standards that regulate such things as electrical hazards, unguarded machinery, confined spaces, heat stress, carcinogens, and access to medical and exposure records in other industries do not apply in agriculture. The hazard communication standards under OSHA with respect to pesticides have been pre-empted by less comprehensive Worker Protection Standards under the purview of the U.S. Environmental Protection Agency. Furthermore, although the enforcement of OSHA standards is generally more limited for businesses that employ 10 or fewer workers, these businesses must nonetheless comply with the standards, while farms that employ 10 or fewer workers and do not have labor camps are exempted altogether from such enforcement. No health and safety justification for the distinction between agricultural and nonagricultural settings appears to exist. It should be a priority to protect the large number of youngsters working in agriculture from the recognized significant risks of such work to the same extent that young workers are protected in other industries.

The committee acknowledges that extending OSHA coverage to agriculture would be a major change in policy with many ramifications, particularly since OSHA regulations have, to date, not distinguished between adult and youth workers. However, the fact that agriculture is one of the most dangerous industries in the country suggests the need to closely examine health and safety issues in agriculture. In this regard, the committee calls on Congress, which annually has passed language that forbids OSHA enforcement on small farms, to commission a study of the potential effects of bringing agriculture generally, and small farms, in particular, into alignment with other businesses under OSHA and to examine the feasibility of such a change. Under OSHA regulations, there are difficulties in singling out a designated group of workers for specific protections. However, in light of the President's Executive Order asking all agencies to consider the effects of their operations and programs on children, the study could investigate the possibility of extending occupational health and safety protections in agriculture to those under the age of 18, rather than to all workers on small farms.

In addition, such a study should review the application of hazard communication standards developed under OSHA and the standards under the EPA's Worker Protection Rule to identify gaps in the coverage of agriculture.

> **Recommendation: To ensure the equal protection of children and adolescents from health and safety hazards in agriculture, Congress should undertake an examination of the effects and feasibility of extending all relevant Occupational Safety and Health Administration regulations to agricultural workers, including subjecting small farms to the same level of OSHA enforcement as that applied to other small businesses.**

Neither the Occupational Safety and Health Administration nor the Environmental Protection Agency (EPA) have considered, in their standard-setting processes, the special risks to the health and safety of young workers. Based on available research, the committee is particularly concerned about young workers' exposure to carcinogens, reproductive toxins, biohazards, and musculoskeletal hazards, which may cause serious and long-term harm that is not adequately prevented by the current standards. Even if young workers are not especially susceptible to these risks, their ages alone mean that the periods of time over which they may suffer adverse consequences are greater for them than for adults. Although the EPA is mandated by the Food Quality Protection Act to review pesticide standards to determine the safety of children from pesticide residues on food, the act does not address the health and safety of minors who are exposed to pesticides or treated crops in the course of working. In light of Executive Order 13045 (issued in April 1997), in which President Clinton identified the need for special attention to environmental health and safety risks to children and called upon all federal agencies to identify and assess those risks, it seems particularly timely for the issues of exposures to working children to be addressed.

Recommendation: The National Institute for Occupational Safety and Health, in consultation with the Occupational Safety and Health Administration and the Environmental Protection Agency, including the latter's Office of Child Health Protection, should report on the extent to which existing occupational health and safety and pesticide standards take into consideration special risks for young workers. In addition, the Task Force on Environmental Health Risks and Safety Risks to Children, created by Executive Order 13045, should ensure that its definition of children include older children and adolescents and includes exposures to children and adolescents at work.

Enforcement

Various studies have documented the widespread inconsistencies among the states regarding the enforcement of child labor laws and the penalties for violating them. Budget cuts have limited federal and state compliance, and only 3 states have more than 50 compliance officers to investigate violations of the labor laws regarding adults and children. Targeted inspections, when used, have been particularly effective in drawing attention to child labor violations by some employers and in deterring others from similar conduct. The penalties for such violations have historically been so low (penalties ranging from $5 to $10,000 per violation, with many states collecting nothing) that fines alone appear to have little deterrent effect on employers. Although federal penalties were increased to $10,000 for any violation that leads to the serious injury or death of a minor, few states have adopted that level of penalty. The Department of Labor has no mechanism to penalize egregious wage and hour violations or child labor cases that involve violations of occupational health and safety rules.

Recommendation: The Wage and Hour Division and the Occupational Safety and Health Administration enforcement systems should establish special-emphasis programs to increase the level and effectiveness of the inspections of industries that entail particularly high risks and employ large numbers of children. Such programs should also target noncompliant owners who endanger children by willfully or repeatedly disregarding the law. The Department of Labor should evaluate the effectiveness of penalty multipliers and other approaches to increased penalties for serious, willful, and repeated violations of wage and hour regulations and health and safety rules involving children at work.

Identifying violators serves two valuable functions: It provides information to young workers, their parents, educators, and others—enabling them to make informed choices about places to work—and it serves as a deterrent to employers, reminding them of their obligations. Publicizing violations of child labor laws is analogous to a public health agency's identifying restaurants found in violation of proper food handling procedures, and it is likely to have the same deterrent effect. To prevent unwarranted punishment, only serious, willful, or repeated violators should be so identified. This recommendation is made with the understanding that it represents a direct reversal of policy in some states, which explicitly prohibits the identification of violators.

Recommendation: State and federal agencies responsible for enforcing regulations governing the health and safety of working minors should actively publicize serious, willful, and repeated violators and violations.

Although a memorandum of understanding exists between the Wage and Hour Division and OSHA, little has actually occurred, in terms of cross-training of inspectors, referrals, or collaborative inspections, that would be efficient and effective in identifying and penalizing all child labor and health and safety violations in workplaces that employ minors. The number of inspectors or compliance officers available to each agency is insufficient and cannot be expected to permit either agency to regularly inspect all workplaces. If the inspectors were cross trained, however, either agency's inspectors would be able to identify serious violations of the other agency's regulations.

Recommendation: Interagency cross-training of inspectors should be developed and collaborative multiagency inspections should be increased to ensure that employers comply with all applicable child labor and occupational health and safety standards.

Workers' Compensation

There has been no systematic study of the adequacy and effectiveness of the workers' compensation system in dealing with the work-related injuries and illnesses sustained by young people. The committee's review indicates that young workers may be less likely than others to make use of the workers' compensation system, but the reasons for this remain speculative. Minors working in agriculture continue to be totally excluded from workers' compensation in most states. The model of indemnification for adult workers—lost wages and medical expenses—does not adequately compensate young workers for their unique losses, such as lost school time (which could have adverse effects on their educational attainment).

Recommendation: The National Institute for Occupational Safety and Health and the Occupational Safety and Health Administration, with the assistance of representatives from state workers' compensation programs, should study and report on the adequacy of current workers' compensation coverage, utilization, and indemnification for young workers. The study should consider examples of effective activities by states and other options for reforming the system to protect and compensate young people for the full range of loss, specifically including the adverse educational consequences of workplace injuries and illnesses.

Work Permits and Registration Systems

Work permits, like other child labor regulations, vary widely among the states in content and requirements. FLSA regulations encourage, but do not require, work permits for minors. These systems offer opportunities to identify young workers in need of training, as well as opportunities for collecting data about young workers. However, state permit systems generally fail to facilitate the training of minors on health and safety issues. The systems seldom make use of the permits to track young people's employment to identify and prevent work-related injuries and illness or violations of hazardous orders or rules regarding wages and hours. One alternative that the committee considers worthy of serious consideration for adoption by states is to require the employers who want to hire minors to obtain permits first. The states of Washington and Oregon have adopted such systems, which enables their labor departments to set and enforce working conditions.

Recommendation: The Department of Labor, in collaboration with NIOSH, should report on the existing and potential work permit or registration systems for young workers and for employers who intend to hire young workers. The report should examine the cost, use, and effectiveness of permits or registration for health and safety education, surveillance, enforcement, and reduction of workplace injuries and illnesses.

OTHER RESEARCH

The committee identified several critical areas in which additional research is needed for the adequate protection of young workers. Because so many young people in the United States are working, it is important to determine the strategies that will best serve to make their work experiences safe and healthful. Such research requires increased knowledge about the risk factors (hazards, level of training and supervision, fatigue, and so on) that lead to workplace injuries and illnesses among children and adolescents, as well as evaluation of injury prevention efforts. Agencies that fund research on children and adolescents should be provided sufficient resources to fund the following types of initiatives:

• Longitudinal studies of how individuals who have worked in their youth function as adolescents and adults and how various outcomes are associated with the quality of the work experiences. Research on working children and adolescents has primarily focused on the effects of the numbers of hours worked. Little attention has been paid to the quality of the work environment and its effect on development, workplace injuries, and educational goals.

• Research to determine whether the developmental characteristics of children and adolescents put them at increased risk from factors in the work environment, including chemical, physical, ergonomic, and psychosocial conditions (such as stress or type of supervision). Very little research has focused on the interaction of developmental characteristics of children and adolescents and risks in the workplace. Recently, the susceptibility of very young children to environmental and chemical toxins has received significant attention. This attention needs to be extended to older children and adolescents to discover at what ages susceptibility reaches a level no different from that for adults. Furthermore, the potential for harm to the musculoskeletal system caused by the physical demands of different types of work during the growth periods of adolescence needs greater attention.

• Research on the most efficient and effective strategies to protect working children and adolescents, with an emphasis on primary prevention of injury and other negative outcomes.

References

CHAPTER 1

Aronson, P.J., J.T. Mortimer, C. Zierman, and M. Hacker
  1996   Generational differences in early work experiences and evaluations. In *Adolescents, Work, and Family: An Intergenerational Developmental Analysis*, J.T. Mortimer and M.D. Finch, eds. Newbury Park, Calif.: Sage.
Bachman, J.G., and J. Schulenberg
  1992   Part-Time Work by High School Seniors: Sorting Out Correlates and Possible Consequences. Monitoring the Future Occasional Paper 32. Institute for Social Research, University of Michigan.
  1993   How part-time work intensity relates to drug use, problem behavior, time use, and satisfaction among high school seniors: Are these consequences or merely correlates? *Developmental Psychology* 29(2):220-235.
Bingham, E.
  1992   The Occupational Safety and Health Act. Pp. 1325-1331 in *Environmental and Occupational Medicine, 2nd edition*, W.N. Rom, ed. Boston: Little, Brown and Co.
Castillo, D.N., D.D. Landen, and L.A. Layne
  1994   Occupational injury deaths of 16- and 17-year-olds in the United States. *American Journal of Public Health* 84(4):646-649.
Derstine, B.
  1996   Job-related fatalities involving youths, 1992-1995. *Compensation and Working Conditions* (December):1-3.
Greenberger, E.
  1984   Children, family, and work. Pp. 103-122 in *Children, Mental Health, and the Law*, N.D. Repucci, L.A. Weithorn, E.P. Mulvey, and J. Monahan, eds. Beverly Hills, Calif.: Sage.

Greenberger, E., and L. Steinberg
  1986   *When Teenagers Work: The Psychological and Social Costs of Adolescent Employ-
         ment.* New York: Basic Books.
Heinzman, M., S. Thoreson, L. McKenzie, M. Cook, D. Parker, and W. Carl
  1993   Occupational burns among restaurant workers—Colorado and Minnesota. *Mor-
         bidity and Mortality Weekly Report* 42(37):713-716.
Heptinstall, E., K. Jewitt, and C. Sherriff
  1997   *Young Workers and Their Accidents.* London, U.K.: Child Accident Prevention
         Trust.
Hull, D.
  1993   *Opening Minds, Opening Doors: The Rebirth of American Education.* Waco,
         Tex.: Center for Occupational Research and Development.
International Labour Office
  1996   *Yearbook of Labour Statistics, 1996.* 55th Edition. Geneva, Switzerland: Interna-
         tional Labour Office.
Johnston, L., J. Bachman, and P. O'Malley
  1982   *Monitoring the Future: Questionnaire Responses From the Nation's High School
         Seniors, 1981.* Ann Arbor: Institute for Social Research, University of Michigan.
Kett, J.F.
  1977   *Rites of Passage: Adolescence in America: 1790 to the Present.* New York: Basic
         Books.
Layne, L.A., D.N. Castillo, N. Stout, and P. Cutlip
  1994   Adolescent occupational injuries requiring hospital emergency department treat-
         ment: A nationally representative sample. *American Journal of Public Health*
         84(4):657-660.
Light, A.
  1995   High School Employment. National Longitudinal Survey Discussion Paper, Report
         No. NLS 95-27. Bureau of Labor Statistics. Washington, D.C.: U.S. Department
         of Labor.
Massachusetts Department of Public Health
  1995   Two Massachusetts news carriers killed: Struck by cars while delivering from bi-
         cycles. *FACE Facts* 1(2).
Meltzer, M.
  1994   *Cheap Raw Material: How Our Youngest Workers Are Exploited and Abused.*
         New York: Viking Child Books.
Mortimer, J.T., M.D. Finch, S. Ryu, M.J. Shanahan, and K.T. Call
  1996   The effects of work intensity on adolescent mental health achievement, and behav-
         ioral adjustment: New evidence from a prospective study. *Child Development*
         67:1234-1261.
National Research Council
  1994   *Preparing for the Workplace: Charting a Course for Federal Postsecondary Train-
         ing Policy*, J.S. Hansen, ed. Committee on Postsecondary Education and Training
         for the Workplace, Commission on Behavior and Social Sciences and Education,
         National Research Council. Washington, D.C.: National Academy Press.
Parnell, D.
  1985   *The Neglected Majority.* Washington, D.C.: Community College Press.
Phillips, S., and K.L. Sandstrom
  1990   Parental attitudes towards youth work. *Youth and Society* 22:160-183.

Resnick, M.D., P.S. Bearman, R.W. Blum, K.E. Bauman, K.M. Harris, J. Jones, J. Tabor, T. Beuhring, R.E. Sieving, M. Shew, M. Ireland, L. Bearinger, and J.R. Udry
  1997   Protecting adolescents from harm: Findings from the National Longitudinal Study on Adolescent Health. *Journal of the American Medical Association* 278(10):823-832.
Rom, W.N.
  1992   The discipline of environmental and occupational medicine. Pp. 3-6 in *Environmental and Occupational Medicine, 2nd edition*, W.N. Rom, ed. Boston: Little, Brown and Co.
Ruhm, C.J.
  1997   Is high school employment consumption or investment? *Journal of Labor Economics* 15(4):735-776.
Scribner, S.
  1984   Studying working intelligence. In *Everyday Cognition: Its Development in Social Context*, B. Rogoff and J. Lave, eds. Cambridge, Mass.: Harvard University Press.
Steinberg, L., and E. Cauffman
  1995   The impact of employment on adolescent development. *Annals of Child Development* 11:131-166.
Steinberg, L., S. Fegley, and S.M. Dornbusch
  1993   Negative impact of part-time work on adolescent adjustment: Evidence from a longitudinal study. *Developmental Psychology* 29(2):171-180.
Steinberg, L., B.B. Brown, and S.M. Dornbusch
  1996   *Beyond the Classroom: Why School Reform Has Failed and What Parents Need to Do*. New York: Simon and Schuster.
U.S. Department of Education
  1996   *Youth Indicators 1996: Trends in the Well-Being of American Youth*. NCES-96-027. National Center for Educational Statistics. Washington, D.C.: U.S. Department of Education.
U.S. Department of Labor
  1998   *Child Labor Fact Sheet*. February 1998. Wage and Hour Division, Employment Standards Administration. Washington, D.C.: U.S. Department of Labor.
Yeatts, J.
  1994   Which Students Work and Why? Master's thesis. Department of Economics, University of North Carolina, Greensboro.

CHAPTER 2

Ahituv, A., M. Tienda, and V.J. Hotz
  1997   Transition From School to Work: Black, Hispanic, and White Men in the 1980s. June 1997. Unpublished paper. Available from Population Research Center, University of Chicago.
Bachman, J.G., and J. Schulenberg
  1992   *Part-Time Work by High School Seniors: Sorting Out Correlates and Possible Consequences*. Monitoring the Future Occasional Paper 32. Ann Arbor: Institute for Social Research, The University of Michigan.
Benz, M.R., P. Yovanoff, and B. Doren
  1997   School-to-work components that predict postschool success for students with and without disabilities. *Exceptional Children* 63(2):151-165.

Bureau of Labor Statistics
  1997 *Employment and Earnings.* January 1997. Washington, D.C.: U.S. Department of
        Labor.
Children's Defense Fund
  1988 *A Children's Defense Budget FY 1989: An Analysis of Our Nation's Investment in
        Children.* Washington, D.C.: Children's Defense Fund.
D'Amico, R.
  1984 Does employment during high school impair academic progress? *Sociology of Edu-
        cation* 57(July):152-164.
  1986 Why does work in high school matter. In *Pathways to the Future, Volume 6*, R.
        D'Amico, ed. Columbus: Center for Human Resources, Ohio State University.
D'Amico, R., and P. Baker
  1984 The nature and consequences of high school employment. Pp. 1-49 in *Pathways to
        the Future, Volume 4*, P. Baker, ed. Columbus: Center for Human Resources
        Research, Ohio State University.
Freeman, R.B., and J.L. Medoff
  1982 Why does the rate of youth labor force activity differ across surveys? Pp. 75-105 in
        The Youth Labor Market Problem, R.B. Freeman and D.A. Wise, eds. Chicago:
        The University of Chicago Press.
Golub, A.
  1997 Employment Information Available From Drug Use Forecasting Data. Paper pre-
        sented to the Committee on the Health and Safety Implications of Child Labor.
        Available from National Development and Research Institutes, New York.
Griliches, Z.
  1980 Schooling interruptions, work while in school and the returns from schooling. *Scan-
        dinavian Journal of Economics* 82:291-303.
Jasso, G.
  1997 Immigrant Children and Work. Paper presented to the Committee on the Health
        and Safety Implications of Child Labor. Department of Sociology, New York Uni-
        versity.
Kablaoui, B.N., and A. Pautler
  1991 The effects of part-time work experience on high school students. *Journal of Ca-
        reer Development* 17:195-211.
Kruse, D.
  1997 Illegal Child Labor in the United States. Paper prepared for the Associated Press,
        November 1997. Available from Douglas Kruse, School of Management and Labor
        Relationships, Rutgers University, or online at http://wire.ap.org/APpackages/alex/
        background/study1 [1998, January 19].
Light, A.
  1994 Transitions from School to Work: A Survey of Research Using the National Longi-
        tudinal Surveys. NLS Discussion Paper, Report No. NLS 94-18, Bureau of Labor
        Statistics. Washington, D.C.: U.S. Department of Labor.
  1995 *High School Employment.* National Longitudinal Survey Discussion Paper, Report
        No. NLS 95-27, Bureau of Labor Statistics. Washington, D.C.: U.S. Department of
        Labor.
Lillydahl, J.H.
  1990 Academic achievement and part-time employment of high school students. *Journal
        of Economic Education* 21:307-316.
McNeil, J.M.
  1997 Americans With Disabilities: 1994-95. Current Population Reports, P70-61, Au-
        gust. Washington, D.C.: Census Bureau, U.S. Department of Commerce. Available

at http://www.census.gov/hhes/www/disable/sipp/disable9495.html [1998, February 3].

Manning, W.D.
1990   Parenting employed teenagers. *Youth and Society* 22:184-200.

Massachusetts Department of Public Health
1997   *Profile of Brockton Working Teens.* Summer. Brockton Area Protecting Young Workers Project. Boston: Massachusetts Department of Public Health.

Michael, R.T., and N.B. Tuma
1984   Youth employment: Does life begin at 16? *Journal of Labor Economics* 2(October):464-476.

National Institute for Occupational Safety and Health
1997   Child Labor Research Needs: Report of the NIOSH Child Labor Working Group. Publication No. DHHS(NIOSH) 97-143. Cincinnati, Oh.: National Institute for Occupational Safety and Health, U.S. Department of Health and Human Services.

Pallas, A.M.
1995   Federal data on educational attainment and the transition to work. In *Integrating Federal Statistics on Children: Report of a Workshop.* Board on Children, Youth, and Families and the Committee on National Statistics, National Research Council. Washington, D.C.: National Academy Press.

Resnick, M.D., P.S. Bearman, R.W. Blum, K.E. Bauman, K.M. Harris, J. Jones, J. Tabor, T. Beuhring, R.E. Sieving, M. Shew, M. Ireland, L. Bearinger, and J.R. Udry
1997   Protecting adolescents from harm: Findings from the National Longitudinal Study on Adolescent Health. *Journal of the American Medical Association* 278(10):823-832.

Robinson, J.P., and G. Godbey
1997   *Time for Life: The Surprising Ways Americans Use Their Time.* University Park: Pennsylvania State University Press.

Ruhm, C.J.
1997   Is high school employment consumption or investment? *Journal of Labor Economics* 15(4):735-776.

Schoenhals, M., M. Tienda, and B. Schneider
1997   The Educational and Personal Consequences of Adolescent Employment. Unpublished paper. Department of Sociology, University of Chicago.

Stanford Center for the Study of Families, Children, and Youth
1991   *The Stanford Studies of Homeless Families, Children, and Youth.* Stanford, Calif.: Stanford University.

Steel, L.
1991   Early work experience among white and non-white youths: Implications for subsequent enrollment and employment. *Youth and Society* 22:419-447.

Steinberg, L., and E. Cauffman
1995   The impact of employment on adolescent development. *Annals of Child Development* 11:131-166.

Stephenson, S.P.
1979   From school to work. *Youth and Society* 11(September):114-132.
1981a   In-school labour force status and post-school wage rates of young men. *Applied Economics* 13:279-302.
1981b   Young women and labor: In-school labor force status and early postschool labor market outcomes. *Youth and Society* 13(December):123-155.
1982   Work in college and subsequent wage rates. *Research in Higher Education* 17:165-178.

Stern, D., and Y.F. Nakata
  1989   Characteristics of high school students, paid jobs, and employment experience after
          graduation. Pp. 189-234 in *Adolescence and Work: Influences of Social Structure,
          Labor Markets, and Culture*, D. Stern and D. Eichorn, eds. Hillsdale, N.J.:
          Lawrence Erlbaum.
Sweet, J.A.
  no   The World of Work. Respondent report #2, National Survey of Families and House-
  date   holds. Survey Center, University of Wisconsin, Madison.
U.S. Department of Education
  1996   *Eighteenth Annual Report to Congress on the Implementation of the Individuals
          with Disabilities Education Act.* Washington, D.C.: Office of Special Education
          Programs.
U.S. General Accounting Office
  1989   *Sweatshops in New York City: A Local Example of a National Problem.* Report
          #GAO/HRD-89-101BR. Washington, D.C.: U.S. General Accounting Office.
  1991   *Characteristics of Working Children.* Report #GAO/HRD-91BR. June 1991.
          Washington, D.C.: U.S. Government Printing Office.
Wagner, M., R. D'Amico, C. Marder, L. Newman, and J. Blackorby
  1992   *What Happens Next? Trends in Postschool Outcomes of Youth with Disabilities.
          The Second Comprehensive Report from the National Longitudinal Study of Special
          Education Students.* Menlo Park, Calif.: SRI International.
White, P.H.
  1997   Employment Among Disabled Adolescents. Paper presented to the Committee on
          the Health and Safety Implications of Child Labor. Available from Section of Rheu-
          matology, Children's National Medical Center, Washington, D.C.
White, P.H., and E.S. Shear
  1992   Transition/Job readiness for adolescents with juvenile arthritis and other chronic
          illnesses. *Journal of Rheumatology* 19(S33):23-27.
White, P.H., D.G. Gussak, B. Fisher, and D. Hixson
  1990   Career maturity in adolescents with chronic illnesses and disabilities. *Journal of
          Adolescent Health Care* 11:S777.
Yates, G., R. MacKenzie, J. Pennbridge, and E. Cohen
  1988   A risk profile comparison of runaway and non-runaway youth. *American Journal
          of Public Health* 78:820-821.

CHAPTER 3

Anders, T.F., M.A. Carskadon, W.C. Dement, et al.
  1978   Sleep habits of children and the identification of pathologically sleepy children.
          Child Psychiatry and Human Development 9:56-63.
Baker, S.P., B. O'Neill, M.J. Ginsburg, and G. Li
  1992   *The Injury Fact Book.* 2nd edition. New York: Oxford University Press.
Banco, L., G. Lapidus, and M. Braddock
  1992   Work-related injury among Connecticut minors. *Pediatrics* 89(5):957-960.
Band, J., and D. Pismire
  1984   Correlates of coal mining accidents and injuries: A literature review. *Accident
          Analysis and Prevention* 16:37-45.
Bell, C.A., N.A. Stout, T.R. Bender, C.S. Conroy, W.E. Crouse, and J.R. Myers
  1990   Fatal occupational injuries in the United States, 1980 through 1985. *Journal of the
          American Medical Association* 263:3047-3050.

Belville, R., S.H. Pollack, J.H. Godbold, and P.J. Landrigan
   1993   Occupational injuries among working adolescents in New York State. *Journal of the American Medical Association* 269(21):2754-2759.

Bernard, B.P.
   1997   *Musculoskeletal Disorders (MSDs) and Workplace Factors: A Critical Review of Epidemiologic Evidence for Work-Related Musculoskeletal Disorders of the Neck, Upper Extremity, and Low Back.* Second printing, July 1997. DHHS Publication No. 97-141. Cincinnati, OH: National Institute for Occupational Safety and Health Publications Dissemination. Available at http://www.cdc.gov/niosh/ergosci1.html [1997, August 26].

Billiard M., A. Alperovitch, C. Perot, and A. Jammes
   1987   Excessive daytime somnolence in young men: Prevalence and contributing factors. *Sleep* 10:297-305.

Bowling, M.
   1996   Teens at Risk: The Youth Exposure to Occupational Hazards Study. Paper presented at the 1996 American Public Health Association's Annual Meeting, New York City, November, 1996. Available from Injury Prevention Research Center, University of North Carolina, Chapel Hill.

Bowling, J.M., C. Runyan, C. Miara, L. Davis, H. Rubenstein, L. Delp, and M.G. Arroyo
   1998   Teenage Workers' Occupational Safety: Results of a Four School Study. Paper presented at the 4th World Conference on Injury Prevention and Control, Amsterdam, The Netherlands, May 17-20. Available from Injury Prevention Research Center, University of North Carolina, Chapel Hill.

Brooks, D.R., and L.K. Davis
   1996   Work-related injuries to Massachusetts teens, 1987-1990. *American Journal of Industrial Medicine* 29:153-160.

Brooks, D.R., L.K. Davis, and S.S. Gallagher
   1993   Work-related injuries among Massachusetts children: A study based on emergency department data. *American Journal of Industrial Medicine* 24:313-324.

Broste, S.K., D.A. Hansen, R.L. Strand, and D.T. Stueland
   1989   Hearing loss among high school farm students. *American Journal of Public Health* 79(5):619-622.

Bureau of Labor Statistics
   1996   *Fatal Workplace Injuries in 1994: A Collection of Data and Analysis.* Report No. 908. Washington, D.C.: Bureau of Labor Statistics, U.S. Department of Labor.
   1997a *BLS Handbook of Methods.* Washington, D.C.: Bureau of Labor Statistics, U.S. Department of Labor. Available electronically at http://stats.bls.gov/homhome.htm.
   1997b Table 4. Fatal occupational injuries and employment by selected worker characteristics, 1996. Available electronically at http://stats.bls.gov/news.release/cfoi.t04.htm.

Bush, D., and R. Baker
   1994   *Young Workers at Risk: Health and Safety Education and the Schools.* Berkeley: University of California at Berkeley.

Carskadon, M.A.
   1990   Patterns of sleep and sleepiness in adolescents. *Pediatrician* 17:5-12.
   1997   Sleep Patterns During Adolescent Development. Presentation to the Committee on the Health and Safety Implications of Child Labor, National Research Council, Washington, D.C., June 25. Available from Department of Psychiatry and Human Behavior, Brown University Medical School.

Carskadon, M.A., K. Harvey, P. Duke, T.F. Anders, I.F. Litt, and W.C. Dement
   1980   Pubertal changes in daytime sleepiness. *Sleep* 2(4):453-460.

Carskadon, M.A., J. Mancuso, and M.R. Rosekind
  1989   Impact of part-time employment on adolescent sleep patterns. *Sleep Research*
          18:114.
Carskadon, M.A., C. Vieira, and C. Acebo
  1993   Association between puberty and delayed phase preference. *Sleep* 16(3):258-262.
Carskadon, M.A., C. Acebo, G.S. Richardson, B.A. Tate, and R. Seifer
  1997   An approach to studying circadian rhythms of adolescent humans. *Journal of Bio-*
          logical Rhythms 12(3):278-289.
Case, R.
  1985   *Intellectual development: Birth to Adulthood.* New York: Academic Press.
Castillo, D.N., and B.D. Malit
  1997   Occupational injury deaths of 16- and 17-year-olds in the United States: Trends
          and comparisons with older workers. *Injury Prevention* 3(December):277-281.
Castillo, D.N., D.D. Landen, and L.A. Layne
  1994   Occupational injury deaths of 16- and 17-year-olds in the United States. *American*
          Journal of Public Health 84(4):646-649.
Centers for Disease Control and Prevention
  1983   Surveillance of occupational injuries treated in hospital emergency departments.
          Morbidity and Mortality Weekly Report 32(2SS):31SS-37SS.
  1996   Work-related injuries and illnesses associated with child labor, United States, 1993.
          Morbidity and Mortality Weekly Report 45(22):464-468.
Chi, M.T.H., R. Glaser, and E. Rees
  1982   Expertise in problem solving. In *Advances in the Psychology of Human Intelli-*
          gence, Vol. 1, R.J. Sternberg, ed. Hillsdale, N.J.: Erlbaum.
Coleman, P.J., and L.M. Sanderson
  1983   Surveillance of occupational injuries treated in hospital emergency rooms—United
          States 1982. *Morbidity and Mortality Weekly Report* 32(2SS):31SS-37SS.
Cooper, S.P., and M.A. Rothstein
  1995   Health hazards among working children in Texas. *Southern Medical Journal* 88(5):
          550-554.
Dahl, R.E.
  1996   The impact of inadequate sleep on children's daytime cognitive function. *Seminars*
          in Pediatric Neurology 3(1):44-50.
Davis, L.K., and E. Frank
  1997   Work-Related Injuries to Massachusetts Adolescents: Findings From the Massachu-
          setts SENSOR Program. Paper presented at the National Occupational Injury Sym-
          posium, Morgantown, West Virginia, October. Massachusetts Department of Pub-
          lic Health.
Derstine, B.
  1996   Job-related fatalities involving youths, 1992-1995. *Compensation and Working*
          Conditions (December):1-3.
Doeringer, P.B., and M.J. Piore
  1971   *Internal Labor Markets and Manpower Analysis.* Lexington, Mass.: D.C. Heath.
Dunn, K.A., and C.W. Runyan
  1993   Deaths at work among children and adolescents. *American Journal of Diseases of*
          Children 147:1044-1047.
Dunn, K.A., C.W. Runyan, L.R. Cohen, and M.D. Schulman
  1998   Teens at work: A statewide study of jobs, hazards and injuries. *Journal of Adoles-*
          cent Health Care 22(1):19-25.

Fingar, A.R., R.S. Hopkins, and M. Nelson
  1992　Work-related injuries in Athens County, 1982-1986: A comparison of emergency department and workers' compensation data. *Journal of Occupational Medicine* 34:779-787.
Fischhoff, B., P. Slovic, and S. Lichtenstein
  1981　Lay foibles and expert fables in judgments about risk. In *Progress in Resource Management and Environmental Planning*, T. O'Riordan and R.K. Turner, eds. New York: John Wiley & Sons.
Garrick, J.G.
  1992　Sports injuries and the osteochondroses. Pp. 759-766 in *Textbook of Adolescent Medicine*, E.R. McAnarney, R.E. Kreipe, D.P. Orr, and G.D. Comerci, eds. Philadelphia: W.B. Saunders Co.
Glaser, R.
  1984　Education and thinking: The role of knowledge. *American Psychologist* 39:93-104.
Greenberger, E., and L. Steinberg
  1986　*When Teenagers Work: The Psychological and Social Costs of Adolescent Employment.* New York: Basic Books.
Hayden, G.J., S.G. Gerberich, and G. Maldonado
  1995　Fatal farm injuries: A five-year study utilizing a unique surveillance approach to investigate the concordance of reporting between two data sources. *Journal of Occupational and Environmental Medicine* 37(5):571-577.
Hayes-Lundy, C., R.S. Ward, J.R. Saffle, R. Reddy, G.D. Warden, and W.A. Schnebly
  1991　Grease burns at fast-food restaurants: Adolescents at risk. *Journal of Burn Care and Rehabilitation* 12(2):203-208.
Heinzman, M., S. Thoreson, L. McKenzie, M. Cook, D. Parker, and W. Carl
  1993　Occupational burns among restaurant workers, Colorado and Minnesota. *Morbidity and Mortality Weekly Report* 42(37):713-716.
Heyer, N.J., G. Franklin, F.P. Rivara, P. Parker, and J.A. Haug
  1992　Occupational injuries among minors doing farm work in Washington state: 1986 to 1989. *American Journal of Public Health* 82(4):557-560.
Hunting, K.L., and J.L. Weeks
  1993　Transport injuries in small coal mines: An exploratory analysis. *American Journal of Industrial Medicine* 23(3):391-406.
Jacobs, J.A., and R.J. Steinbery
  1990　Compensating differentials and the male-female wage gap: Evidence from the New York State comparable worth study. *Social Forces* 69:439-468.
Jensen, R., and E. Sinkule
  1988　Press operator amputations: Is risk associated with age and gender? *Journal of Safety Research* 19:125-133.
Keating, D.P.
  1990　Adolescent thinking. Pp. 54-89 in *At the Threshold: The Developing Adolescent.* S.S. Feldman and G.R. Elliott, eds., Cambridge, Mass.: Harvard University Press.
Keyserling, W.M.
  1995　Occupational safety: Prevention of accidents and overt trauma. In *Occupational Health: Recognizing and Preventing Work-Related Disease, 3rd edition,* B.S. Levy and D.H. Wegman, eds. Boston: Little, Brown and Company.
Knight, E.B., D.N. Castillo, and L.A. Layne
  1995　A detailed analysis of work-related injury among youth treated in emergency departments. *American Journal of Industrial Medicine* 27:793-805.
LaFlamme, L. E. Menckel, and L. Lundholm
  1996　The age-related risk of occupational accidents: The case of Swedish iron-ore miners. *Accident Analysis and Prevention* 28(3):349-357.

Layne, L.A., D.N. Castillo, N. A. Stout, and P. Cutlip
  1994   Adolescent occupational injuries requiring hospital emergency department treat-
         ment: A nationally representative sample. *American Journal of Public Health*
         84(4):657-660.
Leigh, J.P.
  1986   Individual and job characteristics as predictors of industrial accidents. *Accident
         Analysis and Prevention* 18(3):209-216.
Lumley, M., T. Roehrs, D. Asker, F. Zorick, and T. Roth
  1987   Ethanol and caffeine effects on daytime sleepiness/alertness. *Sleep* 10:(4)306-312.
Macy, N.J.
  1992   Orthopedics. Pp. 1116-1131 in *Comprehensive Adolescent Health Care*, S.B. Fried-
         man, M. Fisher, and S.K. Schonberg, eds. St. Louis, Mo.: Quality Medical Publish-
         ers, Inc.
Mann, L., R. Harmoni, and C.N. Power
  1989   Adolescent decision making: The development of competence. *Journal of Adoles-
         cence* 12(3):265-278.
Marks, A., and M.I. Cohen
  1978   Developmental processes of adolescence. *The Volta Review* 80(5):275-285.
Marshall, W.A., and J.M. Tanner
  1969   Variations in pattern of pubertal changes in girls. *Archives of Diseases of Child-
         hood* 44:291-303.
  1970   Variations in pattern of pubertal changes in boys. *Archives of Diseases of Child-
         hood* 45:13-23.
Massachusetts Department of Public Health
  1996   Enhancing Young Worker Health and Safety: Focus Group Report. Unpublished
         report, January 19. Available from Brockton Area Protecting Young Workers
         Project, Massachusetts Department of Public Health, Boston.
  1997   *Profile of Brockton Working Teens*. Brocton Area Protecting Young Workers
         Project. Boston: Massachusetts Department of Public Health.
  1998   Work-related injuries to teens. *Newsletter from the Teens at Work: Injury Surveil-
         lance and Prevention Project* (Spring). Boston: Massachusetts Department of Pub-
         lic Health.
Mendeloff, J.M., and B.T. Kagey
  1990   Using Occupational Safety and Health Administration accident investigations to
         study patterns of work fatalities. *Journal of Occupational Medicine* 32(11):1117-
         1123.
Miller, M.
  1995   *Occupational Injuries Among Adolescents in Washington State, 1988-1991: A Re-
         view of Workers' Compensation Data*. Technical Report Number 35-1-1995
         (March). Safety and Health Assessment and Research for Prevention. Olympia,
         Wash.: Washington State Department of Labor and Industries.
Mitchell, L.V., F.H. Lawler, D. Bowen, W. Mote, P. Asandi, and J. Purswell
  1994   Effectiveness and cost-effectiveness of employer-issued back belts in areas of high
         risk for back injury. *Journal of Occupational Medicine* 36:90-94.
Mitchell, O.S.
  1988   The relation of age to workplace injuries. *Monthly Labor Review* 111(July):8-13.
Mueller, B.A., D.L. Mohr, J.C. Rice, and D.I. Clemmer
  1987   Factors affecting individual injury experience among petroleum drilling workers.
         Journal of Occupational Medicine 29(2):126-131.
National Center for Health Statistics
  1990   1988 summary: National Hospital Discharge survey. *Advance Data* 185:4-8.

1995   Unpublished mortality data. [Online.] Available: http://www.cdc.gov/nchswww/datawh/statab/unpubd/mortabs/gmwki.htm [1998, April 20].

1996   *Healthy People 2000 Review, 1995-96.* Hyattsville, Md.: Public Health Service, U.S. Department of Health and Human Services.

1997   *Healthy People 2000 Review, 1997.* Hyattsville, Md.: Public Health Service, U.S. Department of Health and Human Services.

National Institute for Occupational Safety and Health

1988   *National Occupational Exposure Survey Analysis of Management Interview Responses.* DHHS(NIOSH) Pub. No. 89-103. Cincinatti, Oh.: U.S. Department of Health and Human Services. Available at http://www.cdc.gov/niosh/89-103.html [1998, August 8].

1995   *NIOSH ALERT: Preventing Deaths and Injuries of Adolescent Workers.* DHHS (NIOSH) Pub. No. 95-125. Washington, D.C.: U.S. Department of Health and Human Services.

1996   Violence in the workplace: Risk factors and prevention strategies. *Current Intelligence Bulletin 57*(June).

1997   Child labor research needs: Report of the NIOSH Child Labor Working Group.

1998   Surveillance for nonfatal occupational injuries treated in hospital emergency departments—United States, 1996. *Morbidity and Mortality Weekly Report* 47(15):302-306.

National Research Council

1987   *Counting Injuries and Illnesses in the Workplace: Proposals for a Better System,* E.S. Pollack and D.G. Keimig, eds. Panel on Occupational Safety and Health Statistics, Committee on National Statistics, National Research Council. Washington, D.C.: National Academy Press.

1989   *Improving Risk Communication.* Committee on Risk Perception and Communication, Commission on Behavioral and Social Sciences and Education and Commission on Physical Sciences, Mathematics, and Resources, National Research Council. Washington, D.C.: National Academy Press.

National Safety Council

1995   *Accident Facts.* Chicago: National Safety Council.

Nelson, M.A.

1992   Sports medicine. Pp. 1132-1151 in *Comprehensive Adolescent Health Care,* S.B. Friedman, M. Fisher, and S.K. Schonberg, eds. St. Louis, Mo.: Quality Medical Publishers, Inc.

Osterman, P.

1982   Employment structures within firms. *British Journal of Industrial Relations* 20(3):349-361.

1988   *Employment Futures: Reorganization, Dislocation, and Public Policy.* New York: Oxford University Press.

Parker, D.L., W.R. Carl, L.R. French, and F.B. Martin

1994a   Characteristics of adolescent work injuries reported to the Minnesota Department of Labor and Industry. *American Journal of Public Health* 84(4):606-611.

1994b   Nature and incidence of self-reported adolescent work injury in Minnesota. *American Journal of Industrial Medicine* 26:529-541.

Pendergrast, R.A., Jr., and W.B. Strong

1992   Sports medicine. Pp. 767-772 in *Textbook of Adolescent Medicine,* E.R. McAnarney, R.E. Kreipe, D.P. Orr, and G.D. Comerci, eds. Philadelphia: W.B. Saunders Co.

Perkins, R.

1995   Evaluation of an Alaskan marine safety training program. *Public Health Reports* 110(6):701.

Petta, D., M.A. Carskadon, and W.C. Dement
    1984   Sleep habits in children aged 7-13 years. *Sleep Research* 13:86.
Pilcher, J.J., and A.I. Huffcutt
    1996   Effects of sleep deprivation on performance: A meta-analysis. *Sleep* 19(4):318-326.
Pollack, S., R. McConnell, M. Gallelli, J. Schmidt, R. Obreron, and P. Landrigan
    1990   Pesticide Exposure and Working Conditions Among Migrant Farmworker Children
            in Western New York State. Paper presented at the Annual Meeting of the Ameri-
            can Public Health Association (November). Available from Kentucky Injury Pre-
            vention and Research Center, University of Kentucky, Lexington.
Reskin, B.
    1993   Sex segregation in the workplace. *Annual Review of Sociology* 19:241-270.
Resnick, L.B.
    1986   *Education and Learning to Think.* Committee on Research on Mathematics, Sci-
            ence, and Technology, Commission on Behavioral and Social Sciences and Educa-
            tion, National Research Council. Washington, D.C.: National Academy Press.
Ries, P.W.
    1978   Episodes of persons injured: United States, 1975. *Advance Data* 18:1-12.
Robinson, J.
    1988   Workplace hazards and workers' desires for union representation. *Journal of Labor
            Research*, 9(Summer)(3):237-249.
    1991   *Toil and Toxics: Workplace Struggles and Political Strategies for Occupational
            Safety and Health.* Berkeley: University of California Press.
Roehrs, T., M. Lumley, D. Asker, et al.
    1986   Ethanol and caffeine effects on daytime sleepiness. *Sleep Research* 15:41.
Rosa, R.R.
    1995   Extended workshifts and excessive fatigue. *Journal of Sleep Research* 4:51-56.
Rosenberg, H.M, S.J. Ventura, J.D. Maurer, et al.
    1996   Births and Deaths: United States, 1995. Table 16. *Monthly Vital Statistics Report*
            45(3, supp 2):31. Available electronically at http://www.cdc.gov/nchwww/datawh/
            statab/pubd/453s216h.htm.
Runyan, C.W., R. Zakocs, K.A. Dunn, M.D. Schulman, and C. Evensen
    1997   Teen Workers' Training and Concerns About Job Safety. Paper presented at the
            American Public Health Association annual meeting, Indianapolis, Ind., November
            12. Available from Injury Prevention Research Center, University of North Caro-
            lina, Chapel Hill.
Ruser, J.
    1998   Denominator choice in the calculation of workplace fatality rates. *American Jour-
            nal of Industrial Medicine* 33(2):151-156.
Schober, S.E., J.L. Handke, W.E. Halperin, M.B. Moll, and M.J. Thun
    1988   Work-related injuries in minors. *American Journal of Industrial Medicine* 14:585-
            595.
Schulman, M.D., C.T. Evensen, C.W. Runyan, L.R. Cohen, and K.A. Dunn
    1997   Farm work is dangerous for teens: Agricultural hazards and injuries among North
            Carolina teens. *Journal of Rural Health* 13(4):295-305.
Shannon, H.S., V. Walters, W. Lewchuck, J. Richardson, L.A. Moran, T. Haines, and D.
            Verma
    1996   Workplace organizational correlates of lost-time accident rates in manufacturing.
            American Journal of Industrial Medicine 29:258-268.
Slovik, P.
    1987   Perception of risk. *Science* 236(4799):280-285.

Stout, N.A., and C.A. Bell
  1991 Effectiveness of source documents for identifying fatal occupational injuries: A synthesis of studies. *American Journal of Public Health* 81:725-728.
Stueland, D.T., B.C. Lee, D.L. Nordstrom, P.M. Layde, and L.M. Wittman
  1996 A population based case-control study of agricultural injuries in children. *Injury Prevention* 2:192-196.
Suruda, A.
  1992 Work-related deaths in construction painting. *Scandinavian Journal of Work and Environmental Health* 18:3-13.
Suruda, A., and W. Halperin
  1991 Work-related deaths in children. *American Journal of Industrial Medicine* 19:739-745.
Tilly, C.
  1991 Reasons for the continuing growth of part-time employment. *Monthly Labor Review* (March):10-18.
  1996 *Half a Job: Bad and Good Part-Time Jobs in a Changing Labor Market.* Philadelphia, Pa.: Temple University Press.
Toscano, G., and J. Windau
  1994 The changing character of fatal work injuries. *Monthly Labor Review* (October):17-28.
  1995 National Census of Fatal Occupational Injuries, 1994. Compensation and Working Conditions. Bureau of Labor Statistics. Washington, D.C.: U.S. Department of Labor.
Tversky, A., and D. Kahneman
  1974 Judgment under uncertainty: Heuristics and biases. *Science* 185:1124-1131.
  1981 The framing of decisions and the psychology of choice. *Science* 211:453-458.
U.S. Department of Health and Human Services
  1996 Work-related injuries and illnesses associated with child labor—United States, 1993. *Morbidity and Mortality Weekly Report* 45(22):464-468.
U.S. Department of Labor
  1992 *Training Requirements in OSHA Standards and Training Guidelines.* OSHA 2254. Washington, DC: Occupational Safety and Health Administration, U.S. Department of Labor.
U.S. General Accounting Office
  1990 *Child Labor: Increases in Detected Child Labor Violations Throughout the United States.* GAO/HRD-90-116. Washington, D.C.: U.S. General Accounting Office.
U.S. Office of Technology Assessment
  1985 *Preventing Illness and Injury in the Workplace.* OTA-H-256, April, 1985. Washington, D.C.: U.S. Government Printing Office. Available at http://www.wws.princeton.edu:80/~ota/ns20/pubs_f.html [1997, December 6].
Van Zelst, R.H.
  1954 The effect of age and experience upon accident rate. *Journal of Applied Psychology* 38(5):313-319.
Venning, P.J., S.D. Walter, and L.W. Stitt
  1987 Personal and job-related factors as determinants of incidence of back injuries among nursing personnel. *Journal of Occupational Medicine* 29:820-826.
Weiss, H.B., L.J. Mathers, S.N. Forjuoh, and J.M. Kinnane
  1997 *Child and Adolescent Emergency Department Visit Databook.* Pittsburgh, Pa.: Center for Violence and Injury Control, Allegheny University of the Health Sciences. Available at http://www.pgh.auhs.edu/childed (1998, April 21).

Weiss, R.
1997   Wake up, sleepy teens. *Washington Post*, September 9:Health 7-9.
Zwyghuizen-Doorenbos, A., T. Roehrs, J. Lamphere, F. Zorick, and T. Roth.
1988   Increased daytime sleepiness enhances ethanol's sedative effects. *Neuropsychophar-macology* 1:279-285.

CHAPTER 4

Ahituv, A., M. Tienda, L. Xu, and V.J. Hotz
1994   Initial Labor Market Experiences of Minority and Nonminority Men. Paper presented at the 46th annual meeting of the Industrial Relations Research Association, Boston, Massachusetts. Industrial Relations Research Association, University of Wisconsin, Madison.
Angrist, J.D., and A.B. Krueger
1991   Does compulsory school attendance affect schooling and earnings? *Quarterly Journal of Economics* 106(4):979-1014.
Aronson, P.J., J.T. Mortimer, C. Zierman, and M. Hacker
1996   Generational differences in early work experiences and evaluations. Pp. 25-62 in *Adolescents, Work, and Family: An Intergenerational Developmental Analysis*, J.T. Mortimer and M.D. Finch, eds. Newbury Park, Calif.: Sage.
Bachman, J.G.
1983   Premature affluence: Do high schools students earn too much? *Economic Outlook USA* 10:64-67.
Bachman, J.G., and J. Schulenberg
1993   How part-time work intensity relates to drug use, problem behavior, time use, and satisfaction among high school seniors: Are these consequences or merely correlates? *Developmental Psychology* 29(2):220-235.
Baker, F., and G.M. Green
1991   Work, health, and productivity: Overview. Pp. 3-29 in *Work, Health and Productivity*, G.M. Green and F. Baker, eds. New York: Oxford University Press.
Barling, J., K.A. Rogers, and E.K. Kelloway
1995   Some effects of teenagers' part-time employment: The quantity and quality of work make the difference. *Journal of Organizational Behavior* 16:143-154.
Benz, M.R., P. Yovanoff, and B. Doren
1997   School-to-work components that predict postschool success for students with and without disabilities. *Exceptional Children* 63(2):151-165.
Bills, D.B., L.B. Helms, and M. Ozcan
1995   The impact of student employment on teachers' attitudes and behaviors toward working students. *Youth and Society* 27(2):169-193.
Bureau of the Census
1993   Education: The Ticket to Higher Earnings. Statistical Brief No. SB/93-7. Washington, D.C.: U.S. Department of Commerce.
Call, K.T.
1996a   The implications of helpfulness for possible selves. Pp. 63-96 in *Adolescents, Work, and Family: An Intergenerational Developmental Analysis*, J.T. Mortimer and M.D. Finch, eds. Newbury Park, Calif.: Sage.
1996b   Adolescent work as an "area of comfort" under conditions of family discomfort. Pp. 129-166 in *Adolescents, Work, and Family: An Intergenerational Developmental Analysis*, J.T. Mortimer and M.D. Finch, eds. Newbury Park, Calif.: Sage.

Call, K.T., J.T. Mortimer, and M. Shanahan
  1995 Helpfulness and the development of competence in adolescence. *Child Develop-ment* 66:129-138.
Cameron, S., and J. Heckman
  1992 The role of family, labor markets, and public policy in accounting for minority schooling attainment. Unpublished paper, December. Department of Economics, University of Chicago.
Carr, R.V., J.D. Wright, and C.J. Brody
  1996 Effects of high school work experience a decade later: Evidence from the National Longitudinal Survey. *Sociology of Education* 69(January):66-81.
Carskadon, M.A.
  1990 Patterns of sleep and sleepiness in adolescents. *Pediatrician* 17:5-12.
Carskadon, M.A., J. Mancuso, and M.R. Rosekind
  1989 Impact of part-time employment on adolescent sleep patterns. *Sleep Research* 18:114.
Chaplin, D., and J. Hannaway
  1996 High school enrollment: Meaningful connections for at-risk youth. Paper presented at the Annual Meeting of the American Educational Research Association, New York. Urban Institute, Washington, D.C.
D'Amico, R.J.
  1984 Does employment during high school impair academic progress? *Sociology of Education* 57:152-164.
DiPrete, T.A., and P.A. McManus
  1996 Education, earnings gain, and earnings loss in loosely and tightly structured labor markets: A comparison between the United States and Germany. Pp. 201-221 in *Generating Social Stratification: Toward a New Research Agenda*, A.C. Kerckhoff, ed. Boulder, Colo.: Westview Press.
Elder, G.H. Jr.
  1974 *Children of the Great Depression*. Chicago: University of Chicago Press.
Finch, M.D., M.J. Shanahan, J.T. Mortimer, and S. Ryu
  1991 Work experience and control orientation in adolescence. *American Sociological Review* 56:597-611.
Finch, M.D., J.T. Mortimer, and S. Ryu
  1997 Transition into part-time work: Health risks and opportunities. Pp. 321-344 in *Health Risks and Developmental Transitions during Adolescence*, J. Schulenberg, J. L. Maggs, and K. Hurrelman, eds. New York: Cambridge University Press.
Freeman, R.B., and D.A. Wise
  1979 *Youth Unemployment*. Cambridge, Mass.: National Bureau of Economic Research.
Greenberger, E.
  1984 Children, family, and work. Pp. 103-122 in *Children, Mental Health, and the Law*. N.D. Repucci, L.A. Weithorn, E.P. Mulvey, and J. Monahan, eds. Beverly Hills, Calif.: Sage.
  1988 Working in teenage America. Pp. 21-50 in *Work Experience and Psychological Development*, J.T. Mortimer and K.M. Borman, eds. Boulder, Colo.: Westview.
Greenberger, E., and L. Steinberg
  1986 *When Teenagers Work: The Psychological and Social Costs of Adolescent Employ-ment*. New York: Basic Books.
Greenberger, E., L.D. Steinberg, A. Vaux, and S. McAuliffe
  1980 Adolescents who work: Effects of part-time employment on family and peer rela-tions. *Journal of Youth and Adolescence* 9:189-203.

Hamilton, S.F., and J.F. Claus
1981   Inequality and youth unemployment: Can work programs work? *Education and Urban Society* 14:103-126.
Hamilton, M.A., and S.F. Hamilton
1997   *Learning Well at Work: Choices for Quality.* Washington, D.C.: National School-to-Work Office.
Heckman, J.
1982   Heterogeneity and state dependence. In *Studies in Labor Markets*, S. Rosen, ed. Chicago: University of Chicago Press.
Heckman, J., and B. Singer
1984   A method for minimizing the impact of distributional assumptions in econometric models of duration analysis. *Econometrica* 52:271-320.
Hotz, V.J., L. Xu, M. Tienda, and A. Ahituv
1998   Are There Returns to the Wages of Young Men from Working While in School? Unpublished paper, March. Department of Economics, University of California, Los Angeles.
Johnston, L., J. Bachman, and P. O'Malley
1982   *Monitoring the Future: Questionnaire Responses From the Nation's High School Seniors, 1981.* Ann Arbor: Institute for Social Research, University of Michigan.
Keithly, D.C., and F.A. Deseran
1995   Households, local labor markets, and youth labor force participation. *Youth and Society* 26:463-492.
Kohn, M.L., C. Schooler, J. Miller, K.A. Miller, C. Shoenbach, and R. Shoenberg
1983   *Work and Personality: An Inquiry Into the Impact of Social Stratification.* Norwood, N.J.: Ablex.
Kopp, H., and R. Kazis, with A. Churchill
no   *Promising Practices: A Study of Ten School-to-Career Programs.* Boston: Jobs for
date   the Future.
Lewin-Epstein, N.
1981   *Youth Employment During High School.* Washington, D.C.: National Center for Educational Statistics.
Lowe, G.S., and H. Krahn
1992   Do part-time jobs improve the labor market chances of high school graduates? In *Working Part-time: Risks and Opportunities*, B.D. Warme, ed. New York: Praeger.
Manning, W.D.
1990   Parenting employed teenagers. *Youth and Society* 22:184-200.
Markus, H., S. Cross, and E. Wurf
1990   The role of the self-system in competence. Pp. 205-226 in *Competence Considered*, R.J. Sternberg and J. Kolligan, Jr., eds. New Haven, Conn.: Yale University Press.
Marsh, H.W.
1991   Employment during high school: Character building or subversion of academic goals? *Sociology of Education* 64:172-189.
Meyer, R.M., and D.A. Wise
1982   High school preparation and early labor force experience. Pp. 277-347 in *The Youth Labor Problem: Its Nature, Causes and Consequences*, R.B. Freeman and D.A. Wise, eds. Chicago: University of Chicago Press.
Mihalic, S.W., and D. Elliot
1997   Short- and long-term consequences of adolescent work. *Youth and Society* 28(4):464-498.
Mortimer, J.T., and M.D. Finch
1986   The effects of part-time work on self-concept and achievement. Pp. 66-89 in *Becoming a Worker*, K. Borman and J. Reisman, eds. Norwood, N.J.: Ablex.

Mortimer, J.T., and M.K. Johnson
  1998   New perspectives on adolescent work and the transition to adulthood.   In *New Perspectives on Adolescent Risk Behavior*, R. Jesser, ed.   New York: Cambridge University Press.
Mortimer, J.T., and M.J. Shanahan
  1994   Adolescent work experience and family relationships.   *Work and Occupations* 21:369-384.
Mortimer, J.T., J. Lorence, and D. Kumka
  1986   *Work, Family, and Personality: Transition to Adulthood.* Norwood, N.J.: Ablex.
Mortimer, J.T., M.D. Finch, K. Dennehy, C. Lee, and T. Beebe
  1994   Work experience in adolescence.   *Journal of Vocational Education Research* 19:39-70.
Mortimer, J.T., M.D. Finch, S. Ryu, M.J. Shanahan, and K.T. Call
  1996   The effects of work intensity on adolescent mental health, achievement, and behavioral adjustment: New evidence from a prospective study.   *Child Development* 67:1243-1261.
Murnane, R.J., and F. Levy
  1996   *Teaching the New Basic Skills: Principles For Educating Children to Thrive in a Changing Economy.* New York: Free Press.
O'Regan, K.M., and J.M. Quigley
  1996   Teenage employment and the spatial isolation of minority and poverty households.   *The Journal of Human Resources* 31:692-702.
Orr, M.T.
  1998   Youth apprenticeship program: Delivering on a promise.   Unpublished paper.   Teachers College, Columbia University.
Phillips, S., and K.L. Sandstrom
  1990   Parental attitudes towards youth work.   *Youth and Society* 22:160-183.
Resnick, M.D., P.S. Bearman, R.W. Blum, K.E. Bauman, K.M. Harris, J. Jones, J. Tabor, T. Beuhring, R.E. Sieving, M. Shew, M. Ireland, L. Bearinger, and J.R. Udry
  1997   Protecting adolescents from harm: Findings from the National Longitudinal Study on Adolescent Health.   *Journal of the American Medical Association* 278(10):823-832.
Ruhm, C.J.
  1995   The extent and consequences of high school employment.   *Journal of Labor Research* 16(3):293-303.
  1997   Is high school employment consumption or investment?   *Journal of Labor Economics* 15(4):735-776.
Ruscoe, G., J.C. Morgan, and C. Peebles
  1996   Students who work.   *Adolescence* 31:625-632.
Schoenhals, M., M. Tienda, and B. Schneider
  1997   The Educational and Personal Consequences of Adolescent Employment.   Unpublished paper.   Available from authors, Department of Sociology, University of Chicago.
Schulenberg, J., and J.G. Bachman
  1993   Long Hours on the Job?   Not So Bad for Some Types of Jobs: The Quality of Work and Substance Use, Affect and Stress.   Paper presented at the Biennial Meeting of the Society for Research on Child Development, New Orleans, La.   Survey Research Center, Institute for Social Research, University of Michigan, Ann Arbor.
Secretary's Commission on Achieving Necessary Skills
  1991   *What Work Requires of Schools: A SCANS Report for America 2000.* Washington, D.C.:   U.S. Department of Labor.

Shanahan, M.J.
  1992   High School Work Experiences and Depressed Moods. Paper presented at the American Sociological Association, Pittsburgh, Pa. Department of Human Development and Family Studies, Pennsylvania State University, University Park.
Shanahan, M.J., and J.T. Mortimer
  1996   Adolescent Work Experience and Relations with Peers. Unpublished paper. Department of Human Development and Family Studies, Pennsylvania State University, University Park.
Shanahan, M.J., G.H. Elder, M. Burchinal, and R.D. Conger
  1996a Adolescent earnings and relationships with parents: The work-family nexus in urban and rural ecologies. Pp. 129-166 in *Adolescents, Work, and Family: An Intergenerational Developmental Analysis*, J.T. Mortimer and M.D. Finch, eds. Newbury Park, Calif.: Sage.
  1996b Adolescent paid labor and relationships with parents: Early work-family linkages. *Child Development* 67(5):2183-2200.
Shanahan, M.J., M.D. Finch, J.T. Mortimer, and S. Ryu
  1991   Adolescent work experience and depressive affect. *Social Psychology Quarterly* 54:299-317.
Snedeker, G.
  1982   *Hard Knocks: Preparing Youth for Work*. Baltimore, Md.: Johns Hopkins University Press.
Steel, L.
  1991   Early work experience among white and non-white youths: Implications for subsequent enrollment and employment. *Youth and Society* 22:419-447.
Steinberg, L.D., and E. Cauffman
  1995   The impact of employment on adolescent development. *Annals of Child Development* 11:131-166.
Steinberg, L.D., and S.M. Dornbusch
  1991   Negative correlates of part-time employment during adolescence: Replication and elaboration. *Developmental Psychology* 27:304-313.
Steinberg, L.D., S. Fegley, and S.M. Dornbusch
  1993   Negative impact of part-time work on adolescent adjustment: Evidence from a longitudinal study. *Developmental Psychology* 29:171-180.
Stern, D., and Y.F. Nakata
  1989   Characteristics of high school students, paid jobs, and employment experience after graduation. Pp. 189-234 in *Adolescence and Work: Influences of Social Structure, Labor Markets, and Culture*, D. Stern and D. Eichorn, eds. Hillsdale, N.J.: Lawrence Erlbaum.
Tanner, J., and H. Krahn
  1991   Part-time work and deviance among high school seniors. *Canadian Journal of Sociology* 16(3):281-302.
Tienda, M., and A. Ahituv
  1996   Ethnic differences in school departure: Does youth employment promote or undermine educational attainment? Pp. 93-110 in *Of Heart and Mind: Social Policy Essays in Honor of Sar A. Levitan*, G. Mangum and S. Mangum, eds. Kalamazoo, Mich.: W.E. Upjohn Institute for Employment Research.
Walther, R.H.
  1976   *Analysis and Synthesis of DOL Experience in Youth Transition to Work Programs*. Springfield, Va.: National Technical Information Service.

Wilson, W.J.

1987   *The Truly Disadvantaged: The Inner City, the Underclass, and Public Policy.* Chicago: University of Chicago Press.

1996   *When Work Disappears: The World of the New Urban Poor.* New York: Alfred P. Knopf.

Wofford, S.

1988   *A Preliminary Analysis of the Relationship Between Employment and Delinquency/Crime for Adolescents and Young Adults.* National Youth Survey No. 50. Boulder, Colo: Institute of Behavioral Science, University of Colorado.

Wright, J.P., F.T. Cullen, and N. Williams

1997   Working while in school and delinquent involvement: Implications for social policy. *Crime & Delinquency* 43:203-221.

Yeatts, J.

1994   Which Students Work and Why? Master's thesis. Department of Economics, University of North Carolina, Greensboro.

CHAPTER 5

Aherin, R.A., and C.M. Todd

1989   Developmental stages of children and accident risk potential. Paper presented at the International Winter Meeting of the American Society of Agricultural Engineers. Available at http://www.ag.uiuc.edu/agsafety/devstage.html.

Aherin, R.A., D. Murphy, J. Westaby

1992   Reducing farm injuries: Issues and methods. Report of the American Society of Agricultural Engineers. St. Joseph, Mich.: American Society of Agricultural Engineers.

American Academy of Pediatrics

1988   Rural injuries. Committee on accident and poison prevention. *Pediatrics* 81:902-903.

American Farm Bureau Federation

1998   Farm Bureau opposes OSHA farm change. *Legal Notice* 77(16).

Arroyo, M.G., and L. Kurre

1997   *Young Agricultural Workers in California.* Berkeley, Calif.: Labor Occupational Health Program, School of Public Health, University of California at Berkeley.

Bernard, B.P., ed.

1997   *Musculoskeletal Disorders and Workplace Factors: A Critical Review of the Evidence for Work-Related Musculoskeletal Disorders of the Neck, Upper Extremity, and Low Back.* Second Printing. National Institute for Occupational Safety and Health. Cincinnati, Oh.: U.S. Department of Health and Human Services. Available at http://www.cdc.gov/niosh/ergosci1.html [1997, August 26].

Bureau of the Census

1970   *Historical Statistics of the United States, Colonial Times to 1970.* Bicentennial Edition, Part 2. Washington, D.C.: U.S. Government Printing Office.

1992   *Statistical Abstract of the United States: 1992.* 112th Edition. Washington, D.C.: U.S. Government Printing Office.

California Department of Health Services

1988   Epidemiologic study of adverse health effects in children in McFarland, CA — Phase II report. Berkeley, Calif.: Epidemiological Studies and Surveillance Section.

Carskadon, M.A.
1990   Patterns of sleep and sleepiness in adolescents. *Pediatrician* 17:5-12.
1997   Sleep patterns during adolescent development. Presentation to the Committee on the Health and Safety Implications of Child Labor, National Research Council, Washington, D.C., June 25, 1997.
Carskadon, M.A., K. Harvey, P. Duke, T.F. Anders, I.F. Litt, and W.C. Dement
1980   Pubertal changes in daytime sleepiness. *Sleep* 2(4):453-460.
Council on Scientific Affairs
1988   Cancer risk of pesticides in agricultural workers. *Journal of the American Medical Association* 260(7):959-966.
Dacquel, L.T., and D.C. Dahmann
1993   Residents of farms and rural areas: 1991. Pp. 20-472 in *Current Population Reports*. Bureau of the Census. Washington, D.C.: U.S. Government Printing Office.
Danbom, D.B.
1997   Agricultural history. Pp. 333-337 in *Encyclopedia of Rural America: The Land and People*, G.A. Goreham, ed. Santa Barbara, Calif.: ABC-CLIO.
Davis, S.
1997   Child labor in agriculture. Educational Resource Information Clearinghouse Digest Clearinghouse on Rural Education and Small Schools #ED405159. Charleston, W.Va.: Appalachian Educational Laboratory.
Department of Agricultural Economics
1995   Industrialization of Heartland Agriculture: Challenges, Opportunities, Consequences and Alternatives. Miscellaneous Report No. 176. Conference Proceedings, July 10-11, Minneapolis, Minn. North Dakota State University.
Derstine, B.
1996   Job-related fatalities involving youths, 1992-95. *Compensation and Working Conditions* (December):1-3.
Finney, J., E. Christophersen, P. Friman, I. Kalnina, J. Maddux, L. Peterson, M. Roberts, M. Wolraich
1993   Society of Pediatric Psychology task force report: Pediatric psychology and injury control. *Journal of Pediatric Psychology* 18:499-526.
Fitchen, J.
1995   Why rural poverty is growing worse: Similar causes in diverse settings. In *The Changing American Countryside: Rural People and Places*, E.N. Castle, ed. Lawrence, Kan.: University Press of Kansas.
Gabbard, S., R. Mines, and B. Boccalandro
1994   Migrant Farmworkers: Pursuing Security in an Unstable Labor Market. Based on data from the National Agricultural Workers Survey (NAWS, 1989-91). Research Report No. 5. U.S. Department of Labor, Washington, D.C.
Hahamovitch, C.
1997   *The Fruits of Their Labor: Atlantic Coast Farmworkers and the Making of Migrant Poverty, 1870-1945.* Chapel Hill: University of North Carolina Press.
Hawk, C., J. Gay, and K. Donham
1991   Rural youth Disability Prevention Project Survey: Results from 169 Iowa farm families. *Journal of Rural Health* 7(2):170-179.
Kelsey, T.W.
1991   Farm safety and federal responses to occupational health. *Journal of Rural Health* 7:287-292.
1994   The agrarian myth and policy responses to farm safety. *American Journal of Public Health* 84:1171-1177.

Kelsey, T.W., W.A. Hart, and D.J. Murphy
  1994 Childhood agricultural injuries: Public policy process and measures. *Journal of Agromedicine* 1:47-56.
Landrigan, P.J., S.H. Pollack, J.G. Godbold, and R. Belville
  1994 The health and safety hazards of child labor. Pp. 13-16 in *Child Labor in the 90s: How Far Have We Come?* New York, N.Y.: National Child Labor Committee.
Lee, B.C., L.S. Jenkins, and J.D. Westaby
  1997 Factors influencing exposure of children to major hazards on family farms. *Journal of Rural Health* 13(3):206-215.
Martin, P.
  1988 *Harvest of Confusion: Migrant Workers in U.S. Agriculture.* Boulder, Colo.: Westview Press.
Miller, M.
  1995 *Occupational Injuries Among Adolescents in Washington State, 1988-1991: A Review of Workers' Compensation Data.* Technical Report Number 35-1-1995. March 1995. Olympia, Wash.: Safety and Health Assessment and Research for Prevention, Washington State Department of Labor and Industries.
Miller, T.
  1995 Unpublished tabulation and analysis of 1987-1992 National Health Interview Survey data. Children's Safety Network Economics and Insurance Resource Center, National Public Services Research Institute, Landover Md.
Mills, E.
  1995 The location of economic activity in rural and nonmetropolitan United States. In *The Changing American Countryside: Rural People and Places*, E.N. Castle, ed. Lawrence: University Press of Kansas.
Mines, R., and M. Kearney
  1982 The Health of Tulare County Farmworkers: A Report of 1981. Survey and Ethnographic Research for the Tulare County Department of Health. Department of Labor, Office of the Assistant Secretary for Policy.
Mines, R., S. Gabbard, and A. Stierman
  1997 A Profile of U.S. Farm Workers. Demographics, Household Composition, Income and Use of Services. Based on data from the National Agricultural Workers Survey (NAWS, 1994-95). Prepared for the Commission on Immigration Reform. U.S. Department of Labor, Office of the Assistant Secretary for Policy.
Mobed, K., E.B. Gold, and M.B. Schenker
  1992 Occupational health problems among migrant and seasonal farm workers. In Cross-cultural Medicine—A Decade Later. *Western Journal of Medicine* 157(Special Issue):367-373.
Moses, M.
  1989 Pesticide-related health problems and farm workers. *American Association of Occupation Health Nursing Journal* 37(3):115-130.
Mull, L.D.
  1994 Broken covenant: The future of migrant and seasonal farm worker children and their families in the United States. Testimony presented before the Helsinki Commissions on the human rights violations of migrant workers. Washington, D.C.: Association of Farmworker Opportunity Programs.
Myers, J.R.
  1995 Special analysis of data from the National Institute for Occupational Safety and Health (NIOSH Traumatic Injury Surveillance of Farmers survey). Morgantown, W.Va.: National Institute for Occupational Safety and Health.

Occupational Safety and Health Administration
   1987   Field sanitation: Final rule. 29 C.F.R. Part 1928. *Federal Register* 52(84):16050-
          16096, May 1.
Olenchock, S., and N. Young
   1997a Changing agricultural trends in Wisconsin and beyond. Pp. 173-175 in *Proceedings
          of the Twenty-first Cotton and Other Organic Dusts Research Conference*, P.J.
          Wakelyn, R.R. Jacobs, and R. Rylander, eds. Memphis, Tenn.: National Council.
   1997b Changes in agriculture bring potential for new health and safety risks. *Wisconsin
          Medical Journal* 96(8):10-11.
Palerm, J.V.
   1991   Farm Labor Needs and Farmworkers in California, 1970 to 1989. California Agri-
          cultural Studies, No. 91-2. Sacramento, Calif.: Employment Development Depart-
          ment.
Pless, I.B., and L. Arsenault
   1987   The role of health education in the prevention of injuries to children. *Journal of
          Social Issues* 43:87-103.
Purschwitz, M.
   1990   *Fatal Farm Injuries to Children.* Report for the Office of Rural Health Policy.
          Marshfield, Wisc.: Wisconsin Rural Health Research Center.
Rasmussen, W.D.
   1997   Structure of agriculture. Pp. 44-46 in *Encyclopedia of Rural America, the Land and
          People*, G.A. Goreham, ed. Santa Barbara, Calif.: ABC-CLIO.
Rivara, F.
   1997   Fatal and non-fatal farm injuries to children and adolescents in the United States,
          1990-1993. *Injury Prevention* 3:190-194.
Rosa, R.R.
   1995   Extended workshifts and excessive fatigue. *Journal of Sleep Research* 4:51-56.
Schwartz, D.A., and J.P. LoGerfo
   1988   Congenital limb reduction defects in the agricultural setting. *American Journal of
          Public Health* 78(6):654-657.
Sharp, D.S., B. Eskenazi, R. Harrison, P. Callas, and A.H. Smith.
   1986   Delayed health hazards of pesticide exposure. *Annual Review of Public Health*
          7:441-471.
Shaver, C.S., and T. Tong
   1991   Chemical hazards to agricultural workers. *State of the Art Reviews: Occupational
          Medicine* 6:391-413.
Slesinger, D.P., and E. Muirragui
   1981   The rise and decline of migrant farmworkers: The case of Wisconsin. Research
          Report R3152. College of Agricultural and Life Sciences, University of Wisconsin-
          Madison.
Stallones, L., and P. Gunderson
   1994   Epidemiological perspectives on childhood agricultural injuries within the United
          States. *Journal of Agromedicine* 1(4):3-18.
Stueland, D.T., B.C. Lee, D.L. Nordstrom, P.M. Layde, and L.M. Wittman
   1996   A population based case-control study of agricultural injuries in children. *Injury
          Prevention* 2:192-196.
Tevis, C.
   1994   Downsizing farm chores. *Successful Farming* 92(2):48-50.
Tevis, C., and C. Finck
   1989   We kill too many farm kids. *Successful Farming* 87(3):18A-18P.
U.S. Department of Agriculture
   1997   *Agriculture Fact Book 1997.* Washington, D.C.: U.S. Deparment of Agriculture.

U.S. Environmental Protection Agency
   1993   *A Guide to Heat Stress in Agriculture*. EPA-750-b-92-001. Washington, D.C.:
          U.S. Environmental Protection Agency.
U.S. General Accounting Office
   1993   *Pesticides on Farms: Limited Capability Exists to Monitor Occupational Illnesses
          and Injuries*. GAO/PEMD-94-6, December 15. Washington, D.C.: U.S. General
          Accounting Office.
   1998   *Child Labor in Agriculture*. GAO/HEHS-98-112R, March 20. Washington, D.C.:
          U.S. General Accounting Office.
Wasserstrom, R.F., and R. Wiles
   1985   *Field Duty: U.S. Farmworkers and Pesticide Safety*. Washington, D.C.: World
          Resources Institute.
Wilkening, E., and J. Gilbert
   1987   Family farming in the United States. Pp. 271-301 in *Family Farming in Europe and
          America*, B. Galeski and E. Wilkening, eds. Boulder, Colo.: Westview Press.
Zahm, S.H., and A. Blair
   1993   Cancer among migrant and seasonal farmworkers: An epidemiologic review and
          research agenda. *American Journal of Industrial Medicine* 24:753-766.
Zahm, S.H., M.H. Ward, and A. Blair
   1997   Pesticides and cancer. *Occupational Medicine* 12(2):1-20.

CHAPTER 6

Aherin, R.A., D. Murphy, J. Westaby
   1992   *Reducing farm injuries: Issues and methods. Report of American Society of Agri-
          cultural Engineers*. St. Joseph, Mich.: American Society of Agricultural Engineers.
Baker, R.
   1997   NIOSH Young Worker Community Education Projects: What We Have Accom-
          plished and What We are Learning. Presentation to the NIOSH Child Labor Work-
          ing Team, Washington, D.C., November 18. School of Public Health, University of
          California, Berkeley.
Bartel, A., and L.G. Thomas
   1985   Direct and indirect effects of regulation: A new look at OSHA's impact. *Journal of
          Law and Economics* 28:1-26.
Beyer, D.
   1997   Regulation of Child Labor in the United States: Targeted Analyses, Provocative
          Questions, and Selected Solutions. Unpublished paper presented at committee work-
          shop, June 26. National Child Labor Committee, New York.
Bottoms, G., and D. Sharpe
   no   *Teaching for Understanding Through Integration of Academic and Technical
   date   Education*. Atlanta, Ga.: Southern Regional Education Board.
Bowling, J.M., C. Runyan, C. Miara, L. Davis, H. Rubenstein, L. Delp, and M.G. Arroyo
   1998   Teenage Workers' Occupational Safety: Results of a Four School Study. Paper
          presented at the 4th World Conference on Injury Prevention and Control,
          Amsterdam, The Netherlands, May 17-20. Injury Prevention Research Center, Uni-
          versity of North Carolina, Chapel Hill.
Bureau of the Census
   1994   *1992 Census of Agriculture*. AC92-A-51. Economics and Statistics Administration.
          Washington, D.C.: U.S. Department of Commerce.

REFERENCES

Castillo, D.N., D.D. Landen, and L.A. Layne
1994   Occupational injury deaths of 16- and 17-year-olds in the United States. *American Journal of Public Health* 84(4):646-649.
Cone, J.E., A. Dapone, D. Makofsky, R. Reiter, C. Becker, R.J. Harrison, and J. Balmes
1991   Fatal injuries at work in California. *Journal of Occupational Medicine* 33:813-817.
Department of Labor and Industries
1994   *Changes to the Nonagricultural Child Labor Rules: Impact Analysis.* Report of the Child Labor Rules Research Team. December 22. Olympia, Wash.: Department of Labor and Industries.
Gray, W.B., and J.T. Scholz
1993   Does regulatory enforcement work? A panel analysis of OSHA enforcement. *Law and Society Review* 27(1):177-213.
Greenberger, E., and L. Steinberg
1986   *When Teenagers Work: The Psychological and Social Costs of Adolescent Employment.* New York: Basic Books.
Hamilton, S.F.
1990   *Apprenticeship for Adulthood: Preparing Youth for the Future.* New York: Free Press.
Kett, J.F.
1977   *Rites of Passage: Adolescence in America: 1790 to the Present.* New York: Basic Books.
Keyserling, W.M.
1995   Occupational safety: Prevention of accidents and overt trauma. In *Occupational Health: Recognizing and Preventing Work-Related Disease, 3rd edition,* B.S. Levy and D.H. Wegman, eds. Boston, Mass.: Little, Brown and Company.
Knight, E.B., D.N. Castillo, and L.A. Layne
1995   A detailed analysis of work-related injury among youth treated in emergency departments. *American Journal of Industrial Medicine* 27:793-805.
Komaki, J., A.T. Heinzmann, and L. Lawson
1980   Effect of training and feedback: Component analysis of a behavioral safety program. *Journal of Applied Psychology* 65(3):261-270.
Kopp, H., R. Kazis, with A. Churchill
no date   *Promising Practices: A Study of Ten School-to-Career Programs.* Boston, Mass.: Jobs for the Future.
Leigh, J.P., S. Markowitz, M. Fahs, C. Shin, and P. Landrigan
1996   *Costs of Occupational Injuries and Illnesses in 1992.* Final Report for Cooperative Agreement with ERC, Inc. Cooperative Agreement U60/CCU902886. Washington, D.C.: National Institute for Occupational Safety and Health.
Maples, T.W., J.A. Jacoby, D.E. Johnson, G.L. Ter Haar, and F.M. Buckingham
1982   Effectiveness of employee training and motivation programs in reducing exposure to inorganic lead and lead alkyls. *American Industrial Hygiene Association Journal* 43(9):692-694.
Mintz, B.
1984   *OSHA: History, Law, Policy.* Washington, D.C.: Bureau of National Affairs.
Murphy, P.L., G.S. Sorock, T.K. Courtney, B.S. Webster, and T.B. Leamon
1996   Injury and illness in the American workplace: A comparison of data sources. *American Journal of Industrial Medicine* 30:130-141.
National Committee for Childhood Agricultural Injury Prevention
1996   *Children and Agriculture: Opportunities for Safety and Health, A National Action Plan.* Marshfield, Wisc.: Marshfield Clinic.

National Consumers League
1992   *State Departments of Labor Child Labor Survey.* Washington, D.C.: Child Labor Coalition, National Consumers League.
1993   *1993 State Labor Department Child Labor Survey.* Washington, D.C.: Child Labor Coalition, National Consumers League.
National Institute for Occupational Safety and Health
1994   Comments of the National Institute for Occupational Safety and Health on the Department of Labor, Wage and Hour Division Proposed Rule on Child Labor Regulations, Orders, and Statements of Interpretation (29 CFR part 570, Subpart C). July 12. National Institute for Occupational Safety and Health, U.S. Department of Health and Human Services, Washington, D.C.
1995   *NIOSH ALERT: Preventing Deaths and Injuries of Adolescent Workers.* DHHS (NIOSH) Pub. No. 95-125. Washington, D.C.: U.S. Department of Health and Human Services.
1997   *Child Labor Research Needs: Report of the NIOSH Child Labor Working Group.* Washington, D.C.: U.S. Department of Health and Human Services.
National Research Council
1993   *Pesticides in the Diets of Infants and Children.* Committee on Pesticides in the Diets of Infants and Children, Commission on Life Sciences, National Research Council. Washington, D.C.: National Academy Press.
National School-to-Work-Office
no   *School-to-Work and Employer Liability: A Resource Guide.* Washington, D.C.:
date   National School-to-Work Office. Available at http://www.stw.ed.gov/factsht/emplia.htm [1997, December 3].
Nelson, N.A., J. Kaufman, J. Kalat, and B. Silverstein
1997   Falls in construction: Injury rates for OSHA-inspected employers before and after citation for violating the Washington state fall protection standard. *American Journal of Industrial Medicine* 31:296-302.
Office of Technology Assessment
1985   *Preventing Illness and Injury in the Workplace.* OTA-H-256, April. Washington, D.C.:: U.S. Government Printing Office. Available at http://www.wws.princeton.edu:80/~ota/ns20/pubs_f.html [1997, December 5].
Olson, L.
1997   *The School-to-Work Revolution.* Reading, Mass.: Addison-Wesley.
Parker, D.L., W.R. Carl, L.R. French, and F.B. Martin
1994   Characteristics of adolescent work injuries reported to the Minnesota Department of Labor and Industry. *American Journal of Public Health* 84(4):606-611.
Purschwitz, M.
1990   *Fatal Farm Injuries to Children. Report for the Office of Rural Health Policy.* Marshfield: Wisconsin Rural Health Research Center.
Runyan, C.W., R. Zakocs, K.A. Dunn, M.D. Schulman, and C. Evensen
1997   Teen Workers' Training and Concerns About Job Safety. Paper presented at the American Public Health Association 124th Annual Meeting, November 12. Indianapolis, Indiana. Available from Injury Prevention Research Center, University of North Carolina, Chapel Hill.
Scholz, J.T., and W.B. Gray
1997   Can government facilitate cooperation? An informational model of OSHA enforcement. *American Journal of Political Science* 41(3):693-717.
Shutske, J.M.
1994   An educator's perspective on childhood agricultural injury. *Journal of Agromedicine* 1(4):31-46.

Sigler, J.A., and J.E. Murphy
  1988   *Interactive Corporate Compliance: An Alternative to Regulatory Compulsion.* New
         York: Quorum Books.
Steinberg, L.
  1996   *Adolescence, 4th edition.* New York: McGraw-Hill.
Steinberg, L., B.B. Brown, and S.M. Dornbusch
  1996   *Beyond the Classroom: Why School Reform Has Failed and What Parents Need to
         Do.* New York: Simon and Schuster.
Stern, D., and D. Stevens
  1992   Analysis of Unemployment Insurance Data on the Relationship Between High School
         Cooperative Education and Subsequent Employment. Paper prepared for the Na-
         tional Assessment of Vocational Education, School of Education, University of Cali-
         fornia, Berkeley.
Stern, D., N. Finkelstein, M. Urquiola, and H. Cagampang
  1997   What differences does it make if school and work are connected? *Economics of
         Education Review* 16:213-229.
Stern, D., N. Finkelstein, N., J.R. Stone III, J. Latting, and C. Dornsife
  1994   *Research on School-to-Work Transition Programs in the United States.* Berkeley,
         Calif.: National Center for Research in Vocational Education.
Stewart, R.J.
  1979   The impact of OSHA inspections on manufacturing injury rates. *Journal of Human
         Resources* 14:145-170.
Stout, N.A., and C.A. Bell
  1991   Effectiveness of source documents for identifying fatal occupational injuries: A
         synthesis of studies. *American Journal of Public Health* 81(6):725-728.
U.S. Department of Labor
  1990   Child Labor Requirements in Nonagricultural Occupations Under the Fair Labor
         Standards Act: Child Labor Bulletin No. 101, WH-1330, Wage and Hour Division,
         Employment Standards Administration. Washington, D.C.: U.S. Department of
         Labor.
  1997   *Evaluating the Net Impact of School-to-Work: Proceedings of a Roundtable.* Em-
         ployment and Training Administration. Washington, D.C.: U.S. Department of
         Labor.
  no   Workers compensation data. Available at http://www.dol.gov/dol/esa/public/regs/
  date   statutes/stwclaw: *Table 1: Type of Law and Insurance Requirements for Private
         Employment. Table 3: Coverage of Agricultural Workers.*
U.S. Departments of Education and Labor
  1996   *Implementation of the School-to-Work Opportunities Act of 1994: Report to Con-
         gress.* September. Washington, D.C.: National School-to-Work Office. Available
         at http://www.stw.ed.gov/congress [1997, December 19].
U.S. General Accounting Office
  1991   *Characteristics of Working Children.* GAO/HRD-91-83BR, June. Washington,
         D.C.: U.S. Government Printing Office.
Wallerstein, N.
  1992   Health and safety education for workers with low-literacy and limited-English skills.
         American Journal of Industrial Medicine 22(5):751-766.
Wallerstein, N., and M. Weinger
  1992   Health and safety education for worker empowerment. *American Journal of Indus-
         trial Medicine* 22(5):619-636.

Weeks, J.L.
  1991 Occupational health and safety regulation in the coal mining industry: Public health at the workplace. *Annual Review of Public Health* 12:195-207

Zohar, D., A. Cohen, and N. Azar
  1980 Promoting increased use of ear protectors in noise through informational feedback. *Human Factors* 22(1):69-79.

Appendices

APPENDIX
A

Sources of Information

The committee thanks the people listed below who, through presentations, conversations, interviews, and the submission of written materials, provided important information for our work. Affiliations are those at the time of contact.

Darlene Adkins, The Child Labor Coalition
Sean Barnes, Maryland
Dorianne Beyer, National Child Labor Committee
Dara Carrera, Arlington, Virginia
Mary Carskadon, Brown University
Dawn Castillo, National Institute for Occupational Safety and
    Health
Duncan Chaplin, Urban Institute
Shelley Davis, Farmworkers Justice Fund
Pierre D'Hemecourt, Boston Children's Hospital
William Fern, Wage and Hour Division, U.S. Department of Labor
Susan Gallagher, Children's Safety Network
Linda Golodner, National Consumers League
Andrew Golub, National Development and Research Institutes
Kathie Harris, University of North Carolina at Chapel Hill
Alesha Henry, Bowie, Maryland
Michael Horrigan, Bureau of Labor Statistics

J.D. Hoye, National School-to-Work Office
Marjorie Ireland, University of Minnesota
James Jaccard, State University of New York at Albany
Guillermina Jasso, New York University
Richard Jessor, University of Colorado, Boulder
Bruce Johnson, National Development and Research Institutes
Jo Jones, University of North Carolina at Chapel Hill
Kevin Keaney, Office of Pesticide Programs, U.S. Environmental
    Protection Agency
Art Kerschner, Jr., Wage and Hour Division, U.S. Department of
    Labor
Jens Levy, Massachusetts Department of Public Health
Laura Lull, Association of Farmworker Opportunity Programs
Paul Martin, National Restaurant Association Education
    Foundation
Keith Mestrich, American Federation of Labor-Congress of
    Industrial Organizations
Diane Mull, Association of Farmworker Opportunity Programs
Tom Nardone, Bureau of Labor Statistics
Mary Overpeck, National Institute on Child Health and Human
    Development
David Parker, Minnesota Department of Health
Linda Rosenstock, National Institute for Occupational Safety and
    Health
Carol Runyan, Injury Prevention Research Center, University of
    North Carolina
John Ruser, Bureau of Labor Statistics
Barbara Schneider, National Opinion Research Center
Carol Stack, University of California at Berkeley
Diane Wagener, National Center for Health Statistics
William Weil, Michigan State University
Patience White, George Washington University and National
    Children's Medical Center
Derek Williams, Bowie, Maryland

B

Descriptions of Longitudinal Surveys

Dataset Name:	**National Education Longitudinal Study of 1988 (NELS:88)**
Principal Investigator:	Aurora D'Amico, Jeffrey Owings
Investigator's Institution:	National Center for Education Statistics
Data Collection Organization:	National Opinion Research Center (NORC) of the University of Chicago

Purpose

The National Education Longitudinal Study of 1988 (NELS:88) is the most recent in a series of longitudinal studies conducted by the National Center for Education Statistics at the U.S. Department of Education (also see the write-up on High School and Beyond). NELS:88 is designed to assess trends in secondary school education, focusing on the transition into and progress through high school, the transition into postsecondary school and the world of work, and family formation experiences. Data from this study can be used to examine educational issues such as tracking, cognitive growth, and dropping out of school.

269

Design

NELS:88 is a longitudinal study of a national probability sample of eighth graders. The base year student population excluded students with severe mental disabilities, students whose command of the English language was insufficient to understand survey materials, and students with physical or emotional problems that would limit their participation.

The survey used a two-stage stratified, clustered sample design. The first stage, selection of schools, was accomplished by a complex design involving two sister pools of schools. The second stage included selection of about 24 to 26 students per school. At the second stage, 93 percent of 26,435 selected students agreed to participate. Hispanic and Asian students were oversampled.

Data were collected via questionnaires from 24,599 students from 1,057 public and private schools from all 50 states and the District of Columbia in the base year. Eighth graders participated in group sessions at their schools where they completed student questionnaires and cognitive tests. School administrator data were collected from the senior school administrator (usually the principal or headmaster). For base year teacher data, each school was randomly assigned two of four subject areas of interest (English, math, science, social studies) and teachers were chosen who could provide data for each student respondent in these two subjects. Parent data were obtained through the mail.

For the first (1990) follow-up, all students were surveyed in schools containing ten or more eligible NELS:88 respondents. Only a sub-sample of students was surveyed in schools with fewer than ten students. Because 90 percent of students changed schools between eighth and tenth grade, it was necessary to sub-sample schools in this way. The 1990 sample size was more than 19,000 students, and the 1992 sample size is about the same.

The sample was freshened in 1990 and 1992 to give 1990 tenth graders and 1992 twelfth graders who were not in the eighth grade in 1988 some chance of selection into the NELS:88 follow-up. Such students included primarily those who had skipped or repeated a grade between 1988 and the follow-up year, and those who had moved to the U.S. after 1988. This freshening was conducted so that the first and second follow-up samples were representative of U.S. tenth graders in 1990 and U.S. twelfth graders in 1992.

Periodicity

Base year data were collected in 1988 and included questionnaires from students, school administrators, and parents; teacher ratings of students; and students' achievement test scores.

The first follow-up of NELS:88 was conducted in 1990. At this time, data was collected by way of a student questionnaire (including a brief new student questionnaire for new students who were brought into the sample to preserve representativeness), a dropout questionnaire (of base-year respondents who had since left school), a student achievement test, a teacher questionnaire, and a school administrator questionnaire.

A second follow-up was conducted in 1992. Data come from student (original and new) questionnaires, dropout questionnaires, student achievement test scores, school administrator and teacher questionnaires, and a parent questionnaire focusing on the financing of postsecondary education. In the second follow-up, only math and science teachers for each student were surveyed. Academic transcripts were collected for each student. The 3rd follow-up was conducted in 1994, when the students were approximately two years out of high school. Education, work, and family formation characteristics were included in this wave of the survey. The fourth and final follow-up will take place in 1997.

Content, Policy, and Research Issues

School administrator questionnaire: school, student and teaching staff characteristics, school policies and practices (e.g., admissions, discipline, grading and testing structure), school governance and climate, and school problems.

Teacher questionnaire: impressions of the student, student's school behavior and academic performance, curriculum and classroom instructional practices, school climate and policies, and teacher background and activities. The teacher questionnaire for the second follow-up was only given to math and science teachers, who were asked to rate their own professional qualifications and preparation.

Student questionnaire: family background and characteristics (including household composition, ethnicity, parental education, economic status), relationship with parents, unsupervised time at home, language use, opinions about self, attitudes, values, educational and career plans, jobs and chores, school life (including problems in school, discipline, peer relations, school climate), school work (homework, course enrollment, attitudes toward school, grade repetition, absenteeism), and extracurricular activities. First follow-up included similar content, as well as information about significant life events, family decision making, and substance abuse. The second follow-up contained similar material, as well as plans for the future, money and work, and an early graduate supplement which contained items about reasons for graduating early and current employment and enrollment. The third follow-up includes information on education, work, and family experiences.

Dropout questionnaire: reasons for leaving school, school attitudes and experiences, current activities (employment and education), family background, future plans, self-opinion and attitudes, substance abuse, money and work, family composition and events, and language use.

Parent questionnaire: marital status, household composition, employment, ethnicity, religion, child's school experiences and attendance, child's family life (activities, rules and regulations) and friends, opinion about and contact with child's school, child's disabilities, educational expectations for child, financial information, and educational expenditures. The second follow-up questionnaire included additional brief questions about neighborhood quality and some supplemental questions for parents new to NELS:88.

Student achievement tests: reading, math, science, and history/citizenship tests were administered in all waves.

New student supplement: provides brief information about language, ethnicity, objects in the home, parents' employment, and grade repetition.

School effectiveness study (SES): was added to the first follow-up to provide a probability sample of tenth-grade schools, with a sizable and representative within-school sample of students, through which longitudinal school-level analysis could be conducted. Two hundred and forty-eight schools participated in the first follow-up SES, and the second follow-up SES returned to 247 of those schools.

Transcript files and course offerings: in the second follow-up, complete high school records were collected for 1) students attending sampled schools in the spring of 1992; 2) all dropouts, dropouts in alternative programs, and early graduates, regardless of school affiliations; and 3) triple ineligibles enrolled in the twelfth grade in the spring of 1991, regardless of affiliation. Triple ineligibles are 1988 eighth grades who were ineligible for the base year, first follow-up, and second follow-up surveys due to a mental or physical disability or language barrier. The course offering component provides curriculum data from second follow-up school effectiveness study schools.

Because questionnaires were not identical at each wave, all of the information described above and indicated in the checklist is not available for every wave.

The longitudinal design of this study permits the examination of change in young people's lives and the role of schools in promoting growth and positive life outcomes. For example, NELS:88 data can be used to investigate the transition from middle school to secondary school, the students' academic growth over time, the features of effective schools, the process of dropping out of school as it occurs from eighth grade on, the role of the school in helping disadvantaged students, the school experiences and academic performance of language minority students, and factors associated with attracting students to the study of mathematics and science.

Contact

Aurora D'Amico
National Center for Education Statistics
555 New Jersey Avenue, N.W.
Washington, D.C. 20208
(202) 219-1365
Aurora_D'Amico@ed.gov

Source: National Research Council Workshop on Longitudinal Research on Children, September 12-13, 1997, Washington, D.C.

Dataset Name:	**National Longitudinal Study of Adolescent Health (Add Health)**
Principal Investigator:	J. Richard Udry
Investigator's Institution:	University of North Carolina at Chapel Hill
Data Collection Organization:	National Opinion Research Center (NORC) of the University of Chicago

Purpose

The National Longitudinal Study of Adolescents was designed to assess the health status of adolescents and explore causes of their health-related behaviors, focusing on multiple contexts or environments (both social and physical) in which they live. The study was predicated on the idea that adolescents' health is a result of social environment, health-related behaviors, and individual strengths and weaknesses. Each of these areas are explored in the study.

Design

Add Health is a longitudinal study of adolescents in grades 7 through 12. The study used a school-based clustered sampling design. Using a stratified, random sample of all high schools (defined as schools that included 11th grade and had at least 30 students) in the United States, 80 high schools were selected. A feeder school— a school that sent graduates to the high school and that included a 7th grade—was also recruited in each community. Because some high schools spanned grades 7 to 12, and therefore, acted as their own feeder schools, the core study had a total sample of 134 schools.

A self-administered questionnaire was filled out by all students present on the day of administration at each of the 134 schools during the 1994-1995 school year. Over 90,000 adolescents completed an in-school questionnaire.

A nationally-representative core sample of 12,105 adolescents was selected from the students in the selected schools for in-home interviews. Special oversamples of blacks, Chinese, Cubans, Puerto Ricans, disabled, and siblings also received in-home interviews. In addition, all students in two large schools and 14 small schools were interviewed at home. A total of 21,000 in-home interviews were completed in the 1994-1995 school year. Data were also collected from school administrators and parents.

A second wave of follow-up in-home interviews was conducted in the spring of 1996.

Periodicity

The baseline in-school questionnaires and school administrator questionnaires were completed between September 1994 and April 1995. The first wave of in-home interviews and the parent questionnaires were completed between April and December 1995. A second wave of school administrator questionnaires were completed between May and June 1996. The second wave of in-home interviews took place between April and August 1996.

Content, Policy, and Research Issues

In-school questionnaire: social and demographic characteristics of respondents, education and occupation of parents, household structure, risk behaviors, expectations for the future, self-esteem, health status, friendships, school-year extracurricular activities.

In-home interview: health status, health facility utilization, nutrition, peer networks, decision-making processes, family composition and dynamics, educational aspirations and expectations, employment experience, the ordering of events in the formation of romantic partnerships, sexual partnerships, substance use, and criminal activities. An abridged version of the Peabody Picture Vocabulary Test was also administered.

School administrator questionnaire: school policies and procedures, teacher characteristics, health service provision or referral, student body characteristics, dress codes, and security procedures.

Parent questionnaire: inheritable health conditions; marriages and marriage-like relationships; neighborhood characteristic;, involvement in volunteer, civic, or school activities; health-affecting behaviors; education and employment; household income and economic assistance; parent-adolescent communication and interaction;

and parent's familiarity with adolescent's friends and friends' parents.

Neighborhood/Community context: demographic and household characteristics; labor force participation and unemployment; income and poverty; social integration/disintegration; availability and utilization of health services; social programs and policies; and crime. This information was gathered from a variety of sources, such as U.S. Census, the Centers for Disease Control and Prevention, the National Center for Health Statistics, the Federal Bureau of Investigation, the National Council of Churches, and other published data bases.

Contact

J. Richard Udry
Kenan Professor of Maternal and Child Health and Sociology
Carolina Population Center
University of North Carolina
Chapel Hill, NC 97516-3997
udry@unc.edu

or

Jo Jones
Project Manager
Carolina Population Center
University of North Carolina at Chapel Hill
jo_jones@unc.edu

Research collaborators include:

Karl E. Bauman, Health Behavior and Health Education, University of North Carolina, Chapel Hill
Peter S. Bearman, Sociology, University of North Carolina, Chapel Hill
John O.G. Billy, Battelle, Seattle
Robert W. Blum, Pediatrics, University of Minnesota
William R. Grady, Battelle, Seattle
Kathleen Mullen Harris, Sociology, University of North

Carolina, Chapel Hill
James J. Jaccard, Psychology, State University of New York at Albany
Michael D. Resnick, Public Health and Pediatrics, University of Minnesota
David C. Rowe, Family Studies, University of Arizona

Source: Bearman, P.S., J. Jones, and J.R. Udry. 1997. *Longitudinal Study of Adolescent Health: Research Design.* Available at http://www.cpc.unc.edu/projects/addhealth/design.html; also available at http://www.cpc.unc.edu/projects/addhealth/addhealth_home. html.

Dataset Name: **National Longitudinal Survey of Youth, 1979 (NLSY)**
Sponsoring Organization: Bureau of Labor Statistics, U.S. Department of Labor
Program Director: Michael Horrigan
Data Collection Organization: National Opinion Research Center (NORC) of the University of Chicago

Purpose

To study in detail the life course experience of a large, nationally-representative sample of young Americans, and to allow analysis of the differences in life course experiences of such groups as women, Hispanics, blacks, and the economically disadvantaged.

Design

The NLSY has three subsamples: a cross-sectional sample of 6,111 youth designed to be representative of the noninstitutionalized civilian segment of young people living in the United States in 1979 and born between January 1, 1957 and December 31, 1964; a supplemental sample of 5,295 youth designed to oversample Hispanic, black, and economically disadvantaged youth living in the United States in 1979 and born between January 1, 1957 and December 31, 1964; and a sample of 1,280 youth designed to represent the population born between January 1, 1957 and December 31, 1961 and who were enlisted in the military as of September 30, 1978.

Personally-administered interviews were conducted annually from 1979 through 1986. Due to budget constraints in 1987, a more limited telephone interview was conducted that year. Personal interviews resumed in 1988. In 1993, paper and pencil interview instruments were replaced with computer-assisted interviewing.

Periodicity

Annually. The first interviews were conducted in 1979.

Content, Policy, and Research Issues

Initial survey (1979): family background, knowledge of the world of work, a retrospective evaluation of labor market experience, the influence of significant others, and an abbreviated Rotter locus of control scale.

Subsequent surveys: job search methods, migration, attitudes towards work, educational/occupational aspirations and expectations, school discipline, self-esteem, child care, pre- and post-natal health behaviors, drug and alcohol use, delinquency, time use, AIDS knowledge, childhood residence, and neighborhood problems. Respondents have also been the subjects for a number of special surveys.

Major data elements available in NLSY: demographic and family background characteristics, household composition, educational status and attainment, high school experiences, aptitude and intelligence scores, nongovernment vocational/technical training, government training and jobs, military experience, labor market activity and transitions, detailed work histories, marital history, fertility, child care, income and assets, health, alcohol and substance use, illegal activities, attitudes and aspirations, geographic information, detailed geocode data files, and geographic proximity/mobility matches.

Contact

Michael W. Horrigan
National Longitudinal Surveys
Suite 4945
2 Massachusetts Avenue NE
Washington, DC 20212-0011

Source: NLSY79 Overview. Available at http://stats.bls.gov/nlsyouth.html.

Dataset Name:	**National Longitudinal Survey of Youth 1997**
Sponsoring Organization:	Bureau of Labor Statistics, U.S. Department of Labor
Data Collection Organization:	National Opinion Research Center
Program Director:	Michael Horrigan

Purpose

To provide information about young people making the transition into the labor market and into adulthood and career and family formation. The data will improve understanding of how different youths negotiate the transition and help researchers identify the antecedents and causes for youths who experience difficulties making the transition from school to work.

Design

A representative national sample of approximately 10,000 youth ages 12-16 years old on December 31, 1996. Black and Hispanic persons will be oversampled to permit racial and ethnic comparisons.

Periodicity

Annually. First round of interviews from February to September, 1997.

Content, Policy and Research Issues

Data are collected on the cognitive, social, and emotional development of young people. In the initial survey both a parent and a youth interview are administered. Questions are asked about family background, marital and employment history, health, income and assets. Both interviews have self-administered portions providing data on issues such as smoking, drinking, dating, religious beliefs, depression, and expectations. Information will also be obtained from school administrators and from school transcripts. A math test will be administered to ninth graders in the survey. The Armed Services Vocational and Aptitude Battery will be used to assess the respondents aptitude, achievement and career interests.

Contact

Michael W. Horrigan
National Longitudinal Surveys
Suite 4945
2 Massachusetts Ave. N.E.
Washington, DC 20212-0011

Source: National Research Council Workshop on Longitudinal Research on Children, September 12-13, 1997, Washington, D.C.

Dataset Name:	Monitoring the Future: A Continuing Study of the Lifestyles and Values of Youth
Principal Investigator:	Jerald G. Bachman, John Schulenberg
Investigator's Institution:	Institute for Social Research, The University of Michigan
Data Collection Organization:	Survey Research Center, Institute for Social Research, The University of Michigan

Purpose

To assess the changing lifestyles, values, and preferences of youth in the United States on a continuing basis. Study results are used to monitor trends in substance use and abuse, monitor progress toward Goal 7 (safe, disciplined, and alcohol- and drug-free schools) of the Goals 2000 National Education Goals, and to monitor progress toward national health goals.

Design

A multi-stage random sampling procedure is used to select a representative nationwide sample of 8th, 10th, and 12th grade students. Data are collected in the spring of each year in approximately 420 public and private high schools and middle schools to provide a representative cross-section of students in the coterminous United States at each grade level. Each year current 8th, 10th, and 12th graders are presented with the same set of questions to see how answers change over time. A sample from each 12th grade class has been followed biannually since 1976 using a mail questionnaire.

The design permits examination of four kinds of change: changes in particular years reflected across all age groups; developmental changes that show up consistently from year to year; consistent differences among class cohorts over time; and changes linked to environment or role transitions.

Periodicity

Annually. Beginning in 1975, approximately 16,000 high school seniors were surveyed each year. In 1991, 8th and 10th grade students were added to the sample for annual surveys. Subsamples of seniors from previously participating classes receive follow-up questionnaires by mail biannually.

Content, Policy, and Research Issues

Drug and alcohol use, attitudes towards drugs, availability of drugs, cigarette use, attitudes towards cigarettes, availability of cigarettes, demographic information, grades, hours of work per week, amount of pay for work, parents' education, college plans, high school curriculum, sleep, breakfast eating, exercise, dating, delinquency, life satisfaction, truancy, interpersonal aggression, victimization, and self-esteem.

Contact

Monitoring the Future
Institute for Social Research
The University of Michigan
P.O. Box 1248
Ann Arbor, MI 48106

Source: The Monitoring the Future Study. Available at http://www.isr.umich.edu/src/mtf/purpose.html.

Dataset Name:	Panel Survey of Income Dynamics
Principal Investigator:	Sandra L. Hofferth, Frank P. Stafford
Investigator's Institution:	University of Michigan
Data Collection Organization:	Survey Research Center, Institute of Social Research, The University of Michigan
Sponsoring Organizations:	National Science Foundation; Office of the Assistant Secretary for Planning and Evaluation, Department of Health and Human Services; Department of Labor; the National Institute on Aging; and the National Institute of Child Health and Human Development

Purpose

The study, begun in 1968, gathers information on the dynamic aspects of economic and demographic behavior of a representative sample of U.S. individuals (men, women, and children) and the family units in which they reside.

Design

The study's original 5,000 households constitute a national probability sample of U.S. households as of 1967. In 1990, a representative national sample of 2,000 Latino households, differentially sampled to provide adequate numbers of Puerto Rican, Mexican-American, and Cuban American households, was added to the sample. All members of these original households are tracked, including those who leave to form separate family units. Children born to members of an original-sample member are classified as sample members and are eligible for tracking as separate family units when they set up their own households. Ex-spouses and other adult sample members who move out of a PSID family unit are also tracked to their new family unit. This procedure replicates the population's family-building activity and produces a dynamic sample of families each year. This design is responsible for the increase in the number of family units studied from 7,000 in 1990 to almost 8,700 in 1995. Information is gathered about all persons residing in the family unit, but in most waves there is only one respondent per family unit. As of 1995, information had been collected about more than 50,000 individuals spanning as much as 28 years of their lives.

Periodicity

Annually.

Content, Policy, and Research Issues

The general design and content of the study has remained largely unchanged, with a central focus on economics and demographic events. The major core topics covered are income sources and amounts, poverty status, public assistance, other financial matters, family structure and demographic measures (e.g., marital status, births and adoptions, children forming households), labor market participation, housework time, housing, geographic mobility, socioeconomic background, and general health. Beginning in 1985, comprehensive retrospective fertility and marriage histories of individuals in the households have been assembled. Supplemental topics have been investigated in depth in various years. Supplemental topics include education, military combat experience, health, kinship networks, and wealth.

Contact

PSID Staff
Institute of Social Research
University of Michigan
Ann Arbor, MI 48106
PSID_Staff@umich.edu

Source: PSID homepage. Available at http://www.isr.umich.edu/src/psid/.

Dataset Name:	**National Survey of Families and Households**
Sponsoring Organization:	National Institute of Child Health and Human Development, U.S. Department of Health and Human Services
Program Director:	V. Jeffrey Evans, National Institute of Child Health and Human Development

Data Collection Organization:

Purpose

To study family processes and transitions, viewing family relationships in the context of other adult roles and opportunities.

Design

The original 1987-88 sample included 13,000 households. Double samples were taken from black and Hispanic households, single-parent families, cohabiting and newly married couples, and households with stepchildren. In person interviews were conducted with a randomly chosen adult over age 18. Self-administered surveys were given to the respondent and the respondent's spouse or partner. In the 1993-94 follow-up survey, brief interviews were also completed with children who age 5 or older in the initial survey. Selected children and parents who had divorced or left the original family were followed and surveyed.

Periodicity

First wave of interviews in 1987 to 1988. Follow-up interviews in 1993 to 1994. No future follow-ups are currently planned, however the families are being tracked to allow for further study.

Content, Policy, and Research Issues

Childhood family experience, cohabitation and marital histories, current living arrangements, husband-wife relationships, and parent-child relationships.

Contact

V. Jeffrey Evans
Demographic and Behavioral Sciences Branch
National Institute of Child Health and Human Development
6100 Executive Boulevard
Bethesda, MD 20892-7510

Sources: National Research Council, 1995, *Integrating Federal Statistics on Children: Report of a Workshop*. Washington, D.C.: National Academy Press.

Demographic and Behavioral Sciences Branch, National Institute of Child Health and Human Behavior, 1995, *Report to the NACHHD Council*, January 1995. Available at http://www.nih.gov/nichd/html/report/Jan95.htm.

Dataset Name:	**New Immigrant Pilot Survey (NIPS)**
Sponsoring Organization:	National Institutes of Health Immigration and Naturalization Service National Science Foundation
Data Collection Organization:	National Institutes of Health U.S. Immigration and Naturalization Service
Principal Investigator(s):	Guillermina Jasso, New York University Douglas S. Massey, University of Pennsylvania Mark R. Rosenzweig, University of Pennsylvania James P. Smith, Rand Corporation

Purpose

The NIS Pilot Study has three aims: (1) to assess the cost-effectiveness of alternative methods for locating and maximizing the initial response rates of sampled immigrants; (2) to explore the costs, feasibility, and effectiveness of alternative methods of tracking over time sampled immigrants after their initial contacts that will permit a longitudinal survey of a highly mobile population with minimal attrition; and (3) to obtain immediately useful information from the NIS pilot that would both aid in the design of survey instruments for the full survey and that would provide new and important information on recently-admitted immigrants.

Design and Periodicity

The NIS Pilot Study consists of a baseline survey, a three-month follow-up of half of the original sample, a six-month follow-up of all original sample members, and a one-year follow-up, also of all original sample members.

The sampling frame for the NIS Pilot Study consists of all persons who were admitted to legal permanent residence during the months of July and August of 1996. Because children are quite numerous among immigrants and because employment-based immigrants, in whom there is great interest, are a relatively small category, a stratified random sample was drawn, undersampling children and oversampling the employment-based.

Content

There are two types of data that are pertinent. The first is data on the usual sociodemographic and economic characteristics and activities, so that immigrants and their children can be compared with native-born persons. The second is data on characteristics and behavior unique to immigrants. The first type of data include marital and employment histories, and the second type include migration and language-acquisition histories.

Contact

Guillermina Jasso
Department of Sociology
New York University
Mail Code 0831
269 Mercer Street, #412
New York, NY 10003

Source: National Research Council Workshop on Longitudinal Research on Children, September 12-13, 1997, Washington, D.C.

Biographical Sketches of
Committee Members and Staff

DAVID H. WEGMAN, M.D. (*chair*), is professor and chair, Department of Work Environment at the University of Massachusetts at Lowell. His research focuses on epidemiological studies of occupational respiratory disease, musculoskeletal disorders, and cancer. He has also written on public health and health policy issues, such as hazard and health surveillance, methods of exposure assessment for epidemiologic studies, the development of alternatives to regulation, and the use of participatory methods to study occupational health risks. He is coeditor with Barry Levy of one of the standard textbooks in the field, *Occupational Health: Recognition and the Prevention of Work-Related Disease*, the third edition of which was published in 1995. His recent work has focused on developing methods to study subjective outcomes, such as respiratory or irritant symptom reports, and on the health and safety risks among construction workers. He received a B.A. degree from Swarthmore College and M.D. and M.Sc. degrees from Harvard University.

JAMES V. BRUCKNER is professor of pharmacology and toxicology, College of Pharmacy, and director of the Interdisciplinary Program in Toxicology at the University of Georgia. His primary responsibilities include implementation of an active research program and promotion of the development of a graduate program in toxicology. His current research concerns the basic questions which impact on toxicity risk and assessment using physiologically based pharmacokinetics models. He holds B.S. and M.S. degrees from the University of Texas at Austin College of Pharmacy and a Ph.D. degree from the University of Michigan.

MICHAEL I. COHEN is professor and chair of the Department of Pediatrics at Albert Einstein College of Medicine/Montefiore Medical Center. He held a postdoctoral fellowship from the National Institutes of Health at Einstein before beginning his career in exploring the issues of adolescent development. He is the former president and chief executive officer of the Montefire Medical Center in New York, served on the Council on Adolescent Development of the Carnegie Corporation of New York, and was vice-chair of an advisory committee on adolescent health to the Office of Technology Assessment, U.S. Congress. He is a member of the Institute of Medicine, and a trustee of Foundation for Child Development. He has an M.D. degree from Columbia University and did his pediatric training at Babies Hospital in New York.

NANCY A. CROWELL (*study director*) is a staff officer with the Commission on Behavioral and Social Sciences and Education of the National Research Council/National Academy of Sciences. She serves on the staff for the Board on Children, Youth, and Families and the Committee on Law and Justice, and she previously staffed National Research Council studies on violence against women, family violence, risk communication, and policy implications of greenhouse warming. Training as a pediatric audiogist, Crowell worked in a demonstration project for preschool hearing impaired children and their families at Ball State University. She also worked on several political campaigns and for a political polling and consulting firm prior to joining the National Research Council staff. She holds B.S. degrees in mathematics and French from St. Lawrence University and an M.A. in audiology from Vanderbilt University.

LETITIA K. DAVIS is director of the Occupational Health Surveillance Program in the Massachusetts Department of Public Health, where she works to develop state-based surveillance systems for work-related illnesses and injuries. She has overseen the formation of a physician reporting system for occupational disease, the Massachusetts Occupational Lead Registry, a comprehensive surveillance system for traumatic occupational fatalities, and an experimental surveillance system for work-related injuries to children and adolescents. She has also conducted a number of epidemiological studies and oversees a variety of health and safety educational activities, including a pilot community-based intervention project to enhance the health and safety of young workers. She serves as a visiting lecturer on occupational health at the University of Massachusetts at Lowell, is a member of the Board of Scientific Counselors of the National Institute for Occupational Safety and Health, and has recently served on the Massachusetts Attorney General's Task Force on Child Labor. She holds a B.A. degree from the University of California at Berkeley, an Ed.M. degree from the Harvard School of Education, and a Sc.D. degree from the Harvard School of Public Health.

PETER DORMAN is a faculty member at Evergreen State College. His teaching experience includes micro- and macroeconomic theory and environmental and resource economics. He has published various book and articles on markets and economics, including *Markets and Mortality: Economics, Dangerous Work, and the Value of Human Life* and *The Effect of Free Trade on Contingent Work in Michigan* (with K. Roberts and D. Hyatt). His current research concerns trade, international labor standards, and global labor markets; occupational safety and health in contingent employment; and the information structure of organizations and economic regulation. He holds a B.A. degree from the University of Wisconsin and a Ph.D. degree from the University of Massachusetts.

SANFORD M. DORNBUSCH is a Reed-Hodgson Professor of human biology, sociology, and education, emeritus, at Stanford University, where he currently serves as chair of the Advisory Board of the Stanford Center on Adolescence. He previously was on the faculty of the University of Washington and Harvard University. He was the first sociologist to be chair of three sections of the American Sociological Association (social psychology, methodology, and education) and was the first nonpsychologist to be elected president of the Society for Research on Adolescence. At Stanford he won the

Gores Award for excellence in teaching and has been elected president of the Academic Senate, Advisory Board, and the Bookstore and Faculty Club.

STEPHEN F. HAMILTON is professor of human development at Cornell University and codirector of the Cornell Youth and Work Program. His primary concerns are with adolescent development and education, particularly the interaction of school, community, and work during the transition from adolescence to adulthood. His study of Germany's apprenticeship system led *Apprenticeship for Adulthood: Preparing Youth for the Future*, which contrasted the transition from school to career of non-college youth in the United States and Germany and recommended adaptation of elements of apprenticeship in the United States. To test those recommendations, he initiated a youth apprenticeship demonstration project in Broome County, New York. The book and demonstration project helped to shape the School-to-Work Opportunities Act of 1994. He received a B.A. degree in history from Swarthmore College and a Master of Arts in Teaching degree from Harvard, then taught for 3 years in a Washington, D.C., vocational high school before returning to Harvard, where he received a Ph.D.

BARBARA C. LEE is a senior scientist with the Marshfield Medical Research Foundation in Wisconsin, where she directs programs dedicated to child safety for the National Farm Medicine Center. She is the director of the National Children's Center for Rural and Agricultural Health and Safety, funded by the National Institute for Occupational Safety and Health and the federal Maternal and Child Health Bureau. She chaired the National Committee for Childhood Agricultural Injury Prevention, which developed a national action plan that was endorsed and supported by the U.S. Congress in 1996, and she serves on several advisory boards and committees. With funding from private and public sources, she is responsible for a number of research, education, public policy and program evaluation initiatives that address health and safety for children and adolescents who live, play, and work in rural and agricultural settings. She is a past president of the National Institute for Farm Safety. She holds nursing degrees from the College of St. Teresa (B.S.N.), the

University of Wisconsin-Eau Claire (M.S.N.), and the University of Wisconsin-Milwaukee (Ph.D.).

JEYLAN T. MORTIMER is professor of sociology at the University of Minnesota and director of the Life Course Center. She has conducted a series of longitudinal research projects related to the social psychology of work, including studies of occupational choice, vocational development in the family and work settings, psychological change in response to work, job satisfaction, work involvement, and the link between work and family life. Since 1987 she has directed the Youth Development Study, an ongoing longitudinal examination of the effects of early work experience on students and its implications for mental health, adjustment, and achievement as they mature. The interrelations of adolescent work and family life are examined in her book, *Adolescents, Work, and Family: An Intergenerational Development Analysis* (with M. Finch). She is now studying the effects of adolescent work on the timing and patterning of markers of transition to adulthood. She is past chair of the Social Psychology Section and current chair of the Sociology of Children Section of the American Sociological Association and a fellow of the American Association for the Advancement of Science. She holds a B.A. degree from Tufts University and M.A. and Ph.D. degrees from the University of Michigan.

LINDA RAE MURRAY is a practicing physician in the Division of Occupational Medicine at Cook County Hospital in Chicago. She previously served as medical director of the Near North Health Service Corporation in Chicago. She is on the Board of Health and Medicine Policy Research Group and a member of the American Public Health Association. She holds a B.S. degree from the University of Illinois, a Master of Public Health degree from the School of Public Health, University of Illinois, and an M.D. degree from the Abraham Lincoln School of Medicine.

SUSAN H. POLLACK is an assistant professor in the Department of Pediatrics and Preventive Medicine and Environmental Health and at the Kentucky Injury Prevention and Research Center at the University of Kentucky College of Medicine. She is principal and research associate for the Behavioral Research Aspects of Safety Health

Working Group. She serves as chair for the Pediatric and Adolescent Injury Committee, Injury Control, and Emergency Health Services Section and on the National Committee for Childhood Agricultural Injury Prevention. She holds a B.S. degree from Smith College, an M.S. degree from Georgetown University, and an M.D. degree from Eastern Virginia Medical School.

MICHAEL A. SILVERSTEIN is assistant director for Industrial Safety and Health with the Washington State Department of Labor and Industries, a job that includes responsibility for the state's occupational safety and health programs. He recently completed a 2-year assignment as director of Policy for the Occupational Safety and Health Administration in Washington, D.C. Prior to these government positions, Silverstein worked for 15 years on a wide range of issues with the United Automobile Workers Union in Detroit, Michigan, as assistant director for occupational safety and health. Silverstein is a member of the editorial board of the *Journal of Occupational and Environmental Medicine* and has authored numerous articles in the areas of occupational edpidemiology and occupational safety and health policy. A board-certified specialist in occupational medicine, he holds degrees from Harvard College, Stanford Medical School, and the School of Public Health at the University of Michigan.

DORIS P. SLESINGER is a professor in the Department of Rural Sociology, University of Wisconsin-Madison, and an extension sociologist in University of Wisconsin-Extension. She has served as chair of the department and codirector of the Applied Population Laboratory. She has served on the Health Services Developmental Grants Review Committee of the Agency for Health Care Policy and Research and on the editorial board of the *Journal of Rural Health*. Her research and publications include medical utilization patterns and health status of rural and minority populations, including farm families, migrant farmworkers, and the Amish. She has published a monograph on mothercraft and infant health and numerous demographic works on various minority populations in Wisconsin. Her current research concerns health and injuries, including pesticide exposure, among migrant farmworkers and their children and access to health insurance of Wisconsin farm families and the self-employed.

She holds degrees in sociology from Vassar college (A.B.), the University of Michigan (M.A.), and the University of Wisconsin (Ph.D).

LAURENCE STEINBERG is a professor in the Department of Psychology at Temple University and director of the MacArthur Foundation Research Network on Adolescent Development and Juvenile Justice. His research has focused on psychological development, education, and mental health during adolescence and on the part-time employment of school-aged youth. A fellow of the American Psychological Association and president of the Society for Research on Adolescence, he has served on the editorial boards of *Child Development* and *Developmental Psychology* and as a consultant to the Carnegie Council on Adolescence. He is the author of numerous articles on adolescent development and behavior and the coauthor (with Ellen Greenberger) of *When Teenagers Work: The Psychological and Social Costs of Adolescent Employment* and *Beyond the Classroom: Why School Reform Has Failed and What Parents Need to Do.* He holds an A.B. degree in psychology from Vassar College and a Ph.D. in developmental psychology from Cornell University.

ANTHONY J. SURUDA is director of occupational medicine and associate professor in the Department of Family and Preventive Medicine at the University of Utah School of Medicine. He directs the Occupational Medicine Clinic and provides patient care consultations and recommendations to employees and unions concerning work-related illnesses and injuries. Licensed in Utah and Colorado, he is a member of the American College of Occupational and Environmental Medicine and the American Public Health Association. He holds degrees from St. Peters College (B.S.), Johns Hopkins University School of Hygiene and Public Health (M.P.H.), and Johns Hopkins University School of Medicine (M.D.).

ELLEN G. WIDESS is the executive director of Lead Safe California, a nonprofit, public interest organization dedicated to preventing childhood lead poisoning. Previously, she directed the Pesticide Unit of California's Occupational Safety and Health Administration and the Texas Pesticide Regulatory Program. She has also taught environmental and occupational health law at the University of California-Berkeley and at the University of Texas Law School. Her writing includes a chapter on pesticide poisoning and regulation in *Occupation Disease and Injury* (1991) and a chapter on neurotoxic pesticides and farmworker exposure in *Neurotoxicity: New Developments in Neuroscience* (1990). She is on the board of directors of the Alliance to End Childhood Lead Poisoning and a member of the Task Force on Lead Based Paint Hazard Reduction and Financing of the U.S. Department of Housing and Urban Development. She is a member of the California Bar, the California Public Health Association-North, and the American Public Health Association. She received an A.B. degree from the University of California at Berkeley and a J.D. degree from the university's Boalt Hall School of Law.

Index

S

Other Reports from the Board on Children, Youth, and Families

From Generation to Generation: The Health and Well-Being of Children in Immigrant Families (1998)

New Findings on Poverty and Child Health and Nutrition: Summary of a Research Briefing (1998)

Educating Language-Minority Students (1998)

Violence in Families: Assessing Prevention and Treatment Programs (1998)

Welfare, the Family, and Reproductive Behavior: Report of a Meeting (with the NRC Committee on Population) (1998)

Improving Schooling for Language-Minority Students: A Research Agenda (1997)

New Findings on Welfare and Children's Development: Summary of a Research Briefing (1997)

Youth Development and Neighborhood Influences: Challenges and Opportunities: Summary of a Workshop (1996)

Paying Attention to Children in a Changing Health Care System: Sum-

maries of Workshops (with the Board on Health Promotion and Disease Prevention of the Institute of Medicine) (1996)

Beyond the Blueprint: Directions for Research on Head Start's Families: Report of Three Roundtable Meetings (1996)

Child Care for Low-Income Families: Directions for Research: Summary of a Workshop (1996)

Service Provider Perspectives on Family Violence Interventions: Proceedings of a Workshop (1995)

"Immigrant Children and Their Families: Issues for Research and Policy" in *The Future of Children* (1995)

Integrating Federal Statistics on Children (with the Committee on National Statistics of the National Research Council) (1995)

Child Care for Low-Income Families: Summary of Two Workshops (1995)

New Findings on Children, Families, and Economic Self-Sufficiency: Summary of a Research Briefing (1995)

The Impact of War on Child Health in the Countries of the Former Yugoslavia: A Workshop Summary (with the Institute of Medicine and the Office of International Affairs of the National Research Council) (1995)

Cultural Diversity and Early Education: Report of a Workshop (1994)

Benefits and Systems of Care for Maternal and Child Health: Workshop Highlights (with the Board on Health Promotion and Disease Prevention of the Institute of Medicine) (1994)

Protecting and Improving the Quality of Children Under Health Care Reform: Workshop Highlights (with the Board on Health Promotion and Disease Prevention of the Institute of Medicine) (1994)

America's Fathers and Public Policy: Report of a Workshop (1994)

Violence and the American Family: Report of a Workshop (1994)